7.95

‖‖‖ ‖‖‖‖‖ ‖‖ ‖‖‖ ‖‖ ‖‖‖‖‖‖ ‖‖‖ ‖‖ ‖‖‖
W9-CET-541

4191

E
185
.C82

Coombs
The Black
experience in
America

DATE DUE

28 80			
1 80			
DE 10 84			
MR 02 87			
MR 1 89			
NOV 26 2001			

The Black Experience In America
E185.C82   4191
‖‖‖‖‖‖‖‖‖‖‖‖‖‖‖‖‖‖‖‖
Coombs, Norman
VRJC/WRIGHT LIBRARY

The Immigrant Heritage of America Series

Cecyle S. Neidle, *Editor*

The Black Experience in America

By NORMAN COOMBS

Rochester Institute of Technology

TWAYNE PUBLISHERS

A DIVISION OF G. K. HALL & CO., BOSTON

~~VERNON REGIONAL~~

~~JUNIOR COLLEGE LIBRARY~~

Copyright © 1972, by Twayne Publishers, Inc.
All Rights Reserved

Library of Congress Catalog Card Number: 73-186717
ISBN   0-8057-3208-X

MANUFACTUERD IN THE UNITED STATES OF AMERICA

No people to whom liberty is given can hold it as firmly and wear it as grandly as those who wrench their liberty from the iron hand of the tyrant.

Frederick Douglass

About the Author

Norman Coombs is an associate professor of history at the Rochester Institute of Technology where he has taught since 1961. In 1970 the National Endowment for the Arts and Humanities awarded him a grant to work in Afro-American studies, and it led directly to the writing of this book.

Canadian born, Coombs, after a childhood accident, attended the Ontario School for the Blind. He received the B.S. from the University of Wisconsin — Milwaukee in 1955 and the Ph.D. from the University of Wisconsin in 1961. His work was concentrated in cultural and intellectual history. Coombs spent the year, 1959-60, in London on a Fulbright studying Christian Socialism in the Church of England.

Contents

Contents

Preface

During the last several years, the study of American history has turned in a new direction. Previously, it emphasized how the various immigrant groups in America shed their divergent heritages and amalgamated into a new nationality. More recently, scholars and laymen alike have become more sensitive to the ways in which these newcomers have kept aspects from their past alive, and there is a new awareness of the degree to which ethnicity continues as a force within America.

Most of the original settlers were British, Protestant, and white. Many of the later arrivals differed from them, in one or more ways. History books usually depicted these new waves of immigrants as assimilating almost fully into American society. However, recent writings have put more stress on the ethnic diversities which remain and on the rich variety of contributions which were made to the American scene by each new nationality.

This volume depicts the immigrants from Africa as one among the many elements which created present-day America. On the one hand, they differ from the other minorities because they came involuntarily, suffered the cruelties of slavery, and were of another color. All of this made their experience unique. On the other hand, they shared much in common with the other minorities, many of whom also felt like aliens in their new land.

Throughout most of American history, political power has been held tightly by the white, Anglo-Saxon, Protestant majority. Historical presentations which stressed the political component, thereby tended to leave the later immigrants in the background. However, because these newcomers did not assimilate fully into the mainstream of America, they maintained some of their ethnic identity and made fresh and unique contributions to American life. A socio-cultural approach to history, through highlighting society and culture rather than politics, brings these minorities into proper focus.

This study of Afro-Americans seeks to describe the character and culture which they produced for themselves in America. It also points to the many important contributions which they have made to American cultural life. The spotlight is on what they felt and thought, on the attitudes they developed, and on their increasingly vocal protests against the unfair treatment which they believed was directed at them.

Besides taking a socio-cultural approach to the subject, this book is deliberately interpretive rather than being merely a narrative of events. It is reasonably brief in the hope that it will appeal to interested laymen. At the same time, it contains a number of footnotes so that either scholars or laymen, wanting to check their thoughts against the interpretation presented here, can readily use this book as a guide to further reading.

If at times the treatment of the white majority seems harsh, it is because, in my opinion, it is still necessary for Americans to take a long, cold look at the chilling facts which have too often been ignored. Yet, times and people do change. Race relations in America are not today what they were a century ago. The progress of history may not be the wide highway moving steadily and smoothly upward as many have believed, but the racial picture in America has altered and will continue to do so— sometimes for the better, sometimes for the worse. Nevertheless, it is only by knowing ourselves that we can intelligently face our crises. I hope that this volume will assist the reader as he struggles with this difficult task.

NORMAN COOMBS

September, 1971

Acknowledgments

I would like to express my deep appreciation to the National Endowment for the Arts and Humanities and to the Rochester Institute of Technology for providing me with much of the time which made this research possible. I am also indebted to Professors Benjamin Quarles and Merle Curti for kindly reading and commenting on the manuscript. My thanks are also extended to my father, Earl Coombs, for his invaluable assistance in helping with the hours of painstaking research demanded by such a project. Miss Dorothy Ruhl provided the detailed, careful labor necessary to help prepare the manuscript for the printer, and Mrs. Doris Kist performed the demanding task of proofreading it. I also want to thank Cecyle S. Neidle, the editor of the *Immigrant Heritage of America* series, for her helpful supervision and advice. Finally, I owe a deep debt of gratitude to my wife, Jean, for typing the manuscript, for a host of other miscellaneous tasks and, above all, for her forbearance and encouragement.

N. C.

Introduction

Beginning with Jamestown itself all newcomers to America underwent many stresses. In adjusting to the new life the first settlers had to cope with the Indians while simultaneously trying to scratch a living from the land. Later immigrants, particularly those who came after the Civil War, faced newer problems, including the complicated process of becoming a naturalized citizen. Many of the newer groups, particularly those from Southern Europe, encountered some initial hostility from their predecessors, being regarded as poor stock for "Americanization." These latter-day immigrants could not indefinitely be denied general social acceptance, however, particularly after many of them had become voters and some of them had become well-to-do.

But among all other incoming groups there was one which all the others unchangingly regarded as an out-group, one which they held could never be assimilated. These were the blacks from Africa. Torn from their accustomed ways during the early days of European exploration and settlement in the New World, their roots were deeply imbedded in American soil, with some new and vigorous twentieth century graftings from the British West Indies. But even in the days when the melting pot theory held sway, its proponents did not believe that the black inhabitants were destined to blend into the envisioned homogeneous end product, "this new man," in the phrase of J. Hector St. John (de Crèvecoeur), himself an eighteenth-century transplant from France. The prevailing attitude toward blacks could be characterized as "among us, yet not of us."

The concept of the innate inferiority of the Negro is still very much alive, if diminished in some quarters, but the melting pot theory has become outmoded. Various ethnic groups, while still priding themselves on their true-blue Americanism, no longer feel that they must surrender any distinctive traits or ties they may still retain. Pluralism is now paramount, its watchwords multi-cultural and multi-racial. Hence it follows that diversity, properly bounded by an over-arching unity, is now viewed as the fountainhead of a more encompassing and enriching national culture.

The pluralistic view of our country and its past says unmistakably, if by inference, that the Anglo-Saxon, North European types were not the only ones who contributed to the making of America. Other groups bore their gifts, as we have increasingly become aware of late. Our understanding of one of these hitherto somewhat submerged types is deepened by this fine study, *The Black Experience in America.*

Viewing the Afro-American past from those angles which best illustrate its greatest impact, Coombs gives us a richly interpretive group portrait. He arrests our attention from his opening chapter, one which described the Old World background and heritage of the Negro American and in the process enables the reader to rediscover historical West Africa for himself. This chapter, like each of its successors, has a fresh and imaginative organizational pattern. In war-related chapters, for example, Coombs deals not only with the particular war under survey but also with its fruits, the latter often stunted as far as blacks were concerned. Some chapters, such as "Slavery and Capitalism," an analytical and interpretive essay, could well stand alone, entities in themselves. Another characteristically well worth reading chapter describes the patterns of black leadership in the twentieth century, including those which were self-help oriented, those which were protest-rooted and those which were a combination of both.

The impact of the author's ability to see things from new and unaccustomed angles is heightened by his literary competence. A freshness of approach is combined with a vigor and clarity of expression. Coombs has a flowing, narrative style which is particularly suited to a topic of such broad sweep and contour as this one.

Coombs does not exercise his literary skills at the expense of his judgment. He prefaces his work with a quotation from the great nineteenth century protest figure, Frederick Douglass, and doubtless he prefers a black militant to a black moderate or compromiser. Coombs does not shy away from the unpleasant, and some of his realistic passages may have a chilling effect on new readers in the black experience. But Coombs is first, foremost and always a careful chronicler, portraying man's confusion and terror no less than his courage and his compassion. History as a discipline, no less than history as a Muse, is safe in his sure hands.

BENJAMIN QUARLES

PART ONE

From Freedom to Slavery

CHAPTER 1

African Origins

The Human Cradle

THREE and a half centuries of immigration have injected ever-fresh doses of energy and tension into the American bloodstream. As diverse peoples learned to live together, they became a dynamo generating both creativity and conflict.

One of the most diverse elements in American life was introduced when Africans were forcibly brought to the American colonies. The American experiment had begun and consisted mainly of white men with a European heritage. The African was of a different color, had a different language, a different religion, and had an entirely different world view. But perhaps the most striking contrast was that, while the European came voluntarily in search of greater individual opportunity, the African came in chains. Because the European was the master and thereby the superior in the relationship, he assumed that his heritage was also superior. However, he was mistaken, because the African had a rich heritage of importance both to himself and to mankind. When people interact intimately over a long period of time, the influences are reciprocal. This is true even when their relationship is that of master and slave.

To trace the importance of the African heritage one must go back millions of years. Evidence is accumulating to the effect that Africa is the cradle of mankind. Professor Louis Leakey [1] argues that Africa was important in the development of mankind in three ways. First, some thirty or forty million years ago, the basic stock which eventually gave rise to both man and the ape came into existence in the vicinity of the Nile Valley. Second, some twelve or fourteen million years ago, the main branch which was to lead to the development of man broke away from the line leading to the ape. Third, about two million years ago, in the vicinity of East Africa, true man broke away from his now extinct manlike cousins.

The present species of man—Homo Sapiens—developed through a complex process of natural selection from a large number of different manlike creatures—hominids.

One of the most numerous of the early hominids was Australopithecus Africanus who originated in Africa. Although he also did some hunting, he lived mainly by collecting and eating vegetables. One of the things that identified him as a man was his utilization of primitive tools. He had a pointed stone which may have been used to sharpen sticks, and these sticks were probably used for digging roots to augment his food supply. Leakey believes that Homo Habilis, who lived in East Africa about two million years ago, was the immediate ancestor of man and the most advanced of all the hominids. Although the hominids spread far outside of Africa, it is clear that they originated there and that it was in Africa that true man first emerged. As Darwin predicted a century ago, Africa has been found to be the father of mankind.

For many thousands of years, Homo Sapiens and the other hominids lived side by side in Africa as elsewhere. By ten thousand years ago, however, all the hominids had disappeared. Scholars believe that this was the result of the gradual absorption of all the other hominids by the more biologically advanced Homo Sapiens. This process may explain the appearance of variations within Homo Sapiens. At various times and places, as Homo Sapiens absorbed other hominid strains, differences within Homo Sapiens developed. In any case it is clear that the various types of man came into existence very early. In Africa, this process led to the development of three main types: the brownish-yellow Bushmen in the south, the darker Negroes throughout most of the continent and the Caucasoid Mediterranean types in the north.[2]

Most of the concepts, held even by scholars about the nature and origin of races, are being proven inaccurate. Anthropological literature used to suggest that skin color in some groups was a possible indication of Mongoloid influences or that the thin, straight lips common in another group could be envisioned as a Caucasoid feature. However, it has become increasingly obvious that an analysis based on specific single traits such as these is always a poor indication of either racial origin or of racial contact. In fact, they could just as likely be the result of spontaneous and local variations within a given population grouping. In contrast, recent anthropological research is putting less emphasis on bone measurement and shape and, instead, is turning increasingly to genetic analysis particularly through the examination of blood types.[3]

Making and using tools are what differentiate man from animals. The earliest tools which have survived the wear of time were made of stone. As man's techniques of handling stone improved, so did his tools. The hand axe, a large oval of chipped flint varying in size and weight, came into common usage about half a million years ago, and it has been found in much of Europe, Asia, and Africa. This too seems to have had an African origin. While scholars are not certain about its use, it was probably used for skinning animals and for chopping meat.[4]

The first achievement which radically altered man's condition was the invention of tools. The second achievement was his learning of primitive agriculture which transformed the hunter into the farmer. The domestication of animals and the planting and cultivating of crops had begun in the Near East, but the practice shortly spread to the Nile Valley in Northeast Africa. At the same time, farming communities sprang up throughout the Sahara which, at that time, was going through one of its wet phases.[5] This made it well-suited to early agriculture. Farming permitted men to live together in communities and to pursue a more sedentary way of life. Actually, some Africans had already adopted sedentary community life before the arrival of farming. Making hooks from bones led to the development of a few fishing communities near present-day Kenya.

As the communities along the Nile grew in size and number, they began to develop a complex urban civilization. By 3200 B.C., the communities along the Nile had become politically united under the first of a line of great pharaohs. These early Egyptians undoubtedly were comprised of a racial mixture. The ancient Greeks viewed the Egyptians as being dark in complexion, and it has been estimated that the Egyptian population at the beginning was at least one-third Negro. Herodotus says that it was impossible to tell whether the influence of the Egyptians on the Ethiopians was stronger than that of the Ethiopians on the Egyptians.

What Herodotus and the Greeks referred to as Ethiopia was, in fact, the kingdom of Kush. It was located up the Nile from Egypt. As the Egyptian empire grew in strength and wealth, it strove to expand its power over its neighbors. Egypt sent several military expeditions south along the Nile to try to conquer the black people of Kush. They failed and the Kushites, in turn, endeavored to extend their power over Egypt. In 751 B.C., Kush invaded Egypt and, shortly thereafter, conquered it. This occupation of Egypt lasted for over a hundred years, until both the Kushites and the Egyptians were defeated by an invading army from Assyria in 666 B.C. At that point, the Kushites returned to the safety of their homeland.[6]

The Kushites and the Egyptians had been defeated by a superior technology. While they were fighting with weapons made of copper and bronze, the Assyrians fought with iron. Methods of smelting and working iron had been developed centuries before by the Hittites who lived in Asia Minor. The use of iron spread across the Near East, becoming the basis for the Assyrian power. After their defeat in 666 B.C., the Kushites and the Egyptians rapidly adopted the new iron technology. The coming of the Iron Age to Africa meant the production of better weapons and tools. Better weapons provided safety from hostile foes and protection from ferocious beasts. Better axes meant that man could live in densely forested regions where he had not been able to live before. Better farm implements meant that more food could be grown with less work, this again encouraging the development of denser population centers.

By 300 B.C., Kush had become an important iron-producing center. Its capital, Meroé, located on the upper Nile, developed into a thriving commercial and industrial city. Archeological diggings have unearthed the remains of streets, houses, sprawling palaces, and huge piles of slag left from its iron industry. When scholars are able to decipher the Kushitic writings much more will be known about the culture and way of life of this early black empire. In the first century A.D. a Kushite official, whom the Bible refers to as the Ethiopian eunuch, was converted to Christianity by the apostle Philip while returning from a visit to Jerusalem. Shortly, Christianity spread throughout the entire kingdom. When Kush was defeated by the Axumites, founders of modern Ethiopia, several smaller Nubian, Christian kingdoms survived. Not until the sixteenth century, after almost a thousand years of pressure, did Islam gain supremacy in western Sudan. Ethiopia, shortly after defeating Kush, also became Christianized, and survived as a

Christian island in a Moslem sea. In fact, Ethiopia has remained an independent, self-governing state until the present, with the brief exception of the Italian occupation between 1936 and 1941.[7]

The development of man and civilization in Africa was not limited merely to the area in the Northeast. There is much evidence of cultural contact between people in all parts of the continent. When the Sahara began to dry out about 2000 B.C., the population was pushed out from there in all directions, thereby forcing the spread of both people and cultures. Even then, the Sahara did not become a block to communication as has been thought. There is clear evidence that trade routes continued to be used even after the Sahara became a desert. Scholars also have found that, shortly after the Iron Age reached North Africa, iron tools began to appear throughout the entire continent, and, within a few centuries, iron production was being carried on at a number of different locations. At about the same time, sailors from the Far East brought the yam and the banana to the shores of Africa. These fruits spread rapidly from the east coast across most of the continent, becoming basic staples in the African diet. New tools and new crops rapidly expanded the food supply and thereby provided a better way of life.

West African Empires

Although West Africa had been inhabited since the earliest times, about two thousand years ago several events occurred which injected new vigor into the area. The first event had been the drying of the Sahara, which had driven new immigrants into West Africa and, from the admixture of these new people with the previous inhabitants, a new vitality developed. Then, the introduction of the yam and the banana, as previously noted, significantly increased the food supply. Finally, the developments of iron tools and of iron work further increased the food supply and also provided better weapons. This permitted increased military power and political expansion. These were the necessary ingredients that led to the building of three large and powerful empires: Ghana, Mali, and Songhay. Commerce was another factor which contributed to their development. Governmental control of a thriving trade in both gold and salt provided the wealth and power necessary for establishing these large empires.[8]

Unfortunately, our knowledge about West Africa's early history

VERNON REGIONAL
JUNIOR COLLEGE LIBRARY

is severely limited by the lack of written records from that period. In recent years, archeologists have been unearthing increasing amounts of material which contribute to our knowledge of early Africa. West Africans tended to build their cities from nondurable materials such as wood, mud, and grass. The area does have a rich oral tradition, including special groups of trained men dedicated to its development and maintenance. As oral history is always open to modification and embellishment, with no means available for checking the original version, this material must be used cautiously. Nevertheless, when employed in conjunction with other sources, it does provide a rich source of information.

The earliest written records were provided by the Arabs who developed close contact with West Africa by 800 A.D. After that, West Africans began using Arabic themselves to record their own history. In the middle of the fifteenth century, Europeans began regular contact with West Africa, and they left a wide variety of written sources. While most of these early Europeans were not men of learning, many of their records are still valuable to the student of history.

Ghana was already a powerful empire, with a highly complex political and social organization, when the Arabs reached it about 800 A.D. An Arabic map of 830 A.D. has Ghana marked on it, and other contemporary Arabic sources refer to Ghana as the land of gold. From this time on, a thriving trade developed between Ghana and the world of Islam, including the beginnings of a slave trade. However, this early slave trade was a two-way affair. Al-Bakri, a contemporary Arab writer, was impressed with the display of power and affluence of the Ghanaian king. According to him, the king had an army of two hundred thousand warriors which included about forty thousand men with bows and arrows. (Modern scholars know that the real power of the Ghanaian army was due not to its large numbers as much as to its iron-pointed spears.) Al-Bakri also described an official audience at the royal palace in which the king, the Ghana, was surrounded by lavish trappings of gold and silver and was attended by many pages, servants, large numbers of faithful officials, provincial rulers, and mayors of cities. On such occasions, the king heard the grievances of his people and passed judgment on them. Al-Bakri also describes lavish royal banquets which included a great deal of ceremonial ritual.[9]

The power of the king, and therefore of the empire, was based on his ability to maintain law and order in his kingdom. This permitted the development of a flourishing commerce, and it was by taxing all imports and exports that the king was able to finance his government. The key item in this financial structure was the regulation of the vast gold resources of West Africa, and it was by controlling its availability that the king was also able to manipulate its value. However, after the eleventh century, the Ghanaian empire was continually exposed to harassment from a long series of Arabic holy wars. Over a long period of time, the power of the king was reduced until the empire of Ghana finally collapsed. From its ashes emerged the basis for the creation of a new and even larger empire: the empire of Mali.[10]

Mali, like Ghana, was built on gold. While Ghana had been under attack by the Arabs from outside, various peoples from within struck for their own freedom. The Mandinka people, who had been the middlemen in the gold trade and who had received protection from the king of Ghana, achieved their independence in 1230 A.D. They went on to use their position in the gold trade to build an empire of their own. The peak of their affluence and power was achieved in the early fourteenth century under *Mansa* Kankan Musa who ruled Mali for a quarter of a century. He extended its boundaries beyond those of Ghana to include such important trading cities as Timbuktu and Gao, encompassing an area larger than that controlled by the European monarchs of that day. This empire also was based on its ability to provide stable government and a flourishing economy. An Arab traveler, Ibn Batuta, shortly after Musa's death, found complete safety of travel throughout the entire empire of Mali.[11]

Mansa Musa and, for that matter, the entire ruling class of Mali had converted to Islam. This intensified the contacts between West Africa and the Islamic world. Although several of these kings made pilgrimages to Mecca, the most spectacular was the one by *Mansa* Musa in 1324. On his way there, he made a prolonged visit to Cairo. While there, both his generosity in giving lavish gifts of gold to its citizens and his extravagant spending poured so much gold into the Cairo market that it caused a general inflation. It was estimated by the Arabs that his caravan included some sixty thousand people and some five hundred personal slaves. *Mansa* Musa took a number of Arabic scholars and skilled artisans back to West Africa with him. These scholars enhanced the university of Timbuktu which was already widely known as a center of Islamic studies. Now, besides exchanging material goods, West Africa and the Arabs became involved in a steady exchange of scholars and learning.[12]

The success of Mali in bringing law and order to a large portion of West Africa was responsible for its decline. Having experienced the advantages of political organization, many localities sought self-government. In fact, *Mansa* Musa had overextended the empire. A skilled ruler like himself could manipulate it, but those who followed were not adequate to the challenge. Movements for self-government gradually eroded central authority until by 1500 Mali had lost its importance as an empire. Although the period of its power and prosperity was respectable by most world empire standards, it was short-lived compared to the history of the previous empire of Ghana. Again, a new empire was to emerge from the ruins of the previous one.

The Songhay empire was based on the strength of the important trading city of Gao. This city won its independence from Mali as early as 1375, and, within a century, it had developed into an empire. Songhay carried on a vigorous trade with the outside world and particularly with the Arabic countries. The ruling class, in particular, continued to follow the religion of Islam, but it is generally believed that the masses of the population remained faithful to the more traditional West African religions based on fetishism and ancestor worship. Two of the more powerful rulers were Suni Ali, who began his 28-year reign in 1464, and *Askia* Mohammed, who began his 36-year reign in 1493. *Askia* Mohammed was also known as *Askia* the Great. The security of Songhay was undermined when Arabs from Morocco invaded and captured the key trading city of Timbuktu in 1591. Thus ended the last of the three great empires of West Africa.[13]

It would be a mistake, however, to assume that those parts of West Africa which remained outside of these three empires fulfilled the usual European image of primitive savagery. On the contrary, a number of other small yet powerful states existed throughout the entire period. If this had not been so, the Europeans, as they arrived in the fifteenth century, could have pillaged West Africa at will. Instead, the Europeans were only able to establish trading stations where local kings permitted it. With the exception of a few raiding parties which seized Africans and carried them off as slaves, most slave acquisition was done through a hard bargaining and highly systematized trading process. The Europeans were never allowed to penetrate inland, and they found that they always had to treat the African kings and their agents as business equals. Many of the early European visitors, in fact, were impressed by the luxury, power, trading practices, skilled crafts, and the complex social structure which they found in Africa. Only in some parts of East Africa, where the states were unusually small, were the Portuguese able to pillage and conquer at will. While many Europeans may have thought of Africa as being filled with ignorant savages, those who reached its shores were impressed instead with its vigorous civilization.

The Culture of West Africa

An African should not have to find it necessary to make apologies for his civilization. However, Europeans and Americans have come to believe, at least in their subconscious minds, that civilization can be equated with progress in science and technology. Because the Africans lagged far behind the Europeans in the arts of war and of economic exploitation, the Europeans believed that the Africans must be uncivilized savages. Africa, like the rest of the world outside Europe, had not made the breakthrough in science, technology, and capitalism which had occurred in Europe. Nevertheless, they had their own systems of economics, scholarship, art, and religion as well as a highly complex social and political structure. There are common elements which run throughout the entire continent of Africa, but to gain the best insight into the background of the American slaves, West African culture can be isolated and studied by itself.

The West African economy was a subsistence economy, and therefore people were basically satisfied with the status quo and saw no point in accumulating wealth. Also in a subsistence economy, there is little need for money, and most trade was done through barter. Because there was no money, there was no wage labor. Instead, labor was created either through a system of domestic slavery or through a complex system of reciprocal duties and obligations. However, West African slavery was more like the European system of serfdom than it was like modern slavery.[14]

Within this subsistence economy, each tribe or locality tended to specialize in certain fields of agriculture or manufacture which necessitated a vigorous and constant trade between all of them. However, within the trading centers, money had come into regular use. It usually took the form of cowrie shells, iron bars, brass rings, or other standard items of value. Systems of banking and credit had also been developed, but even those involved in money, banking, and trade had a noncapitalist attitude towards wealth. They enjoyed luxury and the display of affluence, but they had no concept of investing capital to increase overall production.

West Africa also carried on a vigorous trade with the outside world. When the Europeans arrived, they discovered, as had the Arabs before them, that the West Africans could strike a hard bargain. They had developed their own systems of weights and measures and insisted on using them. Europeans who failed to treat the king or his agent fairly, found that the Africans simply refused to deal with them again. Trade was always monopolized by the king, and he appointed specific merchants to deal with foreign businessmen. As previously noted, it was by the control and taxation of commerce that the king financed his government and maintained his power.[15]

The strengths and weaknesses of the West African economy can be seen by a cursory glance at a list of its main exports and imports. West African exports included gold, ivory, hides, leather goods, cotton, peppercorn, olive oil, and cola. While some of these items were only exported for short distances, others found their way over long distances. West African gold, for example, was exported as far away as Asia and Northern Europe. Some English coins of the period were minted with West African gold. West African imports included silks from Asia, swords, knives, kitchenware, and trinkets from the primitive industrial factories of Europe as well as horses and other items from Arabia. Two other items of trade became all important for the future—the exportation of slaves and the importation of guns and gunpowder.

West African manufacturing demonstrated a considerable amount of skill in a wide variety of crafts. These included basket-weaving, pottery making, woodworking and iron-working. Archeological evidence shows that West Africans were making pottery and terra-cotta sculpture as much as two thousand years ago. Three-dimensional forms seem to have held a particular interest for West African artists. During the last century, art critics have gone beyond considering this art as "primitive" and have begun to appreciate its esthetic qualities. In fact, in recent years, African art has had considerable influence on contemporary artists.[16]

The two forms of African art best known outside Africa are music and the dance. African music contrasts with European music in its use of a different scale and in concentrating less on melodic development and more on the creation of complex and subtle rhythmic patterns. Musicians used to view African music as simple and undeveloped, but now musicologists admit that African rhythms are more complex and highly developed than rhythms in European music. Africans like to sing and to develop songs for all occasions: religious songs, work songs, and songs for pleasure. African singing is also marked by the frequent use of a leader and a chorus response technique. African dance, like its music, builds on highly complex rhythmic patterns. It too is closely related to all parts of the African's daily life. There are dances for social and for ritual occasions. The most common use of the dance was as an integral part of African religious rites.

African religion has usually been defined as fetish worship—the belief that specific inanimate objects are inhabited by spirits or endowed with magical powers. While this view of African religion is partly true, it obscures more than it clarifies. The fetish was believed to have some powers of its own, but, in general, it derived them from its close association with a dead ancestor. Behind the fetish was the religion of ancestor worship, and the fetish is better understood as a religious symbol. Ancestor worship was also part of the African's strong family ties and his powerful kinship patterns. Behind the realm of this fetish and ancestor worship lay another world of distant and powerful deities who had control over the elemental natural forces of the universe. While this religion might be described as primitive, it cannot be viewed as simplistic. It involved a series of complex ideas about fetishes, ancestors, and deities which required a high degree of intelligence.[17]

The intricacies of theology, law, medicine, and politics made it necessary to develop a complex system of oral education. Europeans, who tended to identify knowledge with writing, had long assumed that, because there was no written language in early Africa, there could be no body of knowledge. After the arrival of

Islam, Arabic provided a written form within which West African ideas could be set down.

Only recently have scholars become aware of the libraries and the many publications to be found in West Africa. Two of these books were responsible for providing historians with detailed information about the customs and social structure of the area. One was the *Tarikh al-Fattish*, the chronicle of the seeker after knowledge, written by Mahmud Kati in the early fifteenth century. The other was the *Tarikh al-Sudan*, the chronicle of the Western Sudan, written by Abd al-Rahman as-Sadi about the beginning of the seventeenth century.[18]

The society of West Africa was stratified in several different ways. It was divided in terms of differing occupations: farmers, merchants, priests, scholars, laborers, and a wide variety of craftsmen. The social ranking assigned to these occupation divisions varied according to the importance of each occupation.

Society was also divided in terms of clans, families, and villages. At the same time, there was a hierarchical division based on the varying degrees of political power each group exercised within its society. Some had the power to become chiefs and rulers. Some had the right to choose and depose rulers, and others could limit and define the rights of the rulers. However, almost everywhere there was a clear trend toward increasing centralized authority and decreasing popular participation. The centralization of power in West Africa never reached the extremes of absolute monarchy which occurred in Europe, and there was never the same need for revolutionary social changes to revive democratic participation within African society.

In an old Asante ritual, connected with the enthronement of a ruler, the people pray that their ruler should not be greedy, should not be hard of hearing, should not act on his own initiative nor perpetuate personal abuse nor commit violence on his people. While the right to rule was generally passed on from generation to generation within a single family, the power did not immediately and automatically fall on the eldest son within that family. Instead, another family had the power to select the next ruler from among a large number of potential candidates within the ruling family. If the ruler who was selected ruled unwisely and unfairly, he could also be deposed. Here was a distinct limitation on royal absolutism.[19]

In a similar way, there were limitations on the centralization of economic power. While valuable land in Europe had been captured and controlled by private ownership and was the possession of a powerful minority, land in West Africa still belonged to the community. A powerful family had the right to control and supervise the use of the land for the welfare of the community, and, undoubtedly, this power could be misused.[20] Such a family assigned land to its users along with certain tenure safeguards which operated to limit even the power of the family. Those using the land who did not fulfill their obligations to the community by utilizing it properly and wisely, could have the land taken away from them. It might then be given to someone else. Both in economics and in politics, historical custom and precedent has limited minority power and has protected the welfare of the community. Nevertheless, community power and wealth has tended to be divided into two major divisions: the rich and powerful few and the poor and powerless majority. Though the elite ruled and the masses served, rights and obligations which limited the amount of exploitation were always in existence.

One of the signs of the trend toward the increasing centralization of power within the society of West Africa was the development of a professional army. The gigantic armies of Ghana had been conscripted from the common citizenry. As the ruling class in West Africa adopted Islam and as its desire to increase its power continued to undermine local tradition and custom, there was more need for a professional army which would owe its total allegiance to the ruler.

Also, changes in military technology required a skilled and carefully trained army. Horses were expensive and could only be used efficiently by men who were expert riders and who knew how to use a horse in a combat situation. Even more, with the arrival of the Europeans in the fifteenth century, West Africa was introduced to guns and gunpowder. These, too, were expensive and required trained soldiery to make good use of them. While the new military technology had increased the ruler's freedom from popular control, it made him increasingly dependent on and subservient to European interests. The African ruler's desire for guns and the European's desire for slaves went hand in hand.

CHAPTER 2

The Human Market

The Slave Trade

NEITHER slavery nor the slave trade came to West Africa with the arrival of the Portuguese in the middle of the fifteenth century. To the contrary, both institutions had a very long history. A two-way slave trade had existed between the West Africans and the Arabs for centuries. In view of the social structure of both societies, sociologists believe that the Arabs could make use of more slaves than could the West Africans. Therefore, West Africa probably exported more slaves than it imported.

Slaves, besides being common laborers, were often men of considerable skill and learning. Slavery was not a badge of human inferiority. Thus, the first slaves procured by the Europeans from Africa were displayed as curiosities and as proof of affluence. While, especially at the beginning, some slaves were taken by force, most of the African slaves acquired by the Europeans were obtained in the course of a peaceful and regular bargaining process.[1]

When the Portuguese arrived in West Africa, they found a thriving economy which had already developed its own bustling trading centers. Before long, a vigorous trade opened up between the Portuguese and the West Africans. Slaves were only one of a great variety of exports, and guns were only one of a large variety of imports. One of the ways in which the slave trade came to cripple the West African economy was that slaves became almost the exclusive African export. The more the Africans sought to fulfill the Europeans' thirst for slaves, the more they needed guns with which to procure slaves, and to protect themselves from being captured and sold into slavery. Therefore, the Euro-African trade, instead of further stimulating the African economy, actually limited production of many items and drained it of much of its most productive manpower.

The rulers, who had voluntarily and unwittingly involved them-selves in this gigantic trade, soon found themselves trapped. Those who wanted to eliminate or reduce the trade in slaves and who preferred to develop other aspects of a trading economy, found themselves helpless. A ruler who would not provide the Euro-peans with the slaves they desired was then bypassed by all the European traders. Besides losing the revenue from this trade, his own military position was weakened. Any ruler who did not trade slaves for guns could not have guns. Without guns, he would have difficulty in protecting himself and his people. Any ruler or people who could not provide adequate self-defense could be captured and sold into slavery. Once begun, the Africans found themselves enmeshed in a vicious system from which there seemed to be no escape. The only possibility for escape would have been the de-velopment of some kind of African coalition, but each petty ruler was too concerned with his own power to be able to contemplate a federated activity. European greed fed African greed, and vice versa.

In the beginning, African slaves were carried back to Portugal and other parts of Europe to be used as exotic domestic servants. In some cases, they were also used as farm laborers. Parts of Portugal were suffering from a distinct shortage of farm laborers, and Africans filled the void. At the beginning of the sixteenth century, in some sections of rural Portugal as much as one third of the local population was African in origin.[2]

Even so, European labor needs could not support much of a slave trade for long. The enclosure system was under way, chang-ing farming techniques, and it had created a labor surplus. How-ever, at the same time, emerging capitalism financed explorations of Africa, Asia, and the western hemisphere. African sailors were involved in most of these explorations including Columbus's voy-age in 1492. New World gold provided the economic basis for even more rapid European expansion. When the New World came to be viewed by the hungry capitalists as having a potential for agricultural exploitation, New World labor needs expanded astro-nomically. At first these needs were filled by surplus labor from Europe or by exploiting the local Indian populations. When these labor sources proved to be inadequate, the exploitation of slave labor from Africa was the obvious answer.

While the Portuguese were the first to reach the shores of West

Africa and the first to bring African slaves back to Europe, neither they nor the Spaniards ever dominated the slave trade which followed. In 1493, as European exploration of the world moved into high gear, the Pope published a Bull dividing the world yet to be explored into two parts. His intention was to limit competition and conflict between the rulers of Spain and Portugal and to prevent undue hostility between his two main supporters.

However, this left the other European powers, officially, with no room for overseas expansion. While these powers refused to acknowledge the legality of the Bull and soon became involved in exploration and colonization in spite of it, they also tended to become more involved than did Portugal or Spain in some of the by-products of colonization, such as the slave trade. When the Spaniards began to use slaves in their American colonies, the Dutch, French, and British were only too eager to provide the transportation. Before long, they too had colonies and slaves of their own.

The triangular trade between Europe, Africa, and the New World, was one of the most lucrative aspects of the mercantile economy. Mercantilism sought to keep each country economically self-sufficient. Within this framework the role of the colony was to provide the mother country with raw materials which it could not produce for itself and to be a market for the consumption of many of the manufactured goods produced within the mother country.

This triangular trade began in Europe with the purchase of guns, gunpowder, cheap cotton, and trinkets of all kinds. These were shipped to the coast of West Africa and unloaded at a trading station. At key points along the coast, the European nations had made treaties with the local rulers allowing them to set up trading stations and slave factories. At this point, the European traders entered into hard bargaining sessions with the representatives of the local ruler in which the manufactured goods from Europe, especially guns, were traded for African slaves. When the deal was completed, the slaves were loaded on the ship, and the captain set sail for the New World.

Upon arrival in the West Indies, another bargaining process was begun. Here the slaves were traded for local agricultural products which were wanted in Europe. Then the ships were loaded with tobacco, sugar, and other West Indian produce and returned to Europe for still another sale and another profit. At every point along the route, large sums of money were made. A profit of at least one hundred percent was expected. Vast wealth was obtained through the slave trade, and this money was reinvested in the developing industrial revolution. Thereby the Africans unwittingly helped to finance the European industrial revolution which widened the technological gap between Africa and Europe.[3]

The African slave was sometimes a criminal, but, more often than not, he was captured in battle. As the slave trade grew and with it the need for more slaves, the number of these battles increased. Clearly, many battles were being fought solely for the purpose of acquiring slaves who could then be sold to the European traders. Sometimes, too, the slave might have been the political enemy of the ruler or of some other powerful person.

The slaves were then marched to trading stations along the coast where a European agent, who resided at the station, inspected them and negotiated their purchase. The inspection was a humiliating and degrading procedure. Men, women, and children usually appeared stark naked and underwent the close scrutiny of the agent and sometimes a physician. After the trauma of capture and the shame of inspection, the slaves were regimented into crowded quarters at the trading station or "factory" to wait for the next shipment to leave. They had to be supervised very closely as many tried to escape and others tried to commit suicide.

When a ship was ready to sail, the slaves were chained together and marched down to the shore. There they were bundled into large canoes and were paddled through the crashing breakers to where the slave ship was waiting. Slaves have told how they began the voyage in trepidation, being frightened by the sight of the "white devils" who, they had heard, liked to eat Africans. Then, the long voyage commenced. Conditions here were even more crowded than at the "factory." Slaves were generally kept below deck with no sunshine or fresh air. They were crowded so close together that there was never any standing room and often not even sitting room. Again, they had to be supervised closely as many tried to starve themselves to death or to jump overboard. However, the greatest loss of slave property was due to disease. The ship's captain feared that disease would whittle away his profits, and, even more, he worried that it would attack him and his crew. When the passage was completed, and the West Indies had been safely reached, the slave again had to undergo the same kind of degrading inspection and sale which had occurred in Africa, but this time he had to experience the torment in a strange and distant land.

While the economic profits in the slave trade were great, so were the human losses. Statistics concerning the slave trade are often inaccurate or missing. However, it is generally agreed that at least fifteen million Africans, and perhaps many more, became slaves in the New World.[4] About nine hundred thousand were brought in the sixteenth century, three million in the seventeenth century, seven million in the eighteenth century, and another four million in the nineteenth century.

The mortality rate among these new slaves ran very high. It is estimated that some five percent died in Africa on the way to the coast, another thirteen percent in transit to the West Indies, and still another thirty percent during the three-month seasoning period in the West Indies.[5] This meant that about fifty percent of those originally captured in Africa died either in transit or while being prepared for servitude.

Even this statistic, harsh as it is, does not tell the whole story of the human cost involved in the slave trade. Most slaves were captured in the course of warfare, and many more Africans were killed in the course of this combat. The total number of deaths, then, ran much higher than those killed en route. Many Africans became casualty statistics, directly or indirectly, because of the slave trade. Beyond this, there was the untold human sorrow and misery borne by the friends and relatives of those Africans who were torn away from home and loved ones and were never seen again.

Statistics concerning profits in the slave trade are also difficult to obtain. Profits often ran as high as two or three hundred percent, and were an important part of the European economy. These profits provided much of the capital which helped to spur on the industrial revolution.[6] When Queen Elizabeth, in 1562, heard that one of her subjects, John Hawkins, had become involved in the slave trade, she was very critical and commented that he would have to pay a very high price for dealing in human lives. However, when she was confronted with a copy of his profit ledger, her moral indignation softened, and she quickly became one of the members of the corporation. Some merchants were hit hard by the risks accompanying the slave trade and suffered financial disaster. The possible profits were so high, however, that other merchants were always eager to venture into this field and new capital was never lacking.

The industrial revolution, which was partly financed by the slave trade, eventually abolished the need for slavery. The humanitarian outcry against both the slave trade and slavery which occurred at the end of the eighteenth century and swelled in the early nineteenth century, became a significant force as the need for slave labor diminished. In the beginning, as previously noted, the Europeans were not powerful enough to seize slaves at will nor to invade the African kingdoms. But the industrial revolution had immeasurably widened the power gap between Europe and Africa. By the time the slave trade ended, and European adventures had found new ways to achieve gigantic capital gains, Europe had achieved a power advantage sufficient to invade Africa at will.

As European interests in colonizing Africa increased, the European powers, at the middle of the nineteenth century, were almost tearing one another apart in the process of this competitive expansion. In order to avoid further misfortune, the great powers of Europe met at the conference of Berlin in 1885. Without troubling to consult with any Africans, they drew lines on a map of Africa dividing it among themselves. It took only a very few years for a map drawing to become a physical reality. When the Europeans had finished exploiting Africa through the slave trade and had greatly weakened its societies, they invaded Africa in order to exploit its nonhuman material resources.

Caribbean Interlude

Most of the Africans, who were enslaved and brought to the New World, came to the American colonies after a period of seasoning in the Caribbean islands. To the Europeans who had settled in America the Colonies were their new home and they strove to develop a prosperous and secure society in which to live and raise their families. They hesitated to bring their slaves directly from Africa as they believed that Africans were brutal, barbaric savages who would present a real danger to the safety and security of their new homes. Instead, they preferred to purchase slaves who had already been tested and broken.

In contrast to this, Europeans who had gone to the Caribbean islands did not consider the New World as their new home. The island plantations were to be exploited to provide the wealth with which their owners could return to Europe and live like gentlemen. Many of them did not bring their families to the islands, or, when they did, their stay was a temporary one. Therefore, they were more willing than were the Americans to purchase slaves directly from Africa. Moreover, because their sole interest in the islands was economic profit, they could make a double profit by selling their seasoned slaves as well as selling their plantation produce. While the Africans' stay in the Caribbean, obviously, was not part of their African heritage, it was part of the experience which they brought with them to the Colonies. Many of the events which occurred in the Caribbean islands had important repercussions in the American Colonies.[7]

A quarter of a century after Columbus had discovered the New World, the first African slaves were brought to the West Indies to supplement the inadequate labor supply. The Indians who lived on the islands were few in number and had had no experience in plantation agriculture. As the shortage of labor became severe, the plantation owners began to import criminals and were willing to accept the poor and the drunks who had been seized from the streets of European ports.

There was also a continual stream of indentured servants, but this influx was nowhere nearly large enough to fill the growing labor demands. The advantage of African slaves over indentured servants was that they could be purchased outright for life. Moreover, the Africans had no contacts in the European capitals through which they could bring pressure to bear against the abuses of the plantation masters. In fact, African slaves really had no rights which the master was obliged to respect. The supply of African labor seemed to be endless, and many masters found it cheaper to overwork a slave and to replace him when he died, rather than take care of him while he lived. In short, the plantation experience was a brutalizing one.

In the beginning, the major plantation crop had been tobacco. It could be grown efficiently on small plantations of twenty or thirty acres. The tobacco plant needed constant, careful attention throughout the season, and this meant that the number of raw, unskilled laborers that was needed was relatively small.

However, when the new colony of Virginia entered the tobacco field in the early seventeenth century, it was able to produce larger quantities of tobacco at a lower price. The Caribbean islands were hit by a severe economic depression. The Dutch came up with a solution. They had previously conquered parts of northern Brazil from the Portuguese, and there they had learned the techniques of plantation sugar production. It could only be carried on efficiently with plantations of two or three hundred acres, and it required large numbers of unskilled laborers both to plant and harvest the crop and to refine the sugar. The Dutch, then, brought sugar cane to the West Indies. This gave them a new plantation crop, and it also gave them a new outlet for the slave trade which, at that point in history, they had come to dominate.

The development of the sugar cane economy in the West Indies produced a basic social revolution. The small tobacco farmers did not have the capital to develop the large sugar plantations. Some of them went into other occupations, but most of them returned to Europe. The new labor needs were filled by a gigantic increase in the importation of African slaves. The ratio of whites to blacks within the islands changed markedly within a matter of one or two decades. The white population consisted of a handful of exceedingly wealthy plantation owners and another handful of white plantation managers. Many of the slaves soon learned new skills associated with sugar manufacturing, thus reducing the need for white labor even further. The rising demand for slaves meant an expansion of the slave trade, and, as West Indian slaves had a high mortality rate and a low birthrate, this meant a continually thriving slave trade.[8]

As the ratio between whites and blacks widened, the problem of controlling the slaves grew more serious. Brute force was the only answer. The European governments had tried to solve the problem by requiring the plantation owners to hire a specified number of white workers. However, many owners found it cheaper to pay the fine than to comply with this regulation.

In 1667, the British Parliament passed a series of black codes intended to control the slaves in the Caribbean colonies. Other colonial powers followed their example. The law stated that a slave could not be away from the plantation on a Sunday and that he was not permitted to carry any weapons. It also specified that, if he were to strike a Christian, he could be whipped. If he did it a second time, he could be branded on the face. However, if a master, in the process of punishing a slave, accidentally beat him to death, this master could not be fined or imprisoned.[9]

Because the Europeans did not view the islands as their home, there was always a shortage of white women. One of the results of this was the development of an ever-growing class of mulattoes. More and more of them were granted their freedom. While these freedmen did not receive equal treatment with the whites, they were careful to preserve the advantages they held over the slaves. Many of them served in the militia to help keep the slaves under control. However, the threat of slave revolts continued. The greater the possibility of success, the greater the probability that slaves would take the risk of starting a revolt. All of the islands in the West Indies had a history of slave rebellion.

Undoubtedly, the most outstanding slave revolt in the western hemisphere took place in Haiti. During the French revolution, concepts of the rights of man spread from France to her colonies. In Haiti, the free mulattoes petitioned the French revolutionary government for their rights. The Assembly granted their request. However, the French aristocrats in Haiti refused to follow the directives of the Assembly. At this point, two free mulattoes, Vincent Ogé and Jean Baptiste Chavannes, both of whom had received an education in Paris, led a mulatto rebellion. The Haitian aristocrats quickly and brutally suppressed it.

By this time, however, the concepts of the rights of man had spread to the slave class. In 1791, under the leadership of Toussaint l'Ouverture,[10] the slaves began a long and bloody revolt of their own. Slaves flocked to Toussaint's support by the thousands until he had an army much larger than any that had fought in the American revolution. This revolt became entangled with the French revolution and the European wars connected with it. Besides fighting the French, Toussaint had to face both British and Spanish armies. None of them was able to suppress the revolt and to overthrow the republic which had been established in Haiti.

After Napoleon came to power in France, he sent a gigantic expedition under Leclerc to reestablish French authority in Haiti. While he claimed to stand for the principles of the revolution, Napoleon's real interest in Haiti was to make it into a base from which to rebuild a French empire in the western hemisphere. Toussaint lured this French army into the wilderness where the soldiers, who had no immunity to tropical diseases, were hit very hard by malaria and yellow fever.

Toussaint was captured by trickery, but his compatriots carried on the fight for independence. Finally, Napoleon was forced to withdraw from the struggle. One of the results of his failure to suppress the slave revolt in Haiti was his abandonment of his New World dreams and his willingness to sell Louisiana to the United States. Unfortunately, this meant new areas for the expansion of the plantation economy and slavery. In other words, the Haitian revolution was responsible for giving new life to the institution of slavery inside America.

American plantation owners were faced with a dilemma. The Louisiana Purchase, resulting from the revolution in Haiti, greatly expanded the possibilities of plantation agriculture. This meant a greater need for slave labor. However, they were not sure from which source to purchase these slaves. They hesitated to bring raw slaves directly from Africa. They were also loath to bring seasoned slaves from the Caribbean. Events in Haiti had demonstrated that these Caribbean slaves might not be as docile as previously had been believed. Certainly, Americans did not want a repetition of the bloody Haitian revolt within their own borders. Greedy men still bought slaves where they could, but many American slave owners were deeply disturbed and began to give serious thought to terminating the importation of African slaves into America.

CHAPTER 3

Slavery As Capitalism

The Shape of American Slavery

THE slave system in America was unique in human history. Sometimes slaves were treated cruelly; at other times with kindness. They were more often used as a sign of affluence, a way of displaying one's wealth and of enjoying luxury, rather than as the means for the systematic accumulation of wealth. Previously, slavery had existed in hierarchical societies in which the slave was at the bottom of a social ladder, the most inferior in a society of unequals. While each society normally preferred to choose its slaves from alien people, it did not limit its selection exclusively to the members of any one race. Slave inferiority did not lead necessarily to racial inferiority. In contrast to this, slavery in America was set apart by three characteristics: capitalism, individualism, and racism.[1]

Capitalism increased the degree of dehumanization and depersonalization implicit in the institution of slavery. While it had been normal in other forms of slavery for the slave to be legally defined as a thing, a piece of property,[2] in America he also became a form of capital. Here his life was regimented to fill the needs of a highly organized productive system sensitively attuned to the driving forces of competitive free enterprise. American masters were probably no more cruel and no more sadistic than others, and, in fact, the spread of humanitarianism in the modern world may have made the opposite true. Nevertheless, their capitalistic mentality firmly fixed their eyes on minimizing expenses and maximizing profits. Besides being a piece of property, the American slave was transformed into part of the plantation machine, a part of the ever-growing investment in the master's mushrooming wealth.

The development of slavery in America resulted from the working of economic forces and not from climatic or geographic conditions.[3] When the first twenty Africans reached Virginia in 1619, the colony was comprised of small plantations dependent on free white labor. While some historians believe that these immigrants were held in slavery from the beginning,[4] most think they were given the status of indentured servants.[5] English law contained no such category as slavery, and the institution did not receive legal justification in the colony until early in the 1660s. Although the fact of slavery had undoubtedly preceded its legal definition, there was a period of forty years within which the Africans had some room for personal freedom and individual opportunity. Rumors of deplorable working conditions and of indefinite servitude were reaching England and discouraging the flow of free white labor. To counter this, a series of acts were passed which legally established the rights of white labor, but they did nothing to improve the status of the African. In fact, their passage pushed him relentlessly towards the status of slave.[6]

The price of tobacco declined sharply in the 1660s and drove the small white farmer to the wall. Only those with enough capital to engage in large-scale operations could continue to make a profit. In order to fill the need for the huge labor supply required by large-scale agriculture, the colonial legislature passed laws giving legal justification to slavery. At the same time, Charles II granted a royal charter establishing a company to transport African slaves across the ocean and thereby increasing the supply of slaves available to the colonial planter.

Until this time, the number of Africans in the colony had been very small, but thereafter their numbers grew rapidly. The African slaves provided the large, dependable, and permanent supply of labor which these plantations required. The small white planter and the free white laborer found the road to economic success had become much more difficult. To be a successful planter meant that one had to begin with substantial capital investments. Capitalist agriculture substantially altered the social structure of the colony. On one hand, it created a small class of rich and powerful white planters. On the other, it victimized the small white planters, the poor white laborers, and the ever-growing mass of African slaves.[7]

The second unique factor in American slavery was the growth of individualism. While this democratic spirit attracted many European immigrants, it only served to increase the burden of slavery for the African. Instead of being at the bottom of the social ladder, the slave in America was an inferior among equals. A society which represented itself as recognizing individual worth and providing room for the development of talent, rigidly organized the entire life of the slave and gave him little opportunity to develop his skills. In America, a person's worth became identified with economic achievement. To be a success in Virginia was to be a prosperous planter, and white individualism could easily become white oppression leaving no room for black individualism. The existence of slavery in a society which maintained its belief in equality was a contradiction which men strove diligently to ignore.

Perhaps this contradiction can be partly understood by seeing the way in which individual rights had come into being in English society. Instead of springing from a belief in abstract human rights, they were an accumulation of concrete legal and political privileges which had developed since Magna Charta. Viewing it in this light, it may have been easier for the white colonists to insist on their rights while denying them to the slaves. Nevertheless, the existence of slavery in the midst of a society believing in individualism increased its dehumanizing effects.

The third characteristic which set American slavery apart was its racial basis. In America, with only a few early and insignificant exceptions, all slaves were Africans, and almost all Africans were slaves. This placed the label of inferiority on black skin and on African culture. In other societies, it had been possible for a slave who obtained his freedom to take his place in his society with relative ease. In America, however, when a slave became free, he was still obviously an African. The taint of inferiority clung to him.

Not only did white America become convinced of white superiority and black inferiority, but it strove to impose these racial beliefs on the Africans themselves. Slave masters gave a great deal of attention to the education and training of the ideal slave. In general, there were five steps in molding the character of such a slave: strict discipline, a sense of his own inferiority, belief in the master's superior power, acceptance of the master's standards, and, finally, a deep sense of his own helplessness and dependence. At every point this education was built on the belief in white superiority and black inferiority. Besides teaching the slave to despise his own history and culture, the master strove to inculcate his own value system into the African's outlook. The white man's belief in the African's inferiority paralleled African self-hate.[8]

Slavery has always been an evil institution, and being a slave has always been undesirable. However, the slave in America was systematically exploited for the accumulation of wealth. Being a slave in a democracy, he was put outside of the bounds of society. Finally, because his slavery was racially defined, his plight was incurable. Although he might flee from slavery, he could not escape his race.

North American and South American Slavery

Slavery, as it existed in British North America, contained interesting points of comparison and contrast with the slave system operating in Portuguese and Spanish South America. Although both institutions were geared to the needs of capitalistic agriculture, the rights and privileges of the South American planter were restricted and challenged at many points by the traditional powers of the Crown and the Church. On one hand, capitalism, unhampered by other powerful institutions, created a closed slave system which regimented the totality of the slave's life. On the other hand, through the clash of competing institutions, the slave was left with little opportunity in which he could develop as a person.

In the seventeenth century, while the British colonies were being established in North America and their slave system was being created, the English Crown underwent a series of severe shocks including two revolutions. Although it eventually emerged secure, the monarchy managed to survive only by making its peace with the emerging commercial and industrial forces. These same crises undermined the authority of the Church as a powerful institution in society. The nonconformist sects were the stronghold of the merchant class and spread rapidly in the American colonies. There, instead of being a check on the commercial spirit, the Church itself had become dominated by the middle class. Equally important is the fact that in colonial America the level of religious life was very low. Most colonists, with the exception of the original founders who had fled religious persecution, did not come for religious freedom but for economic advancement. When some Virginians, at the end of the seventeenth century, petitioned the government to build a college for the training of ministers, they were told to forget about the cure of souls and, instead, to cure tobacco.[9] The result was that the planter class, unchallenged by any other powerful institutions, was free to shape a slave system to meet its labor needs. In any conflict which arose between personality rights and property rights, the property rights of the master were always protected.

In contrast, the South American planter did not have such a free hand in shaping his own affairs. The Renaissance and Reformation had not made the same impact on Spain and Portugal as they did on the rest of Western Europe. Consequently, secularization and commercialization had not progressed as far in eroding the traditional power and prestige of the Crown and the Church. Although both institutions readily compromised with capitalist interests and strove to develop a working alliance with them, neither the Crown nor the Church in Spain and Portugal had ever been taken over by the commercial interests.

Both Spain and Portugal had had continuous contact with slavery extending back into ancient times. Roman law as well as the Church fathers had concerned themselves with it, and these concepts had been incorporated into Spanish and Portuguese law. Also, slaves continued to exist in both countries down to modern times. Therefore, when Portugal began importing slaves from West Africa in the fifteenth century, the institution of slavery was already in existence. Before long, significant numbers of African slaves were to be found in both Portugal and Spain. When the South American planters began importing slaves, slavery already had a framework and a tradition within which the planter had to operate.[10]

The Spanish Crown devoted a great deal of time and energy to the supervision of its overseas possessions. Instead of permitting considerable local autonomy as the British did, the Spanish Council of the Indies in Madrid assumed a stance of illiberal, paternal, bureaucratic control. From the point of view of the colonial capitalists, the cumbersome royal bureaucracy was always involved in troublesome meddling which impeded their progress. As part of the careful management of its colonies, the Crown strove to control the operation of the slave trade. Similarly, it was concerned with the treatment of the African slaves within the colonies. The Spanish Crown included the slaves among those persons which it ruled instead of relegating them solely to the status of property at the disposal of their owners.[11]

The Church, as a powerful institution, jealously guarded its right to be the guardian and protector of social morality. Besides being concerned with influencing individual behavior, the Church insisted that it was a social institution with the right to interfere in matters relating to public morals. In fact, it was through this role that the Church was able to exercise its worldly powers. While condemning slavery as an evil and warning that it endangered those who participated in it, the Church found it expedient to accept slavery as a labor system. However, it insisted that the African slaves must be Christianized. Missionaries were sent to the trading stations on the African coast where the captives were baptized and catechized. The Church feared that the purity of the faith might be undermined by the infusion of pagan influences. Then, when a slave ship reached the New World, a friar boarded the ship and examined the slaves to see that the requirements had been met. The Church also insisted that the slaves become regular communicants, and it liked to view itself as the champion of their human rights.[12]

The degree to which the individual rights of the slave were either protected or totally suppressed provides a clearer insight into the differences between North American and South American slavery. The laws outlining the rights of slaves have been traditionally placed into four categories: term of servitude, marriage and the family, police and disciplinary powers, and, finally, property and other civil rights.

In both systems the term of servitude was for life, and the child's status was inherited from its mother. Children of slave mothers were slaves, and children of free mothers were free regardless of the status of the father. Inherited lifetime slavery was the norm.

Manumission—granting freedom—was infrequent in British North America. Occasionally, masters who had fathered slave children would later give them their freedom. A few other slaves were able to purchase their own freedom although, strictly speaking, this was a legal impossibility. The slave was not able to own property according to the law, and this meant that the money with which he purchased his freedom had always belonged to his master. Obviously, he could only do this with his master's fullest cooperation.

In South America, however, manumission was much more frequent. This practice received highly favorable social sanction, and masters often celebrated national holidays, anniversaries, birthdays, and other special events by manumitting one or more of their favorite slaves.

The law also defended the right of the slave to purchase his own freedom. He had the right to own property and could accumulate funds with which he might eventually achieve his dream. He also had the right to demand that his master or the courts set a fixed price for his purchase which he could then pay over a period of years. Sundays and holidays were for the slave to use as he saw fit, and, in some cases, he was also guaranteed a couple of hours every day for his own use. During this time he could sell his services and save the proceeds. The law also stated that parents of ten or more children were to be set free. Finally, slaves could be freed by the courts as the result of mistreatment by their masters.[13]

While there was much sentiment in North America supporting marriages among slaves, and there was much animosity against masters who separated families through sale, the law was unambiguous on this point. Slaves were property, and therefore could not enter into contracts including contracts of marriage. Jurists also noted that to prevent the sale of separate members of a family would lower the sale price, and this was to tamper with a man's property. Therefore, property rights had to be placed above marriage rights. In contrast, in South America the Church insisted that slave unions be brought within the sacrament of marriage. The Church also strove to limit promiscuous relationships between slaves as well as between masters and slaves, and it encouraged marriage instead of informal mating. Also, the law forbade the separate sale of members of the family, husband, wife, and children under the age of ten.[14]

The general thrust of the laws outlining police and disciplinary powers in North America was to entrust complete jurisdiction to the master. One judge had laid down the law that the master's power must be absolute in order to render slave obedience perfect, and, although the courts were empowered to discipline slaves in certain situations, the masters generally acted as judges, juries, and dispensers of punishments. In those rare cases where the law did protect the slave against extreme mistreatment, its protection was nullified by the universal proscription against any slave or black person testifying in court against any white. The court also had assumed that it was irrational for a man to destroy his own property, and, therefore, it was impossible for a master to commit premeditated murder against one of his own slaves.

However, in South America the court exercised much more jurisdiction over the slave. Crimes committed by a slave were prosecuted by the court, and, if a slave was murdered, this case was prosecuted by the court as if the victim had been a free man. The law also made a more concerted attempt to protect the slave against mistreatment by his master. A certain type of state lawyer was an official protector of the slaves; he received regular reports on slave conditions from priests as well as from special investigating officials who had been appointed by the state for this purpose. Mistreatment could lead both to the freedom of the slave and to the fining of the master. The law had devised an ingenious system whereby the fine was divided equally between the judge, the informer, and the state treasury.[15]

Finally, the slave in North America could not own property and had absolutely no civil rights. The law clearly stated that he could neither own, inherit, or will property nor engage in buying and selling except at the pleasure of his master. In contrast, the slave in South America could own property, could engage in buying and selling, and was guaranteed Sundays, holidays, and other times in which to work for his own advancement. In short, the law implied that while the master could own a man's labor, he could not own the man as a person.[16]

It is not easy to make a final comparison between these two slave systems. South American masters often evaded the law and could be exceedingly brutal, and North American masters were at times much more lenient than the law required. Conditions of poverty, moreover, were usually more severe in South America, and this fact may have worsened the actual material situation of the South American slave. Nevertheless, in North America the slave was consistently treated as a "thing." In South America there was some attempt to treat him as a man. This fact made a profound difference in the way in which the two systems affected the slave as an individual, and in the way in which they impinged upon the development of his personality.

Slavery and the Formation of Character

The study of American slavery, frequently consisting of a heated debate concerning the institution's merits, has, in recent years, branched into new directions. Scholars have become engaged in the comparative examination of differing slave systems such as those of North and South America. More recently, Stanley M. Elkins has begun an inquiry into the impact of a slave system in forming the individual character of the slaves within that system. In his provocative study, *Slavery: A Problem in American Institutional and Intellectual Life,* he has made some interesting comparisons between the American slave system and the German concentration camps and has endeavored to account for their respective impacts on character formation through the social-psychological theories of personality formation.

In Elkins's thinking, the concentration camps were a modern example of a rigid system controlling mass behavior. Because some of those who experienced them were social scientists trained in the skills of observation and analysis, they provide a basis for insights into the way in which a particular social system can influence mass character. While there is also much literature about American slavery written both by slaves and masters, none of it was written from the viewpoint of modern social sciences. However, Elkins postulates that a slave type must have existed as the result of the attempt to control mass behavior, and he believes that this type probably bore a marked resemblance to the literary stereotype of "Sambo." Studying concentration camps and their impact on personality provides a tool for new insights into the working of slavery, but, warns Elkins, the comparison can only be used for limited purposes. Although slavery was not unlike the concentration camp in many respects, the concentration camp can be viewed as a highly perverted form of slavery, and both systems were ways of controlling mass behavior.[17]

The "Sambo" of American slave literature was portrayed as being docile but irresponsible, loyal but lazy, humble but chronically given to lying and stealing. He was a child figure, often demonstrating infantile silliness and exaggeration, exasperating but lovable and, above all, utterly dependent on and attached to his master. The master explained this behavior as the result of the slave's race or of his primitive African culture.

While assuming that many slaves did approximate the character of "Sambo," Elkins absolutely rejects any racial or cultural explanation. Modern African studies have not led to any evidence of a "Sambo" type in Africa. Similarly, the literature of South America does not contain any figure comparable to him. Apparently, "Sambo" was not merely the result of slavery, but he was the result of the unique form of slavery which developed in North America. Unrestricted in his powers by institutions such as the Crown and the Church, the American slave master had gained total control of his slave property. In a desire to maximize the profits of his investment, he strove to develop the perfect slave. Although the slave might endeavor to conform externally while maintaining his inner integrity, eventually his performance as an ideal slave must have affected the shape of his personality. Modern existentialism has argued that how we behave determines what we are, and it is in this sense that the controlled behavior in the concentration camp and its impact on personality formation provide an illuminating parallel to the study of American slavery.

The experienced gained in the German concentration camps during the Second World War showed that it was possible to induce widespread infantile behavior in masses of adults. Childlike attitudes extended beyond obedience to the guards and showed that a basic character transformation had occurred. Previous social-psychological theory stressed the ways in which an individual's personality was shaped during his earliest childhood years and emphasized the tenacity with which these early traits resisted any attempt at alteration. Personality theory was not achieved in the concentration camps.[18]

The concentration camp experience began with what has become labeled as shock procurement. As terror was one of the primary tools of the system, surprise late-night arrests were the favorite technique. Camp inmates generally agreed that the train ride to the camp was the point at which they experienced the most brutal torture. Herded together into cattle cars, without adequate space, ventilation, or sanitary conditions, they had to endure both horrible crowding and the harassment of the guards. When they reached the camp, they had to stand naked in line and undergo a detailed examination by the camp physician. Then, each was given a tag and a number. These two events were calculated to strip away one's identity and to reduce the individual to an item within an impersonal system.

One's sense of personhood was further undermined by the fact that there was never any privacy. The individual had lost both his identity and his power. Everything was done to him or for him, but nothing was ever done by him. The guards had the power to dispense food, clothing, shelter, punishment, and even death. Prisoners had to request permission to use the sanitary facilities, and permission was not always forthcoming. As the inmates were not sentenced for specified periods of time, they tended to view camp life as having a limitless future.

In a relatively short time, this experience of total dependence developed characteristics of infantile behavior in those prisoners who managed to avoid the extermination chambers. A childish humor and infantile giggling were common. Boasting and lying were widely practiced. Patterns of hero worship emerged, and the guards became the heroes. The prisoners came to accept their values including their German nationalism and anti-Semitism. Some even altered their uniforms to resemble those of the guards, and they slavishly followed orders beyond necessity. Attempts at resistance were very rare, and, when the liberating American forces arrived at the end of the war, they were surprised that there was not some attempt at mass revenge.[19]

In comparison, the African who became an American slave underwent an experience which had some marked similarities to those of the German concentration camp. He too underwent a kind of shock procurement. Although millions of men became slaves, the event was unique to each man. Usually, he had been captured in the course of warfare which, in itself, was a humiliation. After being chained together and marched to the coast, his horror must have increased when he realized that he was being sold to Europeans. It was widely believed by Africans that white men were cannibals. At the coastal station, he also had to endure the humiliation of a naked inspection by a physician. This was followed by a lengthy transoceanic trip which must have exceeded the horrors of the train ride to the concentration camp. The crowded unsanitary conditions in the slave ships were at least as bad as those in the cattle cars, and the Africans also were beaten and harassed to keep them docile.

Moreover, the trip itself was much rougher and longer. After still another inspection, the African was purchased and had to face a lifetime of bondage in an alien environment. He was stripped of his identity, given a new name, and he was taught to envision himself and his African heritage as inferior and barbaric. The white master insisted on total obedience and created a situation of utter dependence. He supplied food, clothing, shelter, discipline, and he was in a position to control the slave's friends and mating. If the "Sambo" of literature mirrored reality, this life of dependency created infantile characteristics in many of the slaves and led them to reject their past while adopting the values of their masters. The American slave system, besides exploiting the African's labor, possessed and violated his person.[20]

Three schools of mass behavior have been suggested as explanations: Freudian psychology, the interpersonal theories of Henry Stack Sullivan, and role psychology. Freudian psychology has put special emphases on early childhood experiences and is the least suited for this purpose. It could be argued that the shock procurement and the total detachment from previous life which it achieved both in the concentration camps and in American slavery had emptied the super-ego or conscience of its contents. Then, the situation of total dependence which followed could have resulted in infantile regression. This would account for the childlike behavior of both "Sambo" and the camp inmates. The slave master and the camp guard, each in his own way, became a father figure, and the respective victims internalized the value system of this symbolic father.[21]

The interpersonal school of psychology states that the determining factor in influencing personality development can be found in the estimation and expectation of "significant others." Those responsible for the physical and emotional security of an individual are his "significant others." For a child these are his parents. As one matures, the number of "significant others" in one's experience increases. This permits one to make decisions of one's own and to develop some individuality.

However, the child has already internalized the estimations and expectations of his parents, and this tends to shape his personality for the rest of his life. Still, acquiring new "significant others" as an adult can be important in reshaping the adult personality. Both the American slaves and the camp prisoners were thrust into situations in which they had a new single "significant other." This was a situation similar to that of childhood, and it could have had the same impact in shaping personality. All previous "significant others" had been made insignificant, and, in each case, the estimations and expectations of this new "significant other" became internalized into the personality of the victims.[22]

Role psychology holds the most promise for explaining the impact of a social situation in determining the development of individual personality. In role psychology the individual and society can be compared to the actor and the theater. Society provides the individual with a number of roles, and the individual's behavior is his performance, the way in which he plays them.

Normally, each individual plays a number of roles simultaneously. While some are pervasive and extensive in scope, others are limited and transitory. The role of man or woman is extensive, but that of customer or student is transitory. Society also endows some roles with considerable clarity, while leaving others open to individual interpretation. The roles people play and the way in which they play them determine personality. Within American slavery as well as within the German concentration camps, the number of roles available were severely limited, and both the slave master and the camp guard defined them very clearly. Both demanded a precise and careful performance. There were those whose performance was faultless in playing their roles. While the concentration camp guard guaranteed its performance through terror and torture, the slave master usually used more subtle means. Besides punishment for missed cues, masters displayed considerable fondness for slaves who played their part well. By restricting role availability and by carefully defining the performance, society could create a group personality type, and, through changing roles, society could change personality.[23]

Although the innovative use of personality types has further illuminated the nature of the American slave system, it has tended to blur the individual experiences and contributions of millions of Africans into a vague amorphous abstraction. The technique has provided important insights into the plight of the slave as the victim of a dehumanizing system, but it tends to obscure the active participation of Africans in American life. Further, it is a crude generalization which, in fact, included many types within it.[24] While most slaves were plantation field hands, there were many whose lives followed different lines and for whom slavery was a very different experience. Some slaves departed sharply enough from the "Sambo" image to become leaders in insurrections. These men were usually urban slaves possessing unusual talents, and thereby escaping much of the emasculation which the typical slave had to endure.[25]

Emphasizing the slave as the victim of the slave system further reduces him to a passive object by insisting that the slave was effectively detached from his African heritage. Many scholars, including Elkins, believe that the attempt to discover Africanism in America by researchers such as Melville J. Herskovits has led to trivial and insignificant results. This belief is reinforced by the example of the German concentration camps. There, people from a wide variety of social and educational backgrounds reacted in highly similar ways. Apparently the individual had been detached from his prior life, and his reactions to the camp were shaped in a standardized manner. Similarly, it is argued, the slave was stripped of his heritage, so that none of his African background could influence his life in America. His personality and behavior were shaped exclusively by the unique form of American slavery.[26]

However, if we apply the experiences gained in the Chinese prisoner-of-war camps during the Korean War, some doubts on this point can be raised. While Americans from a wide variety of social and educational backgrounds behaved with a marked similarity to each other, thereby appearing to prove that their previous experiences were irrelevant to their reactions to the camp, there was, to the contrary, a significant difference between the behavior of the American and Turkish prisoners who had both been fighting in the Korean War. The morale of the American prisoners was easily broken, and each one strove to look out for himself even at the expense of his comrade's life. In contrast, the Turks maintained military discipline and group solidarity. This evidence would seem to indicate that, while individual differences were insignificant, cultural differences did influence adjustment to the camp situation.[27]

There are also grounds to believe that different value systems influenced the way in which contrasting cultures adjusted to slavery. While the African made the adjustment successfully, the American Indian, when he was enslaved, did not. The African's agricultural labor had contained many similarities to the work required on the plantation, but the Indian, accustomed to a migratory hunting existence, was totally unprepared for plantation slavery. He found nothing in it to sustain his values or his will to live, and he was unable to make the adjustment.[28]

If the African's agricultural background helped his adaptation to American slavery, then we must assume that his detachment from his heritage was not complete. Perhaps, besides influencing his life as a slave, his African background may have found its way into other aspects of American society. However, it would seem that because the African came to believe in his own inferiority, there must have been very little conscious attempt to keep his culture alive. Certainly, the recent Black Power movement, intended to revive pride in race and in the past, bears eloquent testimony to the degree to which any conscious link with the African past had been suppressed. Nevertheless, mental and emotional habits can continue without any conscious intention, and habits of this kind are important for the formation of personality. Moreover, it is possible that the image of "Sambo" as an exasperating child may tell as much about the mentality of the white master who perpetuated the picture as it does about the slave whom it depicted. Perhaps the picture of the childlike slave is also a reverse image of the sober, patronizing white master whose life was rooted in austerity. To such a man spontaneity and exuberance might well have seemed infantile.

The life of a slave did not give him much opportunity to create artifacts which could later be catalogued as evidence of African influence. However, he did create a unique music. While Negro spirituals were not imported directly from Africa, they were more than an attempt to copy the master's music. They represent a highly complex fusion of African and European music, of African and European religion, and of African and European emotions. Blues and jazz, which emerged at a later date, represent a similar creative tension. They clearly evolve from the experience of the African in America and include in them elements which can be traced directly to Africa. Jazz is now viewed throughout the world as American music. It demonstrates the fact that the African immigrant was not totally detached from his heritage and that he has made significant contributions to American culture. While American slavery did violate the person of the slave, some Africans, in the face of it all, managed to maintain some sense of individuality and manhood.

Slave Response

Undoubtedly, the slave's most common response to his condition was one of submission. There was no hope of his returning to Africa, and there was no realistic expectation that the situation would be significantly altered. The hopelessness of his plight created a deep sense of apathy. However, even this acceptance of his master's values may have reflected African influences. It was common for a defeated tribe in West Africa to adopt the gods of its victors within the framework of its own religion. This attitude could have facilitated the African's adjustment to slavery in an alien culture.

The majority of slaves worked in the fields on large plantations. Some of them were herded into large work gangs, supervised by an overseer, and carefully directed in the accomplishment of whatever task was necessary for that day. Others were regularly assigned to a specific task without constant supervision and were held responsible for its completion. In this way it was possible for them to develop some sense of initiative. House slaves were usually better off than field hands, but, because they lived in such proximity to their masters, they were much quicker to adopt the master's values and tended to be more obsequious.

Another significant group of slaves, both on the plantation and in the city, developed their talents and became skilled craftsmen: barbers, blacksmiths, carpenters, and a wide variety of other trades. Masters who could not fully utilize the skills of such a craftsman rented their property to their neighbors. In some cases, the master permitted the slave to be responsible for hiring himself out and allowed him to keep some of the profits. The variety of experiences permitted within slavery allowed significant variations in the types of slaves who emerged.[29]

Even apparently submissive slaves developed techniques of passive resistance. The laziness, stealing, lying, and faked illnesses, which were usually attributed to the slave's childlike behavior, may have been deliberate ways of opposing the system. Masters complained that many of their slaves were chronic shirkers. When slaves dragged their feet while working, it was seen as evidence of their inferiority. When white union workers behave similarly, it is labeled a slowdown.

Other slaves appear to have indulged in deliberate mischief, trampling down crops, breaking tools, and abusing livestock. A southern physician, Dr. Cartwright, concluded that this behavior was symptomatic of a mental disease peculiar to Africans. He labeled the disease *Dysaethesia Aethiopica* and insisted that masters were wrong in thinking that it was merely rascality. He also concluded that the slave's chronic tendency to run away was in reality the symptom of yet another African disease, *Drapetomania,* which he believed would eventually be medically cured.[30]

Finally, some slaves engaged in active resistance. Most of the slave insurrections in America were very small, and most were unsuccessful. The three best known insurrections were those led by Gabriel Prosser, Denmark Vesey, and Nat Turner. These revolts will be treated more fully in the next chapter.

The masters consistently refused to see examples of passive or active resistance as signs of manhood. Lying and stealing were never interpreted as passive resistance, but were always attributed to an inferior savage heritage, as was slave violence. Prosser, Vesey, and Turner, instead of being numbered among the world's heroes fighting for the freedom of their people, were usually represented as something closer to savages, criminals, or psychopaths. Modern historical scholarship has been influenced by the interpretation of slave behavior, which stressed the impact of the system on the slave, rather than his response to it. Consequently, it has failed to give proper recognition to African contributions to American life.

CHAPTER 4

All Men Are Created Equal

Slavery and the American Revolution

HOW is it," asked Samuel Johnson, "that we hear the loudest yelps for liberty among the drivers of negroes?" [1] The British author was only one of many Europeans who thought it strange that a nation run by slave owners should be so noisily demanding its own freedom. This same bitter inconsistency was embodied in the death of Crispus Attucks. A mulatto slave who had run away from his Massachusetts master in 1750, he spent the next twenty years working as a seaman and living in constant fear of capture and punishment. In 1770, he, with four others, was killed in the Boston Massacre. Ironically, the first man to die in the Colonial fight for freedom was both an Afro-American and a runaway slave. His death became symbolic of what was to be an underlying question in the years to come: "What place would there be for the African in America once the colonies gained their freedom from the old world?"

The Quakers were the first group in America to attack slavery. In his book *Some Considerations on the Keeping of Negroes*, John Woolman contended that no one had the right to own another human being. In 1758 the Philadelphia yearly meeting said that slavery was inconsistent with Christianity, and in 1775 Quakers played a dominant role in the formation of the Pennsylvania Society for the Abolition of Slavery, the first antislavery society in America.[2]

As the colonists began to agitate for their own freedom, many of them became increasingly aware of the contradiction involved in slaveholders fighting for their own freedom. "To contend for liberty," John Jay wrote, "and to deny that blessing to others involves an inconsistency not to be excused." [3] James Otis maintained that the same arguments which were used to defend the rights of the colonists against Britain could be used with at least equal force against the colonists by their slaves. "It is a clear truth," he said, "that those who every day barter away other men's liberty will soon care little for their own." [4]

In the same vein, Abigail Adams wrote her husband: "It always appeared a most iniquitous scheme to me to fight ourselves for what we are daily robbing and plundering from those who have as good a right to freedom as we have." [5] Perhaps the most radical statement was made by the Reverend Isaac Skillman in 1773. Again, comparing the struggle of the colonists with that of the slaves, he said that it was in conformity with natural law that a slave could rebel against his master.

In 1774 the Continental Congress did agree to a temporary termination of the importation of Africans into the colonies, but, in reality, this was a tactical blow against the British slave trade and not an attack against slavery itself. In an early draft of the Declaration of Independence, the British king was attacked for his involvement in the slave trade, and he was charged with going against human nature by violating the sacred rights of life and liberty. However, this section was deleted. Apparently, Southern delegates feared that this condemnation of the monarch reflected on them as well.

Although neither slavery nor the slave trade was mentioned in the Declaration, it did maintain that all men were created equal and endowed with the right of life, liberty, and the pursuit of happiness. This seeming ambivalence concerning the future of slavery on the part of the Continental Congress left Samuel Johnson's ironic question about American hypocrisy unanswered. From a logical point of view, the Declaration of Independence either affirmed the freedom of the African immigrant, or it denied his humanity. Because each state continued almost as a separate sovereign entity, the Declaration of Independence became a philosophical abstraction, and the status of the African in America was determined independently by each.

Lord Dunmore, the British governor of Virginia, put teeth into Johnson's bitter question. In 1775 he offered to grant freedom to any slave who ran away from his master and joined the British army. Earlier that year, in spite of the fact that both slaves and free men had served at Lexington and Concord, the colonists had shown an increasing reluctance to have any blacks serving in their Army. The Council of War, under Washington's leadership, had unanimously rejected the enlistment of slaves and, by a large majority, it had opposed their recruitment altogether. However, the eager response of many slaves to Lord Dunmore's invitation gradually compelled the colonists to reconsider their stand. Although many colonists felt that the use of slaves was inconsistent with the principles for which the Army was fighting, all the colonies, with the exception of Georgia and South Carolina, eventually recruited slaves as well as freedmen. In most cases, slaves were granted their freedom at the end of their military service. During the war some five thousand blacks served in the Continental Army with the vast majority coming from the North.[6]

In contrast to later practice, during the Revolution the armed forces were largely integrated with only a few segregated units. While the vast majority of Afro-American troops fighting in the Revolutionary War will always remain anonymous, there were several who achieved distinction and made their mark in history. Both Prince Whipple and Oliver Cromwell crossed the Delaware with Washington on Christmas Day in 1776. Lemuel Haynes, later a pastor of a white church, served at the Battle of Ticonderoga. According to many reports, Peter Salem killed the British major, John Pitcairn, at the Battle of Bunker Hill.

Gradually, the colonies were split into two sections by differing attitudes towards slavery. In 1780 the Pennsylvania Legislature passed a law providing for the gradual abolition of slavery. The Preamble to the legislation argued that, considering that America had gone to war for its own freedom, it should share that blessing with those who were being subjected to a similar state of bondage in its midst.[7] Three years later the Massachusetts Supreme Court decided that slavery was contrary to that state's constitution and that it violated the natural rights of man. Connecticut, Rhode Island, New Jersey, and New York all passed laws providing for gradual emancipation. Although the liberal philosophy of the Revolution did lead these states to end slavery, most Northern citizens were not genuinely convinced that natural law had conferred full equality on their Afro-American neighbors. Racial discrimination remained widespread.

At the same time, the Southern states which were dependent upon slavery for their economic prosperity showed little interest in applying the doctrines of the Declaration of Independence to either the slaves or the free blacks in their midst. If anything, the passage of stiffer black codes increased the rights of the masters while diminishing those of slaves and freedmen. Some Southern states had qualms about the advisability of continuing the slave trade, but this did not mean that they had doubts about the value of slavery. Rather, the number of slave insurrections which swept through South America, highlighted by the bloody revolt in Haiti, led them to fear possible uprisings at home. They had always been cautious about bringing unbroken slaves directly from Africa, and now they were also afraid to import unruly slaves from South America.

In 1783 Maryland passed a law prohibiting the importation of slaves, and in 1786 North Carolina drastically increased the duty on the importation of slaves, thereby severely reducing the flow. The Federal Government finally took action to terminate the slave trade in 1807, but a vigorous, illegal trade continued until the Civil War. The first sectional conflict over slavery had taken place at the Constitutional Convention. Those Northerners who had hoped to see slavery abolished by this new constitution were quick to realize that such a document would never be approved by the South. Most of the antislavery forces concluded that it was necessary to put the Union above abolition.

While the Constitution did not specifically mention slavery, it did legally recognize the institution in three places. First, there was a heated debate over the means of calculating representation to the House. Southern spokesmen wanted as many delegates as possible and preferred that slaves be counted. Northerners, wanting to restrict Southern representation, insisted that slaves not be counted. Some of them pointed out that it was an insult to whites to be put on an equal footing with slaves. The compromise which was framed in Article I, Section 2, was that a slave should be counted as three-fifths of a man.

Second, the antislavery elements tried to make their stand at the convention by attacking the slave trade. However, while many Southern states were opposed to the trade, the issue became entangled in power politics. South Carolina, which had few slaves, believed that the termination of the slave trade would force up the price of slaves and place her at a severe disadvantage in comparison with Virginia which already had a large slave supply. It argued that Virginia would be artificially enriched to the disadvantage of the other Southern states. The states of the North and middle South were again forced to compromise, and, in Article II,

Section 9, they agreed that the trade would be permitted to continue for another twenty years.

The third capitulation occurred in Article IV, Section 2, which was the Fugitive Slave Provision. It stated that a slave who ran away and reached a free state, did not thereby obtain his freedom. Instead, that state was required, at the master's request, to seize and return him.

In fact, the delegates to the Constitutional Convention were afraid that the revolutionary ideology of freedom and equality had unwisely and unintentionally unleashed a social revolution. Southern planters envisioned the end of slavery on which their wealth was based. Northern capitalists were opposed to the liberal and democratic land laws which the people were demanding. The economic leaders in both sections of the country believed that there was a need to protect property rights against these new revolutionary human rights. While the Northern states strove to stabilize society in order to build a flourishing commerce, the Southern states tightened their control over their slaves fearing that insurrections from South America or ideas about freedom and equality from the American Revolution itself might inspire a serious slave rebellion.

Slave Insurrections

From the time that the first African was captured until the completion of Emancipation, slaves struck out against the institution in one way or another. Herbert Aptheker has recorded over two hundred insurrections. Although most slave revolts in America were small and ineffective, there were three in particular which chilled Southern hearts. These were led by Gabriel Prosser, Denmark Vesey, and Nat Turner and occurred within the short span between 1800 and 1831. Toussaint l'Ouverture in Haiti had previously demonstrated that slaves could be victorious over large European armies, and the American colonists had taught by their example in the American Revolution that violence in the service of freedom was justifiable. The gradual abolition of slavery which was occurring in the Northern states gave hope that the institution in America might be terminated altogether. However, the slaves saw little reason to believe that their Southern masters would follow the example of the Northerners in abolishing slavery. Many of the slaves came to accept that if the institution was to be destroyed, it would have to be done by the slaves themselves.

In August, 1800, Gabriel Prosser led a slave attack on Richmond, Virginia. During several months of careful planning and organizing, the insurrectionists had gathered clubs, swords, and other crude weapons. The intention was to divide into three columns: one to attack the penitentiary which was being used as an arsenal, another to capture the powder house, and a third to attack the city itself. If the citizens would not surrender, the rebels planned to kill all of the whites with the exception of Quakers, Methodists, and Frenchman. Apparently, Prosser and his followers shared a deep distrust of most white men. When they had gathered a large supply of guns and powder, and taken over the state's treasury, the rebels calculated, they would be able to hold out for several weeks. What they hoped for was that slaves from the surrounding territory would join them and, eventually, that the uprising would reach such proportions as to compel the whites to come to terms with them.

Unfortunately for the plotters, on the day of the insurrection a severe storm struck Virginia, wiping out roads and bridges. This forced a delay of several days. In the meantime, two slaves betrayed the plot, and the government took swift action. Thirty-five of the participants, including Prosser, were executed. As the leaders refused to divulge any details of their plans, the exact number involved in the plot remains unknown. However, rumor had it that somewhere between two thousand and fifty thousand slaves were connected with the conspiracy. During the trials, one of the rebels said that he had done nothing more than what Washington had done, that he had ventured his life for his countrymen, and that he was a willing sacrifice.[8]

In Charleston, South Carolina, a young slave named Denmark Vesey won $1,500 in a lottery with which he purchased his freedom. During the following years he worked as a carpenter. In his concern over the plight of his slave brethren, he formed a plan for an insurrection which would bring them their freedom. He and other freedmen collected two hundred pike heads and bayonets as well as three hundred daggers to use in the revolt, but, before the plans could be put into motion in 1882, a slave informed on them. This time it was rumored that there had been some nine thousand involved in the plot. Over a hundred arrests were made, including four whites who had encouraged the project, and several of the leaders, including Vesey, were executed.[9]

The bloodiest insurrection of all, in which some sixty whites were murdered, occurred in Southampton County, Virginia, in August, 1831. Nat Turner, its leader, besides being a skilled carpenter, was a literate, mystical preacher. He had discovered particular relevance in the prophets of the Old Testament. Besides identifying with the slave experience of the Israelites, Turner and other slaves felt that the social righteousness which the prophets preached related directly to their situation. The picture of the Lord exercising vengeance against the oppressors gave them hope and inspiration. While the Bible did appear to tell the slave to be faithful and obedient to his master, it also condemned the wicked and provided examples that could be interpreted to prove God's willingness to use human instruments in order to bring justice against oppressors. Turner's growing hatred of slavery and his increasing concern for the plight of his brothers, led him to believe that he was one of God's chosen instruments.

As his conviction deepened, the solar eclipse early in 1831 appeared to him to be a sign that the day of vengeance was at hand. In the following months he collected a small band of followers, and in August they went into action. Unlike Prosser and Vesey, he began with only a very small band which lessened his chance of betrayal. As they moved from farm to farm, slaughtering the white inhabitants, they were joined by many of the slaves who were freed in the process. However, word of the massacre spread. At one farm, they were met by armed resistance. Slaves as well as masters fought fiercely to stop the attack. Some of Turner's men were killed and wounded, and the planned drive towards Jerusalem was thrown off stride. This enabled the militia to arrive and break up the attack. In due time Turner and several of his followers were captured and executed.[10]

White men in both the South and the North saw little similarity between these insurrections and the American Revolution. The Turner massacre was universally depicted as the work of savages and brutes, not of men. Vigilance was tightened, and new laws controlling the slaves were passed throughout the South. Both the violence of the slaves and the verbal abuse of the abolitionists only served to strengthen the South in its defense of the peculiar institution. Slaves who revolted were depicted as beasts who could not be freed because they would endanger society. Submissive slaves were pictured as children in need of paternal protection from the evils of a complex, modern world. They were never seen as men whose rights and liberties had been proclaimed in the Declaration of Independence.

Growing Racism

As Afro-American freedmen sought to claim their rights as men and citizens, they were confronted with constant resistance from whites who were unwilling to accept them. Actually, pressure from the mass of Northern white workers had contributed to the abolition of slavery in those states. In the Northern states slavery was forced to compete with free white labor in a way which was not true of the plantation economy of the South. White workers continually complained that slavery was keeping their wages down and unemployment up, and in 1737 the governor of New York had asked the Legislature to investigate the charges that slave competition contributed to unemployment. While this attack had helped to undermine slavery, it had also exacerbated tension between black and white labor. The continual flow of runaways from the South brought an increasing supply of cheap black labor to compete with white workers, and the friction between the two races continued. While many of the runaways, like Frederick Douglass, had worked as skilled craftsmen in the South, they found economic discrimination in the North limiting them to menial labor.

After 1830, when the tide of European immigration began to swell, the competition for jobs grew even sharper, and blacks found that even menial jobs were being taken over by the new European immigrants. Jobs such as stevedores, coachmen, barbers, and servants, which had traditionally been left to blacks, were now being invaded by the Irish. Whereas in 1830 the vast majority of New York City servants were Afro-American, after 1850 most of them were Irish. This economic competition contributed considerably to the hostility, fear, and discrimination which confronted the Northern freedmen.[11]

In 1816 the American Colonization Society was founded. It was considered the ideal solution to the American racial dilemma. Claiming to be interested in the welfare of the African in its midst, the Society advocated colonizing in Africa or wherever else it was expedient. It comforted slave owners by announcing that it was not concerned with either emancipation or amelioration. Both were outside its jurisdiction. It did imply that slaves might eventually be purchased for colonization. Most of its propaganda tried to demonstrate that the freedman lived in a wretched state of poverty, immorality, and ignorance and that he would be better off in Africa.

The movement received widespread support from almost all sections of the white community including presidents Madison and Jackson. Several state legislatures supported the idea, and Congress voted $100,000 to finance the plan which eventually led to the establishment of the Republic of Liberia.

However, the Afro-American community was not very enthusiastic about the project. In 1817 three thousand blacks crowded into the Bethel Church in Philadelphia and, led by Richard Allen, vehemently criticized colonization. They charged that the Society's propaganda only served to increase racial discrimination since it stressed the poverty and ignorance of the freedman and claimed that he was doomed to continue in his filth and degradation because of his natural inferiority. It also argued that whites would only take advantage of the Afro-American, and that the separation of the two races was the only solution. The participants at the Bethel meeting contended that this propaganda tended to justify racial discrimination.

The claim was also made that the removal of freedmen from America would only serve to make the slave system more secure, and they pledged themselves never to abandon their slave brothers. Besides, while they were African by heritage, they had been born in America, and it was now their home. Most of the fifteen thousand who did return to Africa were slaves who had been freed for this purpose, and the project was acknowledged to be a failure. The Society's own propaganda contributed to the alienation of many freedmen. One of its own leaders admitted that the blacks could read and hear and, when they were spoken of as a nuisance to be banished, they reacted negatively like men.[12]

Widespread racial prejudice, besides creating racial discrimination, resulted in oppressive legislation. In 1810 Congress excluded Afro-Americans from carrying the mail. In 1820 it authorized the District of Columbia to elect white city officials, and it consistently admitted new states to the Union whose constitutions severely limited the rights of freedmen. The office of the Attorney General usually took the position that the Constitution did not grant citizenship to Negroes, and Congress itself had limited naturalization to white aliens in 1790. This point of view was later justified by the Dred Scott decision. With only a few exceptions, the Secretary of State refused to grant passports to those wishing to travel abroad, although it did provide a letter of identification stating that the carrier was a resident of the United States. Finally, Massachusetts granted its own passports to its colored citizens, complaining that they had been virtually denationalized.[13]

Also, many states in the Northwest passed laws prohibiting or limiting the migration of Afro-Americans into their territory. An Illinois law said that anyone who entered the state illegally could be whipped and sold at auction. Many states denied blacks the ballot, prohibited their serving on a jury and legally segregated transportation, restaurants, hotels, theaters, churches, and even cemeteries. Most Northern states did not allow them to testify in court against whites. This meant that, if a white man beat a black, the black had no legal protection unless another white was willing to testify on his behalf.[14]

On several occasions white hostility erupted into violence. Black workmen were harassed, abolitionists beaten, and entire communities terrorized. One of the worst of these events occurred in Cincinnati in 1829. With the rapid growth of "Little Africa," that city's black ghetto, the local citizens decided to enforce the state's anti-integration legislation. Some twenty years before, the state had passed a law requiring blacks entering the state to provide proof of their freedom and to post a bond as guarantee of their good behavior. When the inhabitants of "Little Africa" obtained an extension of the 30-day time limit within which they were to comply with the law, the citizens of Cincinnati were outraged, and they took matters into their own hands. White mobs ransacked the area, indiscriminately and mercilessly beating women and children, looting stores and burning houses. It was estimated that half of the two thousand inhabitants of the area left the city. Many of them emigrated to Canada, and the local paper, which had helped to inflame the mob, lamented that the respectable black citizens had left and only derelicts remained.[15]

At the very point in American history when democracy was sinking its roots deeper into the national soil, the status of the

Afro-American was being clearly defined as an inferior one. The Jacksonian Era brought the common man into new prominence, but the same privileges were not extended to the blacks. In the South, society was strengthening the institution of slavery against any possible recurrences of slave insurrections. The activities of the slaves, especially those of Negro preachers, were being watched even more closely than before. In the North, both state and federal laws denied blacks many of the rights of citizenship.

PART TWO

Emancipation without Freedom

CHAPTER 5

A Nation Divided

Black Moderates and Black Militants

ON the eve of the Revolution there was justification for assuming that slavery in the Northern states was withering away. By 1800 most of the Northern states had either done away with slavery or had made provision for its gradual abolition. Although this might not change the status of an adult slave, he knew that his children, when they reached maturity, would be free. This meant that the important issue in the North was that of identity for Negroes who were not fully accepted as Americans. While whites were willing to grant freedom to the Afro-Americans, they continued to view them as inferiors. Many observers remarked that race prejudice actually increased with the abolition of slavery. Northern freedmen concluded, like their slave brothers in the South, that they would have to work out their own salvation. This compelled them to wrestle with such questions as: "Am I an American?" "Am I an African?" "Am I inferior?" "How can I establish my manhood and gain acceptance?"

In the years immediately preceding the Revolution, there were two slaves who had wrestled with some of these questions: Jupiter Hammon and Phillis Wheatley. They tried to establish their claim to manhood through literary ability. Both were poets and wrote conventional romantic poetry in the spirit of the day. In 1761 Jupiter Hammon, a Long Island slave, published his poem: *An Evening Thought. Salvation by Christ with Penitential Cries.* Twelve years later Phillis Wheatley published a slim volume of her poetry which was written in a style much like that of Alexander Pope. Born in Africa in 1753, she had been brought to America as a child and had served in the Wheatley home in Boston. When she displayed some literary ability, her master granted freedom to her and, to some extent, became her patron. Her volume of poetry was published while she was visiting England and is generally considered superior to the poetry of Jupiter Hammon. Although on one occasion Hammon did suggest that slavery was evil, he instructed slaves to bear it with patience. Neither he nor Phillis Wheatley made any direct challenge to race prejudice. Instead, they strove to gain acceptance as talented individuals who might help others of their race to improve their situation. Unfortunately, white society regarded them only as unusual individual exceptions and contained to maintain its racial views.[1]

Gustavus Vassa was born in Africa in 1745 and was brought to America as a slave. Eventually, after serving several masters, he became the property of a Philadelphia merchant who let him buy his own freedom. After working for some time as a sailor, he settled in England, where he felt he would encounter less racial discrimination. There he became an active worker in the British anti-slavery movement. In 1789 he published his autobiography, *The Interesting Narrative of the Life of Oloudah Equiano, or Gustavus Vassa*, in which he bitterly attacked Christians for participating in the slave trade.

In 1792, Benjamin Banneker, a freedman from Maryland, wrote to Thomas Jefferson complaining that it was time to eradicate false racial stereotypes. While expressing doubts regarding the merits of slavery in his *Notes on Virginia*, Jefferson had expressed his belief in the inferiority of the African. Banneker had educated himself, especially in mathematics and astronomy, and in 1789 he was one of those who helped to survey the District of Columbia. Later, he predicted a solar eclipse. In 1791 he had begun the publication of a series of almanacs, and the next year he sent one of these to Jefferson in an attempt to challenge his racial views. Jefferson was so impressed with the work that he sent it to the French Academy of Science. However, he seemed to view Banneker as an exception rather than as fresh evidence undermining white racial stereotypes.[2]

In Massachusetts Paul Cuffe was rapidly becoming a black capitalist. After having worked as a sailor, he managed to buy a ship of his own. Over the years, he came to own considerable property in Boston, and eventually he had an entire fleet of ships sailing along the Atlantic coast, visiting the Caribbean and crossing the ocean to Africa. During the Revolution, he and his brother, both of whom owned property and paid taxes, raised the question of political rights. Claiming "no taxation without representation," they both refused to pay their taxes because they were denied the ballot. Their protest led Massachusetts to permit blacks to vote on the same basis as whites. Nevertheless, over the years Cuffe developed reservations about the future of the African in America. In 1815, at his own expense, he transported thirty-eight blacks back to Africa. This was one of the first attempts at African colonization. Apparently the costs and other problems surrounding the project were so great that he never pursued it further.[3]

As it became increasingly apparent that the end of slavery would not mean the end of discrimination, cooperative action by Afro-Americans seemed to be the only basis from which to gain acceptance, and in 1775 the African Lodge No. 459, the first Afro-American Masonic lodge in America, was founded. Prince Hall, its founder, was born in Barbados and came to America at the age of 17. Identifying himself with Afro-Americans, he became a minister in the Methodist Church where he dedicated himself to their advancement. However, he concluded that only through working together, through black cooperation, could any progress be made. After being refused recognition by the American Masons, his lodge was legitimized by a branch of the British Masons connected with the army stationed in Boston. Before long African lodges as well as other fraternal organizations sprang up all across the country. Denied access to white society, blacks found it necessary to form various kinds of organizations for their own welfare.[4]

Even within the church which supposedly stressed brotherhood, separate African organizations were emerging. During the revolution, George Liele founded a black Baptist church in Savannah, Georgia. Although similar churches sprang up throughout the South, the independent church movement progressed more rapidly in the Northern states. In 1786 Richard Allen, who had previously purchased his freedom from his Delaware master, began prayer meetings among his own people in Philadelphia. He wanted to found a separate black church, but he was opposed by blacks and whites alike. However, when the officials of St. George's Methodist Church proposed segregating the congregation, events came to a head. Richard Allen, Absalom Jones, and others went to the gallery as directed, but the ushers even objected to their sitting in the front seats of the gallery. When they were pulled from their knees during prayer, Allen and his friends left the church, never to return. They immediately formed the

Free African Society and began collecting funds to build a church. This resulted in the founding of St. Thomas' African Protestant Episcopal Church headed by Absalom Jones. In spite of the behavior of the Methodists, Allen believed that Methodism was better suited to his people's style of worship and gradually he collected a community of followers. In 1794 the Bethel African Methodist Episcopal Church was opened in Philadelphia. In 1816 several A.M.E. congregations met together to form a national organization with Allen as its bishop. Similar events in New York City led to the establishment of the African Methodist Episcopal Zion Church. Early in 1809 a black Baptist Church was founded in Philadelphia, and later in that same year congregations were established in Boston and New York. The New York congregation developed into the Abyssinian Baptist Church.[5]

The African church became the most important organization within the Afro-American community. Besides providing spiritual strength and comfort, it became a community institution, a center for social, political, and economic life. The minister became the most important leader of his people. However, the full potential for organizing protest was overlooked. For the most part, the church taught an other-worldly religion which strove to provide strength with which to endure the sorrows of this life, but it did not try too actively to change the situation. Richard Allen, for example, counseled patience and caution, advising his people to wait for God to work in His own way. In the meantime, the Christian was to practice obedience to God and to his master. Most of the clergy stuck to religious matters and avoided political questions. However, there were those who took an active part in politics, and they became leaders in the abolition movement and in the Negro Convention Movement. They included men like Samuel Ringgold Ward and Henry Highland Garnet.[6]

Another manifestation of group solidarity occurred in the Negro Convention Movement which began in 1830 and continued until the Civil War. These meetings brought together leaders from Afro-American communities throughout the North. They debated important problems, developed common policies, and spoke out with a united voice. They consistently urged the abolition of slavery in the Southern states, and they condemned the legal and social discrimination which was rampant throughout the North. At the 1843 convention in Buffalo, N.Y., Henry Highland Garnet tried

VERNON REGIONAL
JUNIOR COLLEGE LIBRARY

to persuade the movement to declare violence an acceptable tool in the destruction of slavery. However, by a vote of 19 to 18 the movement continued to oppose violence and to limit its power to an appeal based on moral persuasion.[7]

Besides the Convention Movement, there were two other means for achieving broad leadership. This was still an age of oratory. Frederick Douglass, William Wells Brown, Sojourner Truth, and many others traveled from town to town and state to state giving lectures to both black and white audiences. Also, they exploited the press to reach even larger numbers. Some of the more famous autobiographies written at this time were those of Frederick Douglass, William Wells Brown, Austin Steward, and Josiah Henson, all of whom recorded the horrors of slavery as well as the humiliations of racial discrimination.

One of the most vehement attacks against slavery and discrimination was *Walker's Appeal in Four Articles Together with a Preamble to the Colored Citizens of the World But in Particular and Very Expressly to those of the United States of America.* Although his father had been a slave, David Walker himself was born free in North Carolina. His hatred of slavery drove him to Boston, where he became a clothing merchant, but he was unable to forget his brethren who were still in bondage. The result was that in 1829 he published a pamphlet which was both a vehement attack on the institution of slavery and an open invitation for the slaves to rise up in arms.

First, he pointed out that all races of the earth were called men and assumed to be free with the sole exception of the Africans. He denied that his people wished to be white, insisting rather that they preferred to be just as their creator had made them. Urging his brothers not to show fear because God was on their side, Walker contended that any man who was not willing to fight for his freedom deserved to remain in slavery and to be butchered by his captors. Insisting that death was preferable to slavery, he stated that, if an uprising occurred, the slaves would have to be willing to kill or be killed. Moreover, he urged that it was no worse to kill a man in self-defense than it was to take a drink of water when thirsty. Rather, a man who would not defend himself was worse than an infidel and not deserving of pity.

In addressing the American people, Walker foresaw that if they would treat Africans as men, they could all live together in harmony. Georgia offered $10,000 for Walker if taken alive and $1,000 for him dead. A year later Walker died under somewhat mysterious circumstances, and some claimed that he had been murdered. His pamphlet circulated widely throughout the North and the South, and many believed that it helped to encourage slave insurrections.

Freedoms Journal, which had been founded in 1827 by Samuel E. Cornish and John B. Russwurm, was the first in a long series of Afro-American newspapers. Russwurm had been the first of his race to receive a college degree in America. In their first editorial, they proclaimed what was becoming a growing conviction. They said that others had spoken for the black man for too long. It was time that he spoke for himself. They also attacked slavery and racial prejudice. They strove to make the paper a medium for communication and debate within the Afro-American community. They also intended to use the paper to clarify misconceptions about Africa. Like many of their contemporaries, Cornish and Russwurm believed that even those who were friendly to their race were unconsciously steeped in prejudice. Therefore, it was doubly necessary for Afro-Americans to speak out for themselves, to expose the prejudices of bigots and liberals.

However, by 1829 Russwurm had become increasingly bitter about the future of his race in America and came to believe that returning to Africa was the only way to escape prejudice. He believed that the colony which had been established in Liberia was in need of educated leadership, and he went there to become its superintendent of education. Cornish remained behind and continued to work as a minister and as a newspaper editor.[8]

The North Star, later known as Frederick Douglass's paper, was the best known of the black journals. Its editor, Frederick Douglass, was born a slave in Maryland in 1817. His mother was a slave named Harriet Bailey, and the identity of his white father remains unknown. He was raised by his maternal grandmother on a distant farm and almost never saw his mother. Like many slaves, he was denied a father, almost denied a mother and largely denied any meaningful identity. After working for several years as a slave both on the plantation and in the city, he determined to run away. Although an earlier attempt had failed, he now made his way north to New Bedford, Massachusetts. There he was shocked to discover that, while some whites gave him protection and help, race prejudice was still rampant. A skilled craftsman, he was unable to find work. When an employer was willing to accept him, his fellow workers threatened to walk off the job. For the next three years, he worked as servant, coachman, and common laborer earning about a dollar a day.

Then, he met William Lloyd Garrison, the famous white abolitionist, who was impressed with his slave experiences and his ability to describe them. At one meeting, after Douglass had spoken, Garrison asked the audience whether this was a beast or a man. Douglass soon became a regular lecturer in the abolitionist movement. As he traveled throughout the North, he was continually harassed by racial discrimination in trains, coaches, boats, restaurants, hotels, and other public places. In contrast, when he went to England to raise funds for the movement, he was struck by the fact that he could go any place, including places frequented by the aristocracy, and be accepted as a man. He said that wherever he went in England he could always identify an American because his race prejudice clung to him like clothing. While in England, abolitionists raised funds which allowed him to purchase his freedom.

When he returned to America, Douglass settled in Rochester, New York, where he began publication of *The North Star*. Rochester was a thriving city on the Erie Canal, and, because it also had a port on Lake Ontario, it became an important terminal on the Underground Railroad. While many runaways settled in Rochester, others boarded steamers for Canada where they would be beyond the reach of the law. Douglass came to play an important role on the Underground Railroad, in the life of Rochester and, through *The North Star,* among Northern freedmen. Garrison felt double-crossed when his most important cohort in the Afro-American community struck out on his own. Douglass, in agreement with the position previously taken by Cornish and Russwurm, believed that blacks must assume leadership in their own cause.

Before long, *The North Star* was recognized as the voice of the black man in America. Douglass spoke out on all issues through its pages, and he continued to tour the country lecturing before audiences of both colors and discussing matters of policy with other abolitionists. He did not believe in merely exercising patience and obedience. Rather, he believed it was necessary to prick the white man's conscience with moral persuasion. His tactics combined nonviolence with self-assertion. Although the Constitution had indirectly recognized slavery, Douglass believed that its spirit, as well as that of the American Revolution, implied the eventual destruction of that institution. Therefore, political action was a legitimate and necessary tool with which to attack slavery and racial discrimination. From his knowledge of the South, he was convinced that slavery could not be overthrown without violence. However, he insisted that the black man was in no position to take the leadership in the use of physical force. At the same time, he was increasingly aware of the depth of racial prejudice of Northern whites, and he knew that there was a long struggle ahead to gain political, social, and economic freedom.[9]

White Liberals

In 1832 William Lloyd Garrison and eleven other whites founded the New England Anti-Slavery Society which, besides working for the abolition of slavery, fought for the rights of freedmen. Garrison soon became the fiery and controversial leader of the abolitionist movement and the editor of *The Liberator*. The movement included men like Wendell Phillips, Arthur and Lewis Tappan, Theodore Dwight Weld, Gerrit Smith, James Birney, and many others. They condemned the American Colonization Society for sharing the unchristian prejudices of the slaveholders. Although the Northern states had abolished slavery, most whites believed that it was not their business to interfere with the domestic affairs of the Southern states. They also held that freedmen in the North must be kept in their place, and they viewed the abolitionists as a dangerous and radical minority.

The abolition movement itself was weakened by internal fragmentation. Garrison was jealous of anyone who competed with him for leadership. His brand of abolitionism attacked the Constitution as a vicious document giving sanction to slavery. He advocated that the Northern states separate from the South as a means of removing federal protection from slavery. Because the government was based on an unholy document, he concluded that any kind of political action automatically enmeshed one in this evil system. He was vehemently against the use of violence to overthrow slavery and insisted that moral persuasion was the only legitimate tool in the cause. Anyone who did not supoprt his doctrines faithfully was viewed as an enemy. This meant that he did not cooperate with abolitionists who condoned the use of violence or with those who were willing to accept the Constitution and engage in political action.[10]

Ironically, the abolitionist movement was also divided by racial prejudice. While opposing slavery, some refused to believe in political equality. Others were willing to grant political equality, but they resisted the idea of social mixing. A Philadelphia antislavery society spent many meetings debating whether it should extend membership to blacks, and, by a majority of two, it finally voted to drop its color bar.[11]

Black abolitionists became increasingly irritated by the racial attitudes of their white colleagues. Many of the whites were influential businessmen, and they were attacked for their own hiring practices. It was claimed that, when they hired blacks at all, they hired them only in menial positions. Martin R. Delany, abolitionist, journalist, and physician, complained that the blacks had taken a back seat in the movement for too long. He also bitterly attacked the whites for thinking that they knew best what was good for the African. He concluded that both friend and foe shared the same paternalistic prejudices.[12]

The Underground Railroad was another project which involved large numbers of whites. Besides providing financial backing for it, they worked as conductors and stationmasters. They helped lead runaways to safety, and they sheltered escapees. These men wanted to do more than speak out on the issue of slavery; they wanted to take action. Helping runaway slaves was against the law, and these men had such strong convictions that, while they did not think of themselves as criminals, they were willing to deliberately break the law. They participated in a kind of civil disobedience. However, the bravest workers on the Underground Railroad were black. If they were caught, especially in the South, they would have to pay the ultimate price for their heroism. The best known of all the black conductors was a brave runaway slave woman named Harriet Tubman. She ventured deep into the South on several occasions to lead large numbers of slaves to freedom, and she became a national legend. Several states put a price on her head. During the Civil War she served as a Union spy behind Confederate lines.[13]

Gradually the abolitionist movement and the Underground Railroad won the support of ever-increasing numbers of white

Northerners. At the same time, the South became increasingly bitter. Abolitionist literature was banned throughout the South, and most of the abolitionist leaders, because they had circulated literature in violation of this ban, had a price put on their heads. The Underground Railroad was more than a symbolic attack on the institution of slavery. While there is no way of telling how many slaves traveled to freedom with its help, certainly the value of human property lost to the South was very high. A slave was worth about $1,000, and thousands of slaves escaped. The financial and labor drain on the Southern economy was considerable. Also, when Southern masters came north to recapture runaway slaves, Northern consciences were outraged.

Finally, as the new states from the West were being permitted to join the Union, the question as to whether slavery should be legalized in them became important. Even Northern white bigots opposed the extension of slavery into these states. From their point of view, slavery was unfair competition with free labor, and they wanted the new states for the purpose of expansion. As the middle of the century approached, dark clouds of crisis could be seen on the horizon.

Growth of Extremism

During the 1850s American racial attitudes grew more extreme. While slavery continued to flourish throughout the South, discrimination was rampant throughout the North. Instead of gradually withering away as some had expected, the peculiar institution had been thriving and spreading into the Southwest ever since Eli Whitney's discovery of the cotton gin in 1793 had given new life to the growing of cotton. Slavery was booming in Alabama and spreading into Louisiana, Mississippi, and even Texas. At the same time, the North, after experiencing a full decade without slavery, was still steeped in discrimination and prejudice. After several years of freedom, Northern blacks still were not gaining economic advancement, political rights, or social acceptance. As the numbers of European immigrants had increased, job discrimination grew. The Northern states were, at the same time, abolishing the political rights of Afro-Americans. The hopes which had accompanied the end of slavery in those states were fading into despair. The relentless struggle for advancement apparently had failed, and increasing numbers became convinced that more radical action was necessary.

At the same time, white supremacy advocates were uneasy because their views had not been universally accepted, and they were adopting a stronger defense. The Southern justification of slavery was based on four main arguments. First, it was claimed that slavery was indispensable to its economy and that every society, whether slave or free, needed those who must do its menial labor. Although many Northerners might not agree that the need for labor was a justification for slavery, many would concur with the second argument, which was that the Negro was destined for a position of inferiority. Here the racial prejudices of North and South overlapped. The third argument was that Christianity had sanctioned slavery throughout all of history as a means for conversion. This contention had more justification than the religious abolitionists cared to admit. Finally, the South argued that white civilization had developed a unique high culture precisely because slavery removed the burden from the white citizens. Again, while Northerners might not totally agree with this point, many of them did believe in the superiority of white civilization. Although these points convinced few outsiders of the necessity for the existence of slavery, they did underline the widespread belief in black inferiority and white superiority. From this point of view the necessity for defending the glories of white civilization against the corruption of racial degeneration justified more and more radical action.

Besides mounting this vigorous vocal defense of slavery, the South stiffened its resistance to the circulation of antislavery propaganda. State laws were passed banning the publication and circulation of abolitionist materials, and mobs broke into post offices, confiscated literature from the U.S. mail, and publicly burned it. The Compromise of 1850, at the urging of the South, included the Fugitive Slave Act which vastly increased the powers of the slave owner to pursue runaway slaves throughout the North. The law also required that Northern officials cooperate in this process. Afro-Americans who had been living in Northern communities for years and who were accepted as respected citizens were now threatened with recapture by their previous masters. Many of these leaders were forced to flee. Freedmen who lacked adequate identification were also endangered by legal kidnapping and enslavement.

Throughout the North both blacks and whites, with the aid of the Federal Government, were alienated by this new long arm of the peculiar institution which reached deep into their communities. In fact many felt, like Frederick Douglass, that this law made the Federal Government an agent of slavery, and they believed that it forced local governments to become its co-conspirators. Several Northern states passed new civil rights laws in an attempt to protect their citizens. Frequently local vigilance committees tried to prevent the arrest of blacks in their midst. On other occasions mobs tried and sometimes succeeded in freeing those already arrested. In Boston, for example, a federal marshal was killed in a clash with one such mob. The Fugitive Slave Act was a powerful blow at the Afro-American communities in the North. It has been estimated that between 1850 and 1860 some twenty thousand fled to Canada. In the face of this reversal moderation became meaningless.[14]

The involvement of the Federal Government in supporting slavery led to a growing alienation within the Afro-American community. Increasingly militant leaders reevaluated their position on colonization. Henry Highland Garnet and Martin R. Delany, both workers in the abolition movement, reversed their positions and became proponents of emigration. While Garnet favored emigration to Liberia, Delany became an advocate of moving to Central and South America. He said that the United States had violated its own principles of republicanism and equality and that it was keeping Negroes in economic and political bondage. He concluded that Negroes were left with a choice between continued degradation in America or emigration. By 1852 he had come to prefer the latter choice.[15]

In 1854 a colonization convention was held in Cleveland for those who were interested in emigration within the boundaries of the western hemisphere. The convention noted that the Afro-American community was developing a growing sense of racial consciousness and pride. Although blacks were in the minority in Europe and America, it pointed out that most of the world's population was colored. Integration into the mainstream of American life, besides appearing to be impossible, seemed to demand the denial of selfhood for the black man. Therefore, black separatism grew in popularity and became a platform from which to maintain a sense of identity and individual worth.[16]

However, many militants like Frederick Douglass did not approve of black nationalism and colonization. They claimed that they were still Americans and did not constitute a separate nation. Leaders who were not black nationalists, however, could still be militant. Although Douglass did not actively support John Brown's raid on Harpers Ferry, the reason for his decision was that he doubted its effectiveness and not because he opposed its violent technique. In fact, Douglass applauded the attack. He said that Brown had attacked slavery "with the weapons precisely adapted to bring it to the death," and he contended that, since slavery existed by "brute force," then it was legitimate to turn its own weapons against it.[17] Previously the Reverend Moses Dixon had established two fraternal organizations to train blacks for military action. Although nothing substantial came from them, the idea of developing guerrilla forces as the only remaining tool against slavery was gaining support.

Another militant, H. Ford Douglass, concluded that the government had become so tyrannical that it was possible for him to engage in military action against it without his becoming a traitor to his country. He said, "I can hate this government without becoming disloyal because it has stricken down my manhood, and treated me as a salable commodity. I can join a foreign enemy and fight against it, without being a traitor, because it treats me as an ALIEN and a STRANGER, and I am free to avow that should such a contingency arise I should not hesitate to take any advantage in order to procure such indemnity for the future."[18]

Robert Purvis, a Philadelphian, also agreed that revolution might be the only tool left with which to secure redress for grievances. He contended that to support the government and the constitution on which it was based was to endorse a despotic state, and he went on to express his abhorrence for the system which destroyed him and his people. Purvis said that he could welcome the overthrow of this government and he could hope that it would be replaced by a better one.[19]

The alienation of the Afro-American from his government was dramatically underscored and justified in 1857 by the Dred Scott Decision which was handed down by the Supreme Court. A slave who had resided with his master in a territory where slavery was forbidden by act of Congress had claimed his freedom. After returning to slave territory, he sued his master on the grounds that residence in a nonslave territory had made him free. The court said that the Missouri Compromise which had established slave-free territories was unconstitutional, and it went on to state that blacks were not citizens of the United States and therefore could not bring a suit in court. In one single decision the court had lashed out at the Afro-American with two blows. Besides justifying slavery, it had openly supported the spread of the peculiar institution into the West. Then, it castrated the freedmen by denying any political rights to them. They were left with four alternatives: slavery, a freedom rooted in poverty and prejudice, emigration abroad, or revolution.

Suddenly, the terms of the equation were dramatically altered by an obscure white man named John Brown. After beginning his public career in New England as a participant in the abolitionist struggle, Brown became absolutely outraged by the apparent success that the South was having in spreading slavery into the new territories. He became one of the most active leaders in Kansas and rallied support to prevent that state from falling into the hands of proslavery factions. The slavery debates in Kansas exploded into open combat. Brown's outrage became a fiery conviction that God had chosen him to be one of the leaders in the righteous struggle against slavery. He also came to believe that, if God had justified violence in defending righteousness in the Old Testament, it could be used in other places and on a wider scale to topple the peculiar institution.

Brown spent several weeks in Rochester, New York, at the home of Frederick Douglass planning what amounted to a guerrilla campaign against the South. Despite Brown's urging, Douglass refused to join in what he believed to be a futile and desperate gesture. However, he wished Brown the best of luck. The plan was to establish a center of operation in the Virginia hills. Brown did not expect to defeat the South by force of arms. Instead, he believed that he could establish a mountain refuge which would attract ever-increasing numbers of slaves. His hope was that the drain on the slave system, coupled with the masters' fear of attack, would so strain the peculiar institution that, bit by bit, the South would be forced to negotiate some kind of settlement.[20]

However, Brown had to obtain arms and ammunition, and, to

keep the operation going he and his men needed food and other supplies. The result was the raid on the government arsenal at Harpers Ferry, Virginia. The attacking party included five blacks: Lewis Sheridan Leary, Dangerfield Newby, John Anthony Copeland, Osborn Perry Anderson, and Shields Green. Two of them were killed in the attack, two more were later executed, and one escaped. The attack failed, and Brown and several others were executed. Before his execution Brown said that, while they might dispose of him quite easily, the Negro question itself could not be so easily dismissed. His prediction proved correct. Brown's execution made him a martyr and at the end led to the victory for which he had yearned.

CHAPTER 6

From Slavery to Segregation

Blue, Gray, and Black

BROWN'S raid convinced the South that Northern harassment of slavery would continue and that the tactics would become even more desperate. At the same time, the election of Abraham Lincoln was interpreted by the South as a swing of the political pendulum in favor of the abolitionists. This was not true. Both Lincoln and the Republican Party had decided that the antislavery issue was not a broad enough platform on which to win an election. While Lincoln had made it clear that he himself opposed slavery, he also insisted that his political position, as well as that of the party, was to oppose the extension of slavery rather than to abolish it.

Although he emphasized different beliefs in varying localities, he still maintained that, while he opposed the enslavement of human beings, he did not view Africans as equals. He was convinced that there was a wide social gap between whites and blacks, and he indicated that he had grave doubts about extending equal political rights to Afro-Americans. Besides opposing slavery, he believed that racial differences pointed to the necessity for the separation of the two races, and he favored a policy of emigration. However, he had no interest in forcing either abolition or emigration on anyone.

His political goals were to increase national unity, to suppress the extension of slavery, to encourage voluntary emancipation, and to stimulate volitional emigration. He was far from the abolitionist which the South believed him to be. At the same time, abolitionists were almost as unhappy with his election as were slaveholders. His election was clearly an attempt to strike a compromise, but the South was in no mood to negotiate. It was not willing to permit the restriction of slavery to the states in which it already existed. Unwilling to compromise on this point, the Southern states seceded.[1]

Once the Civil War began, Lincoln's primary goal was to maintain or reestablish the union of all the states. His strategy was to operate from a platform which provided the largest numbers of supporters. With these priorities in the foreground, the government took considerable time to clarify its position on emancipation as well as its stand regarding the use of freedmen in the Union forces. Lincoln suspected that he would not get the kind of solid and enthusiastic support from the Northern states which he needed if he did not work towards eventual emancipation. At the same time, if he took too strong a position in favor of emancipation, he feared that the border states would abandon the Union and side with the South. Similarly, the refusal to use blacks in the armed forces might seriously weaken the military cause. Yet, their use might alienate the border states, and it might be so repugnant to the South as to hinder future negotiations.

Early in the war the North was faced with the problem of what to do with the slaves who fled from the South into the Union lines for safety. In the absence of any uniform policy, individual officers made their own decisions. According to the Fugitive Slave Act, Northern officials should have helped in capturing and returning them. When General Butler learned that the South was using slaves to erect military defenses, he declared that such slaves were contraband of war and therefore did not have to be returned. Congress stated that it was not the duty of an officer to return escaped slaves. However, on at least one occasion, Lincoln gave instructions to permit masters to cross the Potomac into Union lines to look for their runaway slaves.[2]

In August, 1861, a uniform policy was initiated with the passing of the Confiscation Act. It stated that property used in aiding the insurrection could be captured. When such property consisted of slaves, it stated that those slaves were to be forever free. Thereafter, slaves flocked into Union lines in an ever-swelling flood. Besides fighting the war, the Union Army found itself bogged down in caring for thousands of escaped slaves, a task for which it was not prepared. In some cases confiscated plantations were leased to Northern whites, and escaped slaves were hired out to work them.

In December of 1862 General Saxton declared that abandoned land could be used for the benefit of the ex-slave. Each family was given two acres of land for every worker in the family, and the government provided some tools with which to work it. However, most of the land was sold to Northern capitalists who became absentee landlords with little or no interest in maintaining the quality of the land or in caring for the ex-slave who did the actual labor. These ex-slaves were herded into large camps with very poor facilities. The mortality rate ran as high as 25 percent within a two-year period. Gradually, a very large number of philanthropic relief associations, many of which were related to the churches, sprang up to help the ex-slave by providing food, clothing, and education. Thousands of school teachers, both black and white, flocked into the South to help prepare the ex-slave for his new life.[3]

In the beginning, Lincoln had been very reticent in permitting the use of slaves or freedmen in the Army. As early as 1861 General Sherman had authorized the employment of fugitive slaves in "services for which they were suited." Late in 1862 Lincoln permitted the enlistment of some freedmen, and, in 1863, their enlistment became widespread. By the end of the war more than 186,000 of them had joined the Union forces. For the first time in American history, however, they were forced to serve in segregated units and were usually commanded by white officers. One of the ironies of the conflict was that the war which terminated slavery was also responsible for initiating segregation within the Armed Forces. In a way this fact became symbolic of the role which racial discrimination and segregation eventually came to play in American society. Besides fighting in segregated units, the Negro soldiers, for about a year, received half pay. The 54th Massachusetts Regiment served for an entire year without any pay rather than to accept discriminatory wages. In South Carolina a group of soldiers stacked their arms in front of their captain's tent in protest against the prejudicial pay scale. Sgt. William Walker, one of the instigators of the demonstration, was court-martialed and shot for this action. Finally, in 1864 all soldiers received equal pay.[4]

The South was outraged by the use of "colored troops." It refused to recognize them and treat them as enemy soldiers, and, whenever any were captured, it preferred to treat them as runaway slaves under the black codes. This meant that they received a much harsher treatment than they would have if they had been treated as prisoners of war. Also, the South preferred to kill them instead of permitting their surrender. As a result more than 38,000 of them were killed during the war.[5]

Many Northerns were also upset by the use of "colored troops." They did not like to have the Civil War considered a war to abolish slavery. Many of them feared that this would only increase job competition. As a result, when white longeshoremen struck in New York and blacks were brought in to take their place, a riot ensued. Many of the white strikers found themselves drafted into the Army, and they did not appreciate fighting to secure the freedom of men who took away their jobs. Even during the war racial tensions continued to run high in the North.[6]

In 1862 General Hunter proclaimed the freedom of all slaves in his military sector: Georgia, Florida, and South Carolina. When Lincoln heard of it, he immediately reversed the decree. He preferred gradual, compensated emancipation followed by voluntary colonization. He persuaded Congress to pass a bill promising federal aid to any state which set forth a policy of gradual, compensated emancipation. Abolitionists said that masters should not be paid for freeing their slaves because slaves were never legitimate property. Congress also established a fund to aid voluntary emigration to either Africa or Latin America. However, few slave owners were interested even in compensated emancipation, and the plan received almost no support. Lincoln finally concluded that emancipation had become a military necessity. In September of 1862 he issued a preliminary decree promising to free all slaves in rebel territory. On January 1, 1863, the Emancipation Proclamation went into effect. However, slavery continued to be legal in a few areas which were not in rebellion. Final abolition of the institution came with the passage of the Thirteenth Amendment in 1865.[7]

By the end of the war the South became so desperate that the use of slaves in the Army was sanctioned, and they were promised their freedom at the end of the conflict. As the end of the war came, some questions had been solved and new ones had been created. Lincoln's belief in the fact that the Union was indissoluble had been vindicated, and it was also evident that national unity could not go hand in hand with sectional slavery. But three new questions were now emerging. How should sectional strife be healed? What should be the status of the ex-slave? Who should determine that status?

Reconstruction and Its Failure

At the close of the war more attention was given to the reconstruction of Southern institutions than to the elevation of the ex-slave. While a handful of the Radical Republicans, such as Sumner and Stevens, were aware that slavery had not prepared the ex-slave for participation in a free competitive society, most liberals assumed that the termination of slavery meant the end of their problems. They believed that blacks could immediately enter into community life on an equal footing with other citizens. Any suggestion that the ex-slave needed help to get started drew considerable resentment and hostility from liberals and conservatives alike. With the abolition of the peculiar institution, the antislavery societies considered their work finished. Frederick Douglass, however, complained that the slaves were sent out into the world empty-handed. In fact, both the war and emancipation had intensified racial hostility. The ex-slave had not yet been granted his civil rights. At the same time, he was no longer covered by property rights. Therefore he was even more vulnerable to physical intimidation than before.

As the war drew to an end, Lincoln initiated a program aimed at the rapid reconstruction of the South and the healing of sectional bitterness. With only the exclusion of a few Confederate officials, he offered immediate pardon to all who would swear allegiance to the Federal Government. As soon as ten percent of the citizens of any state who had voted in 1860 had taken this oath, a state could then hold local elections and resume home rule. Since almost no blacks had voted in the Southern states in 1860, his plan did nothing to encourage extending the franchise to them. However, he did believe that educated blacks could and should be given the right to vote, but this extension of the franchise was apparently to be determined by each state at some future time.[8]

After Lincoln's assassination, Andrew Johnson further accelerated the pace of reconciliation. Granting personal pardons by the thousands, he initiated a plan for restoration which was even more lenient. Southern states resumed home rule, and, in the federal election of 1866, they elected scores of Confederate officials to Congress. At the same time, other Confederate officials were elected to other local posts throughout the South. One of the most urgent tasks taken up by these new home-rule governments was the determination and definition of the status of the ex-slave. State after state passed black codes which bore an amazing resemblance to those of slavery days. Blacks were not allowed to testify in court against whites. If they quit their jobs, they could be imprisoned for breach of contract. Anyone found without a job could be arrested and fined $50. Those who could not pay the fine were hired out to anyone in the community who would pay the fine. This created a new system of forced labor. At the same time, blacks could be fined for insulting gestures, breaking the curfew, and for possessing firearms. This created the kind of supervision of personal life which was similar to that of slavery. Although the Thirteenth Amendment had made slavery unconstitutional, the South was trying to recreate the peculiar institution in law while not admitting it in name.[9]

Radical Republicans in Congress were outraged both at the unrepentant obstinacy of the South and at the leniency of Johnson's plan for restoration. After refusing to seat many of the Southern delegates to Congress, the Radical Republicans went on to pass civil rights legislation which was aimed at protecting the ex-slave from the black codes. President Johnson, however, vetoed these bills as well as the Fourteenth Amendment. An enraged Congress passed the civil rights legislation over his vote and came within one vote of impeaching the President.[10]

Although impeachment failed, Johnson lost his leadership in the government, and Congress, within two years after the end of the war, began Reconstruction all over again. The first large-scale Congressional hearings in American history were held to investigate the conditions in the South. The investigation documented widespread poverty, physical brutality, and intimidation as well as legal discrimination. The committee made a detailed examination of the race riots which had occurred in Memphis and New Orleans in which scores of blacks had been killed. It concluded that the New Orleans riot was, in fact, a police massacre in which dozens of blacks were murdered in cold blood.

Congress removed home rule from the Southern states and divided the area into five military districts. Even those Southerners who had already received federal pardons were now required to swear a stricter oath in order to regain their right to vote. State conventions met to draft new constitutions. These conventions were dominated by a coalition of three groups: new black voters, whites who had come from the North either to make personal fortunes or to help educate the ex-slave, and Southern whites who had never supported the Confederacy. The oath of allegiance required a citizen to swear that he was now and always had been loyal to the Federal Government. This excluded all the Confederate officials. These new Southern reconstruction governments operated under the protection of the Army and with the encouragement of the Federal Government. They strove to reconstruct the South economically, politically, and socially. They established a system of public education, built many new hospitals, founded institutions for the mentally and physically handicapped, and attempted to reform the penal system.

During Reconstruction blacks played a significant political role throughout the South. Besides voting in large numbers, they were elected to local, state, and federal offices. Between 1869 and 1901, two became U. S. Senators and twenty were members of the House of Representatives. Senators Revels and Bruce were elected from Mississippi. P. B. S. Pinchback was elected to the Senate from Louisiana, but he was not permitted to take his seat. He did serve as Lieutenant Governor of Louisiana, and, for three days, was Acting Governor.[11]

White conservatives in the South were outraged, and they were determined to have absolutely nothing to do with a government which permitted Negro participation. They spread the myth that Reconstruction governments were in the grip of intolerably stupid and corrupt black men. Although Negroes were elected to state governments in significant numbers, the fact was that at no time were they in control. Moreover, when the critics themselves came to power, they did nothing to undo the work of the Reconstruction governments. This fact cast doubts on the sincerity of their criticism. The one thing which the white conservatives did when they regained power was to disenfranchise the blacks. This indicated that their real complaint in regard to Reconstruction was the participation of Negroes in government.[12]

With the Federal Government protecting the civil and political rights of the ex-slave, the South was unable to use the law to keep him in his place. The passionate belief in white superiority and a desperate fear of black retaliation caused many whites to resort to physical intimidation to achieve their purposes. The Ku Klux Klan was the most notorious of a large number of similar organizations which spread throughout the South. Negroes and white sympathizers were beaten and lynched. Some had their property burned, and others lost their jobs if they showed too much independence.

In 1869 Congress took action against the Klan and other white-supremacy organizations. The Klan was officially disbanded, but, in fact, it only went underground. Most of these organizations were spontaneous local developments, and this made it difficult for either federal or state governments to find and destroy them. Often their tactics were successful in shaping election results. Their propaganda was also useful in influencing public opinion. They insisted that they were only protecting women, children, and civic morality. They backed the myth that government was in the hands of corrupt officials, and claimed that they had to use unusual tactics to challenge its power. The federal military forces stationed in the South were too small to be effective against such widespread guerrilla activities, and many of the soldiers, though they had fought against slavery, were still in sympathy with white supremacy.[13]

Although Reconstruction did protect some of the political and civil rights of the Afro-American community, it achieved almost nothing in improving the social and economic situation. The concept of social and economic rights was almost nonexistent a century ago. Political rights, however, without economic security could be a mere abstraction. Meaningful freedom had to be more than the freedom to starve. This meant that the ex-slave needed land, tools, and training to provide him with an economic base that would make his freedom real. The ex-slave had limited education, limited experience, a servile slave attitude, and he was in need of social and economic training to compensate for the years of slavery. Without this he could not enter a competitive society as an equal. Emancipation was not enough.[14]

Most slaves had been engaged in plantation agriculture and were destined to continue in some kind of farm work. Sumner and Stevens led the fight in Congress to provide each of them with forty acres and a mule, and this would have provided the basis for their developing into an independent class of farmers. However, they were doomed to remain a subservient mass of peasants. The prewar slave plantation was replaced by share-cropping, tenant farming, and the convict lease system. In some cases the ex-slave was provided with land, tools, and seed by a plantation owner who, in turn, was to get a share of the crop at the end of the season. His share was always so large that the cropper remained permanently in his debt. Similarly, tenant farmers paid rent for their land and were extended loans by the store-keeper for their provisions. Interest rates ran so high that they too remained in permanent bondage. Finally, some plantation owners leased convicts from the state and worked them in chain gangs which most closely resembled the prewar slave system. In every case, the result was that black farm laborers remained members of a permanent peasant class.[15]

The other hope for the advancement of the ex-slave was through the development of industrial skills. At this time the American labor movement was emerging and was striving to protect and elevate the status of industrial workers. If the ex-slave had been integrated into this movement, it would have helped many of them to achieve economic security. At the same time, it would have strengthened the labor movement itself. However, white workers usually saw blacks as job competitors rather than as part of a mass labor alliance. In 1866 the National Labor Union decided to organize black workers within its ranks, but by 1869 it was urging colored delegates to its convention to form their own separate organization. This resulted in the creation of the National Negro Labor Convention. This split between black and white workers tended to push blacks into political action while whites put all their efforts into economic advancement.

The Knights of Labor was formed in 1869, and it did seriously try to organize blacks and whites. In the North it operated mixed locals, and in the South it had separate black and white organizations. It employed both black and white organizers. In 1886 its total membership was estimated at 700,000 of which 60,000 were black. The following year its total membership had shrunk to 500,000, but its black membership had increased to 90,000. The early labor movement which strove to organize the mass of industrial workers was soon replaced by skilled trade unions which aimed at the organization of a labor elite. Although the American

Federation of Labor did not profess racial discrimination as a deliberate national policy, many of its individual trade unions did, and, because of its federated structure, the A. F. of L. had no power over local discriminatory practices. Whites in skilled trades used unions to maintain an exclusive control in those trades, and they deliberately strove to relegate blacks to the lower ranks of industrial labor. Barred from the road to advancement, black labor became a permanent industrial proletariat.[16]

The Freedmen's Bureau was the one federal attempt to raise the social and economic standing of the ex-slave. Along with the American Missionary Association, the Freedmen's Bureau did significant work in education. Hundreds of teachers staffed scores of schools and brought some degree of literacy and job skills to thousands of pupils. However, beyond the field of education, the Bureau did little except to provide temporary help. Begun as a war measure, when the Radical Republicans came into control, they put it on a more permanent footing. Even liberals, however, were not prepared to support a long-term social experiment, and, after some half dozen years, the Bureau was terminated. This left the Afro-American community without the economic base necessary for competing in American society on an equal basis.

The one achievement of Reconstruction had been to guarantee a minimum of political and civil rights to the ex-slave, but white-supremacy advocates were adamant in their intention to destroy this advance. Where terror and intimidation were not successful, relentless economic pressure by landowners, merchants, and industrialists brought most of the ex-slaves into line. Year by year they exerted less influence at the voting booths.

Although the country was aware of this, Northern liberals were growing weary of the unending fight to protect the freedman. Furthermore, masses of Northern whites sympathized with Southern race prejudice. While they did approve of ending slavery, they were not willing to extend social and political equality. The North had begun to put a higher priority on peace than on justice. Industrialists were expanding their businesses rapidly, and they wanted the South to be pacified, so that it would be a safe area for investment and expansion. If this meant returning power to white conservatives, they were willing to pay the price.[17]

The presidential election of 1876 degenerated into chaos and confusion. Samuel J. Tilden, the Democratic candidate, and

Rutherford B. Hayes, the Republican, disputed its results. Democrats and Republicans both claimed twenty electoral votes from Oregon, Louisiana, South Carolina, and Florida. The first returns had shown that Tilden was the victor, but Republicans, especially Army veterans, warned that they would not accept such a result. The Republicans represented themselves as the party of the Union, and they claimed that the Democrats were the party of secession. The debate grew so heated that it appeared war could erupt again. Pessimists warned that it would be the last free election in American history. After months of bickering, a compromise was reached. The South was willing to support Republican Hayes if, when in power, he would remove the troops and restore home rule. The votes were counted again in the four states in question, and all twenty were awarded to Hayes allowing him to win by one electoral vote.[18]

Hayes began on an ambivalent note. On one hand he said that the country must have honest and equal government. This would appear to be a concession to the South which complained vehemently about the supposed corruption of black Reconstruction. On the other hand, he admitted that the rights of blacks must be protected by the Federal Government. In practice, however, by returning the South to home rule, he abandoned the ex-slave. He said that the ex-slave's interest would be best protected by being left in the hands of honest and influential Southern whites.

Hayes had expressed an awareness of the brutality and intimidation which still continued in the South, but he had apparently concluded that federal intervention only aggravated the problem. In his opinion Southern gentlemen were not thieves and cutthroats; they too were educated, civilized, and Christians. The fact that they were not aware of the brutality in their midst and that some of them undoubtedly participated in it, bewildered him. He was willing to proceed on the assumption that, if the Southern whites were left alone, they would, as they asserted, treat the ex-slave honestly and fairly. Hayes seemed unaware that men could be educated, civilized, and claim to be Christians while at the same time behaving as bigots and racists. To satisfy the industrialists in the North and the white conservatives in the South, Hayes buried the last remains of Reconstruction. However, he made a one-sided compromise. While he committed himself to immediate action, the South was only bound by vague promises to be fulfilled at some indefinite date. At the end of his term white supremacy in the South was more firmly rooted than it had been when he took office.[19]

The New Racism

For several years the fate of the Southern Negro hung in the balance. With home rule restored, the South, so it seemed, had achieved its goals. Bourbon whites, the remnant of the plantation aristocracy, dominated the Southern Democratic party and through it controlled state and local governments. There was a growing discontent among small farmers who wanted the state governments to alter the tax burden and interest rates in their favor. Largely spearheaded by the Populist movement, Negro and white farmers came to see that their interests were identical. The Southern Farmers' Alliance grew rapidly, and it encouraged the formation of the colored farmers' organizations with which it was closely allied. In Georgia, Tom Watson led the attempt to form a coalition between Negro and white farmers against the interests of the conservative white aristocracy. Hopes for a genuinely popular government and for a society free from racial tension reached a high level.

Unfortunately, some Negroes continued to back the Democratic party. House servants had always felt close to the gentry, and many of them remembered that poor white farmers had always been particularly prejudiced against them. In turn, conservatives deliberately encouraged racial hatred in order to drive a wedge between poor whites and Negroes within the rising Populist movement. It became evident to both Democrats and Populists that the Negro vote had become the deciding vote in many states. White farmers and white aristocrats both felt uneasy over this state of affairs.

The result was widespread agreement to systematically and legally eliminate Negroes from politics altogether. State constitutions were either amended or rewritten. Literacy tests and poll taxes became standard devices for limiting Negro voting. The "understanding test" required a citizen to interpret a portion of the state constitution to the satisfaction of the registrar. The severity of the test varied invariably with the color of the applicant. The "grandfather clause" prohibited those whose ancestors had not voted from exercising the franchise. Because slaves had not voted, their descendants were disqualified. Although the Fifteenth Amendment had been designed to guarantee the vote to the ex-slave, the South now evaded it. Although both major parties complained about this disenfranchisement and condemned it as being unconstitutional, neither party took any action.[20]

The Supreme Court also played an important part in restricting the freedom of freedmen. In 1883 it declared the 1875 Civil Rights Act to be unconstitutional. This act had made it illegal for individuals to discriminate in public accommodations. Although it had never been enforced, the court's decision, nevertheless, came as a setback, because it was the signal to the South that through Jim Crow legislation Negroes could be kept in "their place." Under slavery there had been considerable social contact between the races. Segregation as a social system was begun in the North prior to the Civil War, but, during the last two decades of the nineteenth century, Southern states made it a legal requirement. Its relentless growth is carefully outlined by C. Vann Woodward in his book *The Strange Career of Jim Crow*. Finally, the South developed two societies with two sets of institutions: separate railroad cars, separate waiting rooms, separate washrooms, separate drinking fountains, separate hospitals, separate schools, separate restaurants, separate cemeteries and, although there was only one judicial system, separate Bibles for taking oaths.

In 1896 the Supreme Court gave its blessing to the Jim Crow system. Plessy, a Louisiana mulatto, insisted on riding in the white car on the train. He was arrested and found guilty of violating the state statute. He appealed to the U. S. Supreme Court, but it upheld his conviction by claiming that "separate but equal" facilities were not a violation of his rights. Because the court did not define what it meant by equal and did not insist on enforcing that equality in concrete terms, its decision was, in fact, a blatant justification for separate and inferior facilities for Negroes. American society and law had turned the Afro-American community into an untouchable class.[21]

Segregation was accompanied by a new wave of race hatred. White Americans came to believe that all Negroes were alike and therefore could be treated as a group. An identical stereotype of the Negro fixed itself on the white mind throughout the entire country. If the Northerner hated this stereotype somewhat less than did the Southerner, it was only because the number of Negroes in the North was considerably smaller. At the end of the century only two percent of the total number of Afro-Americans was to be found in the North. The great northern migration had not yet begun.[22]

Both the Northern press and the genteel literary magazines contained the same vulgar image of the Negro which was to be found in openly racist communities in the South. Whether he appeared in news articles, editorials, cartoons, or works of fiction, he was universally portrayed as superstitious, stupid, lazy, happy-go-lucky, a liar, a thief, and a drunkard. He loved fun, clothes, and trinkets as well as chickens, watermelons, and sweet potatoes. Usually he was depicted as having been a faithful and loving slave before Emancipation, but, unfortunately, he was unable to adjust to his new freedom.[23]

News stories and editorials referred to Negroes in slanderous terms without any apparent sense of embarrassment. Phrases like "barbarian," "Negro ruffian," "African Annie," "colored cannibal," "coon," and "darkie" were standard epithets. Whenever blacks were depicted in cartoons or photographs, the stereotype presented them as having thick lips, flat noses, big ears, big feet, and kinky woolly hair. News items concerning those involved in criminal activities almost always identified them by color. This contributed to the development of the stereotype of the criminal Negro.[24]

Throughout its history, America had been predominantly an Anglo-Saxon and Protestant country. The Afro-American stood out in sharp distinction to this picture both because of his color and his African heritage. By the end of the nineteenth century America was being flooded with immigrants from Southern and Eastern Europe. They too were much darker than the dominant strains of Northern Europe, and many were Catholics. There was a growing feeling that these new immigrants, like the Negroes, were inherently alien and intrinsically unassimilable. Liberals in the progressive movement, who were concerned about protecting the integrity and morality of American society, were in the forefront of those who feared the new hordes of "swarthy" immigrants.

One of those who feared that the large influx of South and East Europeans would undermine the quality of American life was

Madison Grant. In his book *The Passing of the Great Race,* he warned that Nordic excellence would be swamped by the faster-spawning Catholic immigrants. Originally these racial stereotypes had some cultural and historical basis, but they were gaining a new strength and authority from the sociological and biological sciences centering in the concepts of Social Darwinism.[25]

Darwinism and related theories in anthropology and sociology helped to give an aura of respectability to racism in both Europe and America. The same kind of pseudo-scientific thinking which was developed in Europe to justify anti-Semitism was used in America to reinforce prejudices against Negroes as well as against Jews and South Europeans. In the first half of the nineteenth century the American anthropologist Samuel George Morton argued that each race had its own unique characteristics. Racial character, he believed, was the result of inheritance rather than of environment. Because these characteristics found specific environments congenial, each race had gravitated to its preordained geographic habitat.

Darwin's theory of evolution offered another explanation for the existence of differing species in the animal kingdom, and anthropologists concluded that it would also provide an explanation for racial differences in mankind. Early anthropologists and sociologists were preoccupied with dividing humanity into differing races and trying to catalog and explain these differences. Phrenology was another pseudo-science which attempted to construct a system according to which intellectual and moral characteristics would be correlated with the size and shape of the human head. On this basis many tried to divide mankind into physical types and to assign to each its own intellectual and moral qualities.

Another one who believed that human races could be scientifically measured and that their superiority and inferiority could thus be established was Joseph A. de Gobineau, a French anthropologist. Herbert Spencer took Darwin's concept of the survival of the fittest and used it as a scientific justification for the competitive spirit. It became the basis of the explanation why some individuals moved up the social ladder while others remained behind. Racial thinkers applied the concept of human competitiveness to racial conflict instead of to individual competition. In its usual form the Anglo-Saxon or Teutonic race was depicted as superior, and the Semitic and Negroid races as inferior. Human history was explained as the history of race conflict, and racial hostility was justified because, through this conflict, the superior types would survive and human civilization would be elevated. The concept of human equality was reduced to a meaningless abstraction. Scholars like William Graham Sumner insisted that the founding fathers only intended human equality to refer to their own kind of people.

To Thomas Nelson Page, in the *North American Review*, it appeared that the African race had not progressed in human history. It had failed to progress in America, not because it had been enslaved, but because it did not have the faculty to raise itself above that status. He continued to argue that its inability to advance in the scale of civilization was demonstrated by the level of social and political life to be found in Liberia, Haiti, the Dominican Republic, and Brazil. In the same journal, Theodore Roosevelt announced that the African was a member of "a perfectly stupid race" which was kept down by a lack of natural development.[26]

Another one whose views became influential was Josiah Strong. A prominent clergyman at the turn of the century, he was of the opinion that the pressure of population expansion would eventually push the whites, who had superior energy and talent, into Mexico, South and Central America, the islands of the seas, and eventually into Africa itself. This expansion would lead to racial conflict which would culminate in the survival of the fittest through the victory of the white over the colored races of the world.[27] Strong's belief that white racial superiority would naturally lead to racial imperialism and world domination by the white race was shared by many contemporary Americans. A few of those who shared his ideas were Senator Albert Beveridge, Henry Cabot Lodge, John Hay, Admiral Alfred T. Mahan, and Theodore Roosevelt. Racism opened the door to American imperialism.[28]

The new racism could not depend on the existence of slavery in order to reinforce white superiority. Instead, it drew on racial stereotypes and flimsy scientific opinion. The conquest of Africa by Europe and the American acquisition of lands in the Caribbean and Pacific which were inhabited by darker peoples, were taken as clear evidence of racial inequality even in the land which had been founded on the belief in the equality of all men. Second-class citizenship for blacks had become a fact which was accepted by Presidents, Congress, the Supreme Court, the business community, and by labor unions. Segregation was universal. In the North it was rooted in social custom, but in the South it had been made a matter of law. Separate facilities were inferior facilities. The basic political and civil rights of the Afro-American were severely limited in almost every state. Perhaps the clearest and cruelest index of the lowest state to which the black had been relegated was the large number of lynchings which occurred at the end of the century. In the 1890s lynchings of both blacks and whites were common. In that decade one black was lynched almost every two days. It became universally accepted that the American principles of justice, liberty, and equality did not have to be applied equally to whites and blacks.

CHAPTER 7

Racism and Democracy

Fighting Jim Crow

RAYFORD W. LOGAN, in his book *The Betrayal of the Negro* described the turn of the century as the low point in Afro-American history. After Emancipation, he contended, the hopes of the Negroes were betrayed. Again they were pushed down into second-class status. It appeared that democracy was for whites only. Actually, the increasing growth of racism and of legal segregation as well, led inevitably to the development of opposition groups bent on destroying this discrimination. Segregation promoted the creation of Negro institutions which then became the center for this counterattack.

The most prominent of these Afro-American institutions was the Negro church. Like the white church, it was fragmented into many separate denominations. There was the African Methodist Episcopal Church, the African Methodist Episcopal Zion Church, the Colored Methodist Episcopal Church, the National Baptists, and a host of denominational organizations.

However, integrated congregations within the mainly white church groups were almost nonexistent. Those blacks who did belong to such white denominations usually attended all-black congregations within the larger institutional structure. Negro colleges also sprang up throughout the South as well as an occasional one in the North. These included such well-known schools as Howard, Hampton, Tuskegee, and Fisk. The churches and colleges became training grounds for a growing middle-class and for future community leaders. Each in its own way provided a debating center in which racial problems closing in from all sides were considered.

As Negroes were frequently denied employment by whites, they began to develop businesses of their own. Because their capital was almost always small, their task was made more difficult. White-owned banks hesitated to lend money to Negroes, forcing them into developing banks of their own. By 1900 blacks had founded four banks which appealed mainly to a Negro clientele. They had a combined capital of more than $90,000. White-owned insurance companies often refused to sell insurance policies to Negroes. Standardized mortality charts showed that Negroes died at an earlier age than whites. When insurance companies did accept them as clients, they were charged higher rates than were whites. During the nineteenth century, various Negro secret societies attempted to develop insurance programs for their members. In 1898 the National Benefit Insurance Company was opened in Washington. Owned by blacks, it deliberately sought out Negro patronage. In the same year, the Mutual Benefit Insurance Company was opened in North Carolina along similar lines.[1]

White undertakers and beauticians were reluctant to cater to Negro customers. Aside from their personal tastes, they feared that it would alienate their white patrons. A similar situation held true for dentists and doctors. This forced the Afro-American community to develop its own professionals. By 1900, Negroes had invested half a million dollars in undertaking establishments. By that same year, the Afro-American community had produced 1,700 physicians, 212 dentists, 728 lawyers, 310 journalists, and several thousand college, secondary, and elementary school teachers.[2]

Other Negro professionals, finding themselves excluded from existing official affiliations, formed their own professional fraternity in 1904. Two years later, the first Greek letter society for Negroes was established to help its members in coping with the effects of social isolation on largely white college campuses. In 1915, Carter G. Woodson established the Association for the Study of Negro Life and History and began publication of the *Journal of Negro History.*

In 1905, W. E. B. DuBois, John Hope, Monroe Trotter, Kelly Miller, and other outspoken young Negro intellectuals met in Niagara Falls, Ontario, and founded the "Niagara Movement." Unlike the other black institutions mentioned above, the "Niagara Movement" was primarily political in its objectives. On the one hand, it strove to seize the leadership of the Afro-American community, taking it away from the more conciliatory emphasis of

Booker T. Washington. On the other hand, they wanted a platform from which to condemn, loudly and clearly, the white prejudice they found all about them.

The organization deliberately tried to resurrect the spirit of the angry abolitionists immediately preceding the Civil War. The meeting places of their three conventions were chosen for their symbolic value. Niagara Falls was the terminal on the underground railway, the point at which runaways had reached freedom. Harpers Ferry had been the site of John Brown's violent assault on slavery, and Oberlin, Ohio, had been well known as a center of abolitionist activity.

The growth of racism at the turn of the century, besides encouraging the development of Negro institutions, revived the interests of some whites in fighting for racial justice. Whites were particularly upset by racially motivated acts of violence. Lynchings reached a high point in American history at this time. Between 1900 and 1910, there were 846 lynchings, in which 92 victims were white and 754 Negro.[3] Northern whites were especially perturbed as racial violence began to move into the North. Previously they had viewed it as a Southern white man's problem. When a vicious race riot occurred in Springfield, Illinois, in 1908, this illusion was shattered. William English Walling, the journalist, was shocked and wrote an impassioned article, "Race War in the North," which was published in *The Independent*.

Walling's article, which was based on his visit to Springfield, brought several collaborators to his side. In it, he contended that Southern racists were bringing the race war into the North and that the only alternative was to revive the spirit of abolitionism and to fight for racial equality. The following year a group of concerned individuals, black and white, met in New York City and their meeting resulted in the formation of the National Association for the Advancement of Colored People. Those attending this meeting, besides Walling, included Oswald Garrison Villard, the grandson of William Lloyd Garrison, Jane Addams, the founder of Hull House in Chicago, John Dewey, the philosopher, William Dean Howells, the editor of *Harper's* magazine, Mary White Ovington, a New York social worker, and Dr. Henry Moskowitz. The Negro delegation consisted of W. E. B. DuBois and most of the other members of the Niagara Movement. At this meeting it was decided that the achievement of racial equality must be the major target of their attack. In order to achieve this goal it was decided that their immediate priorities should include the enfranchisement of Negroes and the enforcement of the Thirteenth and Fourteenth Amendments. The members also insisted that it was time to launch a concerted attack against lynching and other kinds of mob violence.[4]

The National Association for the Advancement of Colored People was officially established in 1910 with Moorefield Storey as its president. W. E. B. DuBois was the only black on its board and served as its director of publicity and research. Most blacks and whites at the time believed that the N.A.A.C.P. was irresponsible for including so many of the members of the Niagara Movement in its membership. Monroe Trotter and a few others, however, held that an interracial organization such as the N.A.A.C.P. could not be trusted to take a strong enough stand on important issues, and they refused to cooperate with it. The N.A.A.C.P. began publication of its own journal, *Crisis*, which was a basic part of its informational program. *Crisis* was edited by W. E. B. DuBois.

The most important work of the Association was done by its legal department. Its lawyers attacked the legal devices used by some states to disenfranchise Negroes. In 1915, the Supreme Court declared, in *Guinn v. United States*, that the "grandfather clause" in the constitutions of both Maryland and Oklahoma was null and void because it contradicted the Fifteenth Amendment. Two years later, in *Buchanan v. Warley*, the court said that Louisville's ordinance requiring Negroes to live in specified sections of the city was unconstitutional. In 1923, the N.A.A.C.P. came to the defense of a Negro who, it believed, had not received a fair trial. In *Moore v. Dempsey*, the Supreme Court granted the defendant a new trial because the court which had convicted him of murder had exempted Negroes from serving on its jury.

Branches of the N.A.A.C.P. spread all across the country. By 1921 there were more than 400 separate chapters, and the Association was still growing. Its membership, whether white or black, tended to be middle-class and educated. In this respect it bore a marked similarity to the National Urban League which came into existence at about the same time.

The National Urban League grew out of a concern for the employment problems of Negroes in New York City. George Edmund Haynes, a Negro graduate student at Columbia University, was researching the economic conditions of New York City Negroes. He was invited to present his findings to a joint meeting of two city organizations which were probing the same problem. The Committee for Improving Industrial Conditions of Negroes in New York as well as the National League for the Protection of Colored Women had been formed early in the century and were eager to base their efforts on scientific study rather than on mere sentimentality. Haynes's research was later published as *The Negro at Work in New York City.*[5]

This meeting resulted in the establishing of the Urban League which has been concerned primarily with finding employment for Negroes and aiding them in acquiring improved job skills. Haynes and Eugene Kinckle Jones were its executive directors. One of its sponsors was Booker T. Washington, who was more sympathetic with its orientation than he had been with either the Niagara Movement or the N.A.A.C.P., both of which were more political and aggressive. The philanthropist Julius Rosenwald gave the League substantial financial aid. The Urban League soon spread into other major cities and gained increasing importance as ever-growing numbers of Negroes migrated into Northern urban areas and needed assistance in making the adjustment. Negro churches and colleges, along with interracial organizations, began to establish the foundation for the long hard struggle for racial equality which lay ahead.

Making the World Safe for Democracy

While Negroes and some whites were engaged in trying to put American ideals into practice within the country, others were reaching out to spread American democracy to more "underprivileged" peoples. American society had always contained a missionary dynamic. The Puritan Fathers came to America to escape religious oppression and to establish what they believed would be the Kingdom of God. While it appeared that all they wanted was space in which to be left alone, their conviction that they were building God's Kingdom implied a belief that their new society would prosper and spread. If it were really the Kingdom of God, it could not be expected to remain an insignificant settlement on a distant and unimportant continent. For the next two hundred years, this missionary dynamic was absorbed in spreading across the North American continent. While the Americans did not see their expansion into the West as being imperialistic, American Indians saw it otherwise.

With the disappearance of the Western frontier, missionary-minded Americans felt compelled to carry the benefits of their civilization to backward areas of the world. At the same time, European imperialism was gaining new vitality. Businessmen were looking for new markets and for new sources of raw materials. Patriots, in their turn, believed that they were being called upon to assume the "white man's burden" and to civilize and democratize the world. Both drives seemed to coincide. The Berlin Conference in 1885 divided those parts of Africa not yet annexed among the major European nations. The point of the conference was to plan national exploits in such a way as to reduce conflicts. In the course of a very few years, the rest of Africa was colonized by these nations. Africans, of course, were given no voice in the matter. China, though it was not colonized, was also divided into spheres of economic influence. The United States was quick to join in this scramble. Its influence, however, was limited largely to Asia and Latin America.

This new imperialist expansion was not interpreted by its proponents as being exploitative. Instead, they depicted it as bringing the blessing of civilization to the "underprivileged." The concept of the "white man's burden" was particularly common in Britain and America. The prevailing idea was that the white race, especially the Anglo-Saxon and Teutonic branches of it, had been especially blessed by God so that it could achieve industrialization and democratization. It further taught that it was their obligation to carry the benefits to less fortunate peoples.

This new imperialism hid its domination behind paternalism, but it still presented the imperialists as superiors and the colonials as inferiors. Moreover, because in most cases the imperialists were white and the colonials colored, it meant that this imperialist drive also carried racial connotations. The American version of the "white man's burden" was most blatantly presented by Josiah Strong in his book *Our Country*. According to Strong, the superior Anglo-Saxon race in America would multiply rapidly, become powerful and prosperous, and then would spread the blessings of industrialization and democracy south into Mexico and into the Caribbean Islands. At the same time, American commercial interests were searching for new markets and were making increasing investments in these very areas. The merchants were looking for new markets to exploit, but the idealist rhetoric talked only in terms of benevolent paternalism.

These trends came to a head in the Spanish-American War. Conflicts had been increasing in Cuba between the Spanish authorities in control and the local citizens. Americans became interested in several abortive uprisings which occurred on the island. The brutal way in which the Spanish had suppressed them incensed the Americans. The violence in Cuba also endangered American life and property—the result of increasing American investments. The public favored intervention, proposing that their Caribbean neighbors should also share in the benefits of democracy. They viewed the Spaniards as an antidemocratic element from the Old World blocking the road to progress in the western hemisphere.

The battleship *Maine* was sent to the Havana harbor ostensibly on a courtesy visit. Its real object was to protect American interests. It was mysteriously blown up, and many of its crew were killed. The cause of the explosion is still unknown. American chauvinists chose to believe that the ship had been deliberately destroyed, and they demanded retaliation. Before long, American troops were sent to "liberate" the Cubans from Spanish oppression.

Although the number of Negro troops who participated in the Spanish-American War was small, they fought heroically and contributed significantly to the American victory. The Negro participants served in segregated units. These included the 9th and 10th Cavalry and the 24th and 25th Infantry units. In the battle of San Juan Hill, the Negro cavalry opened the way for the Rough Riders' famous charge which was led by Theodore Roosevelt. Later in the day, the 24th Infantry came up from the rear to support the action.[6]

At the end of the war, Spain gave the United States sovereignty over Puerto Rico and, for the payment of a sum of money, the U. S. also gained the Philippines. Spain gave up her sovereignty over Cuba, but its future status was not made clear. American public opinion had become so wed to the cause of democracy in Cuba that the American government felt it could not take direct control of the island. It was deemed necessary to establish a Cuban Republic, but it was obvious that America would exercise considerable influence over it. Early in the century the Platt Amendment was passed by the U. S. Congress, and Cuba was required to include it within her own constitution. This gave the United States authority to intervene in Cuban affairs in order to maintain law and order. The U. S. also obtained Guantanamo Bay as a naval base in Cuba.[7]

In 1916 American marines landed in Santo Domingo to restore law and order there in the wake of a series of local uprisings. Again, Americans wanted to protect their business interests in the island. The American presence, however, only contributed to the total collapse of civil government, and the marines were not withdrawn until 1924. American commercial influence continued and grew even after the soldiers left. Similarly, America intervened in the internal affairs of Haiti. It began with the assumption of financial control of the Haitian government to help it achieve stability and, at the same time, to secure American investments. In an attempt to maintain law and order, American intervention spread to include taking control of the country's police force. In 1917, the U. S. established military rule in Haiti and this was not appreciated by the local citizens. The marines were compelled to shoot some two thousand Haitians in the process of restoring peace. The troops were not finally withdrawn from Haiti until 1934.[8]

In spreading the benefits of her civilization into the Caribbean, America acquired a colored empire which only served to complicate her own racial situation. Blacks, however, played an important role in the acquisition of this territory. American ministers to Haiti were usually Negroes, and Negro soldiers played a significant part in the Spanish-American War. In their attempts to demonstrate their loyalty and patriotism, American Negroes unwittingly helped to bring more colored peoples under the sway of American racism.

America's real involvement in world politics occurred with her entrance into the First World War. The British and French had sought to give the war an ideological flavor in order both to stir up the patriotism of their own citizens and also to draw in support from other nations, especially the United States. The war was portrayed as a conflict between democracy and authoritarianism. When America joined the conflict, President Wilson emphasized even further this posture of idealism. Americans viewed the war as the last war—the war which would make the world "safe for democracy."

The Afro-American community remained oblivious to the hostilities in Europe and was late in becoming aware of the imminence of war. Negroes were preoccupied with the racial harassments confronting them at home and seldom looked beyond the country's borders. Once America became involved in the fighting, however, they were eager to demonstrate that they were patriotic and loyal citizens. Even W. E. B. DuBois, who was as hostile and angry as any, came to support the war effort. In an article which he wrote in *Crisis,* he called for his brothers to close ranks with the rest of American society and to present a solid front against the enemy. This patriotic solidarity came in spite of the fact that segregation was creeping into the Federal Government itself.

President Taft, who had tried to broaden the base of the Republican Party in the South, had made some feeble beginnings at instituting segregation in federal facilities in Washington. In 1913, Wilson, the first Southern Democratic president since the Civil War, vastly expanded the process. The N.A.A.C.P. expressed shock at Jim Crowism becoming an official part of the government in the nation's capital. At the same time, the Civil Service required job applicants to file their photographs with their applications. The N.A.A.C.P. charged that this was part of the spread of discriminatory practices in Washington, but the Civil Service denied it.[9]

When America declared war against Germany in April, 1917, only a few Negroes were members of the standing army. However, many immediately rushed to enlist, but only a few were accepted. Local enlistment officers were dubious about the ability and the loyalty of Negroes. Apparently their previous service record had been forgotten. When Congress passed the Selective Service Act in May, it was made to apply to all citizens alike. During the course of the war, some 367,000 Negroes were called into military service. This was 31 percent of those who had registered. Meanwhile, only 26 percent of the white registrants were called. Once the Selective Service Act went into effect, discrimination had the reverse effect from what it had produced before. Instead of keeping Negroes out of the Army, some Selective Service Boards discriminated against them in terms of the exemptions which were permitted. Throughout the war, the Navy only accepted Negroes in menial jobs, and the Marine Corps barred them altogether.[10]

Training the Negro troops presented another problem. No community welcomed an influx of hundreds or thousands of young Negro men. The South, especially, was outraged when large numbers of "cocky" Negroes from the North descended upon some sleepy, peaceful town. Segregation and discrimination within the military itself caused further irritations and triggered violence at more than one camp. The 92nd, an all-Negro outfit, was trained at seven separate locations, and it was the only American unit never to come together before reaching the front. The 93rd, another all-Negro unit, was never consolidated. When it reached France, it served with various units of the French Army. It had been sent overseas hastily, and its troops received most of their training in Europe. Its men had largely been recruited from New York State, and they were sent to Spartanburg, South Carolina, for their training. The local citizens deliberately picked a fight with the men in order to "put them in their place." A riot was narrowly averted. When they were shipped back north for training, they found themselves sharing a camp with white troops from the South. Another incident almost occurred, and they were immediately sent overseas for training.[11]

Besides serving in segregated units, most of the Negro troops were assigned to menial tasks. One third of the American stevedore force in Europe was Negro. Nevertheless, many of them did become involved in the fighting and distinguished themselves heroically. Besides receiving American awards, they were generously honored by the French. The 369th was the first American unit to reach the Rhine, and the French praised it highly.

Many of the Negro soldiers were surprised by the hospitality which they received in France. Several stayed behind, after the war, to study in European universities. In spite of the fact that many whites warned the French of dangers involved with associating with Negroes, especially white women with Negro men, the French were happy to have them share in the defense. Many invited them into their homes. In the meantime, rumors spread in America that Negro troops were taking unwise liberties with French women. It was also said that the crime of rape was widespread. Americans worried about what would happen when these men returned home. The rumors were so insistent that, finally, the government sent Dr. Moton, the president of Tuskegee Institute, to Europe to investigate the situation. He found that the rumors were totally unwarranted.

When the victors met at Versailles to write the treaty which ended the war, black people around the world, including Afro-Americans, hoped that they would take up the problem of the African peoples as well. The only consideration which was given to Africa, however, was the disposal of the German colonies. These were distributed among the victors. This did nothing to give Africa back to the Africans; it only changed the identity of the European masters. W. E. B. DuBois, who was looking for a way to spotlight the problem of the African peoples, called a Pan-African Congress to meet in Paris simultaneously with the meeting in Versailles. Fifty-seven delegates came, of which most were from Africa and America. While they had no authority and could do little of significance, the Congress did dramatize to the world the plight of the subject peoples of Africa.[12]

Urban Riots

In spite of the fact that Negroes were fighting overseas to defend their country, racial tensions continued at home. In the years immediately preceding the war, racially motivated lynchings and riots, which had been largely confined to the South, began to spread into the North and Midwest.

In Statesboro, Georgia, two blacks, who had been accused and convicted of murder, were seized from the courtroom by an angry mob. After beating and burning them, the mob went on to loot and burn Negro-owned homes in the community. In 1906, a white mob raged out of control for several days in Atlanta, Georgia. In the same year, the 25th Infantry in Brownsville, Texas, became involved in a riot with the white citizens of that town, and Roosevelt dismissed the whole battalion without honor. In 1904, a riot occurred in Springfield, Ohio, much farther north than anyone would have expected. A Negro, who had been charged with killing a white police officer, was seized from jail by an angry mob. After hanging him from a telephone pole, the mob riddled his body with bullets. Then, they went on to destroy large sections of the Negro part of town.

In 1908, Springfield, Illinois, was the scene of the famous riot which helped to motivate the founding of the N.A.A.C.P. There, a white woman claimed to have been raped by a Negro. Although she admitted that she had, in fact, been assaulted by a white man, the angry mob was only further enraged. It ran out of control for several days, and the state's militia was called in to restore order. Besides looting and burning, the mob boldly and deliberately lynched two of the city's responsible Negro citizens. The leaders of the mob, as usual, went unpunished.

Although DuBois had urged the Negroes to close ranks with white America, white racists did not reciprocate. An even worse race riot occurred in East St. Louis, Illinois, in 1917. The white community was afraid that a mass influx of Negroes from the South was about to occur. On one hand, Illinois Democrats played on racial prejudice to further their political interests. They accused Republicans of intending to colonize large numbers of Negroes from the South in order to enlarge the Republican vote.

On the other hand, labor unions feared that Negroes would be imported as strikebreakers. During an attempt to organize a union at the Aluminum Ore Company which led to a strike in April, 1917, this atmosphere increased racial tensions. In 1913, the company had hired no Negro workers at all. By 1916, there were two hundred Afro-American employees. Within three months at the end of 1916 and the beginning of 1917, the company fired some two hundred whites while, at the same time, hiring approximately the same number of Negroes. The city had been totally segregated, and the white citizens intended to keep it that way. The school system had been segregated in spite of a state law of 1874 which forbade segregation in education. Jim Crow was also standard in theaters, restaurants, and hotels in opposition to the 1885 law that had outlawed segregation in public accommodations. Local citizens were afraid that the rumored influx of Negroes would drastically alter the situation. Later investigation showed that the size of the migration had been vastly exaggerated.[13]

Tension surrounding the racial and labor conflict in East St. Louis exploded into a minor riot in May. A Negro had accidentally wounded a white man during a liquor-store holdup, but the story that was circulated was that an innocent young white girl had been shot and killed. The white community, especially the striking workers, became an enraged mob which roamed the streets beating any Negroes it could find. The mob also burned Negro-owned stores and homes. The next day the National Guard arrived and, with the help of the police, searched the Negro community for weapons. In spite of the fact that the mob had been white, it was the Negroes who were disarmed and arrested. East St. Louis became filled with rumors that the Negroes were preparing for revenge.

Late in the evening of July 1, a Ford sedan raced through the Negro section of East St. Louis shooting at doors and windows as it passed. The police heard that Negroes were on a shooting rampage, and they sent a car to investigate. They came in another Ford sedan, and most of the officers were wearing civilian dress. In the meantime, the Negro citizens had prepared for the return of the first car. As the police entered the poorly lit street, they were met by a barrage of bullets. Almost all the officers were either killed or wounded. The white community was outraged at what it believed to be an unprovoked attack, and it wanted revenge.

Although the Guard was called again, the riot lasted for several days. At one point, the white mob set a row of shacks on fire and waited in ambush until its residents were forced to flee the flames. Then, they took great delight in coldly and deliberately shooting them down as they fled. It was reported that some of those who were shot were thrown back into the burning buildings, and others were thrown into the river. Two children, between one and two years old, were found shot through the head. At times, the mob would not let ambulances take away the wounded and dying. For the most part, the Guard and the police stood by. According to some reports, they occasionally participated themselves.

According to official reports thirty-nine Negroes and two whites had been killed, but the police contended that, because so many bodies had been burned, thrown in the river, or buried in mass graves, the figure was really much larger. They estimated the number of dead at a hundred, and the grand jury accepted their calculation. It was also estimated that as many as 750 had been wounded. The Guard held an investigation of the riot, and it exonerated the behavior of its soldiers. However, a Congressional investigation later accused the Guard's colonel of cowardice, and it said that the Guard had exhibited extreme inefficiency. The *Washington Evening Mail* carried a cartoon which depicted Wilson standing before a group of Negroes reading an official document proclaiming that the world should be made safe for democracy. The caption over the cartoon read, "Why not make America safe?"

When the Negro soldiers returned home from Europe, they brought new experiences and changed attitudes with them. As soldiers, they had been taught to stand up and fight like men. In Europe, they had been treated more like men than ever before. The attitude of submissiveness which had been stamped on the Afro-American community by its slave mentality and which had been reinforced by the philosophy of Booker T. Washington was undermined by this new sense of manhood. When a wave of two dozen riots swept America in the summer of 1919, Negroes fought back as they had not done in East St. Louis. Riots occurred in places as diverse as Longview, Texas, Washington, D.C., Omaha, Nebraska, and Chicago, Illinois.

The worst riot of that bloody summer occurred in Chicago. It began when a young Negro boy, swimming in Lake Michigan, crossed into a section of the water which had been traditionally reserved for whites. White youths began throwing stones at him, and he drowned. A later investigation showed that he had not been hit by any of these rocks. Nevertheless, this incident triggered the tense racial situation in Chicago into an explosion. Fighting broke out all over the city. Whites pulled Negroes from streetcars and beat them openly. The fighting raged for thirteen days. At least thirty-eight people were killed. Fifteen of these were white, and twenty-three were Negro. Also, some five hundred people were injured of which the majority were Negro. Many houses were burned, and it was estimated that one thousand families were left homeless.[14]

The Klan Revival

While the nation went to war to make the world safe for democracy, many at home believed that it was still necessary to make America safe first. These people fell into two groups. There were those within the Afro-American community who felt that a country which systematically disenfranchised a large minority group and which also tolerated widespread discrimination, segregation, and violence against that minority was not a secure democratic state. At the same time, those who were responsible for much of this harassment and terror believed that violence was necessary precisely in order to protect democracy. They believed that true democracy sprang from the virtue of a white, Anglo-Saxon, Protestant civilization, and they wanted to protect it against alien subversion.

One of the main "protectors" of white American civilization was the Ku Klux Klan. The original Klan had thrived in the deep South immediately after the Civil War. In 1915, it underwent a revival. Inspired by the migration of Afro-Americans from the South into the North and West as well as by the gigantic immigration of South and East Europeans, the Klan, beginning in Georgia, rapidly spread beyond the South into a national movement. Confidently believing in the superiority of its own democratic way of life, America had thrown open its doors to the hungry and oppressed of Europe. American society took pride in being the world's great melting pot. However, many old-stock Americans did not view their society as being a cultural amalgam, and they expected that the new European immigrants, as well as the Afro-Americans, would want to be assimilated into their society as it already existed. When they promised the newcomers freedom and equality, many of these Americans were offering these benefits expecting that the immigrants would adjust and conform. They did not believe that the values and life style of foreigners were equal to their own, and therefore they did not want to grant the outsiders the freedom to "pollute" American society with alien cultures. When it became evident that American Negroes as well as many of these new immigrants were not able to be absorbed into white, Anglo-Saxon, Protestant America as easily as had been expected, many ardent patriots became panic-stricken over the future of the American way of life. This sense of terror drove them to take extreme action in its defense.

The invisible empire of the Ku Klux Klan was the most militant and best organized of several defenders of this kind of American patriotism. It built its power on a series of appeals which had deep roots throughout American life. During the 1920s, anti-Semitism was widespread, and many respectable hotels and clubs were closed to Jews. Discrimination against foreign-born Americans was prevalent. Many patriotic and artistic societies were exclusively for native-born Americans. Discrimination against Afro-Americans was a national phenomenon, but in the South it was an orthodox social and political creed.

The revival of the Klan in 1915 was closely associated with the release of the famous motion picture *The Birth of a Nation*. D. W. Griffith based his movie on material taken from two novels by Thomas Dixon: *The Leopard's Spots* and *The Klansman*. At first *The Birth of a Nation* was censored in some cities in the North and West for being inflammatory because of its racial attitudes. This angered many who claimed that it was, in fact, a truthful account of the Klan. Concerned by the official opposition to the movie, Dixon contacted an old college friend who was then occupying the White House. President Woodrow Wilson consented to a special White House showing of the picture. After the White House showing, opposition throughout the North and West disintegrated, and the movie went on to become a gigantic success. It grossed eighteen million dollars. While much of this success was undoubtedly due to its appeal to common underlying racial prejudice in the American character, it must also be admitted that much of the popularity was due to the fact that it was the first full-length successful movie and that it had much entertainment value.[15]

Colonel William J. Simmons chose the opening of the movie in Atlanta, Georgia, as the time to launch his Klan revival. His father had been a member of the original Klan. When the revival began in 1915, the Klan was primarily a fraternal, Caucasian-supremacy organization without the violence normally associated with it. But when Simmons later decided to develop it into a larger organization, he found it necessary to adopt more aggressive tactics.

At one meeting, Simmons dramatically portrayed the dynamic, hostile note that helped the organization to spread and appeal to the fears and the hatreds of people throughout the country. In the middle of a speech, he first drew a gun from one pocket and laid it on the table before him. Then, he pulled another gun from another pocket and placed it beside the first one. Opening his jacket, he unfastened a cartridge belt and draped it ostentatiously across the table. Finally, he reached into still another pocket, pulled out a knife and plunged it into the wood between the two guns. With this flamboyant gesture, he issued a challenge to all "niggers," Catholics, Jews, and all others. He warned them that his organization and its supporters were ready to meet them and would protect themselves and the American way of life from any kind of corruption. While the Klan is normally thought of as being an anti-Negro institution, the other major themes on which it built in the 1920s were opposition to Catholicism, dope, bootlegging, gambling, roadhouses, and loose sexual behavior.[16]

For the Klan, the end justified the means. Defending the values of American society was to them so important as to condone the use of violence and murder. By 1921, Klan membership had soared to 100,000, but its real growth had only just begun. As it came under public attack, its popularity increased. Newspapers and Congressmen charged that the Klan had violated the First, Fourth, Fifth, Sixth, and Thirteenth Amendments to the Constitution. The House Rules Committee held hearings on the Klan. However, the committee chairman found that he lost the next election. Newspapers attacked the Klan in lurid headlines which, although they helped to sell copy, only succeeded in making the Klan more attractive to potential members. By 1923, Klan membership was estimated between two and three million.[17]

When it was at its zenith, the Klan used violence, intimidation, and parades to make its presence known in the community. Its members were prominent on police forces, sheriff departments, and various other local branches of government. In the early 1920s, Klan support was responsible for electing a handful of senators and several Congressmen. Finally, in 1924, an attempt was made to capture both political parties on the national level. Failing to get its nominee chosen as Vice President on the Republican ticket, the Klan swung its full attention to the Democratic convention in Madison Square Garden in New York. Anti-Klan forces at the convention were also strong. The convention leadership made the attempt to keep the issue in the background, but a minority report on the platform resulted in forcing the convention to condemn the Klan by name. The convention was split in two. As a result, it took the party nine days and one hundred and twenty-three ballots before it was successful in choosing its national candidates. In the following year, the Klan again tried to make its presence felt on the national scene. It held a march of its members in Washington. Forty thousand robed and hooded Klansmen marched down Pennsylvania Avenue in a display of strength while thousands more cheered and watched.[18]

The violence which, for a short time, had helped the Klan to grow, would eventually contribute to its decline. It appealed to public animosity against Catholics, Jews, and Negroes, but its own vitriolic crusade swung segments of that same public opinion in favor of its victims. The Klan revival was particularly disheartening to Negroes, who had assumed that the Klan was dead. While slavery was gone, brutality and intimidation remained. Half a century after the demise of the original Klan, it had risen again and, this time, had become a nationwide phenomenon. Jim Crow was the law in the South, and racism had become rampant in the North. Slavery had been abolished, but Negroes were aware that they still were not free.

PART THREE

The Search for Equality

CHAPTER 8

The Crisis of Leadership

The Debate over Means and Ends

IN the nineteenth century the problem that faced the Afro-American community was how to destroy the institution of slavery. In the twentieth century the question was how to achieve equality. Frederick Douglass had been in the vanguard of the fight to overthrow the peculiar institution; later, he was among the first to realize that Emancipation had not solved all the problems. It was his belief that the forces of racism and indifference were responsible for relegating the ex-slave to a second-class status. When the Federal Government terminated Reconstruction without providing his people with the tools for competing in American society, Douglass's disappointment was severe.

At the turn of the century the focus of the problems facing Afro-Americans had changed. Slavery had been abolished, but not race prejudice. The elimination of this scourge became the basis for a new drive. Douglass, who for a half century had been looked upon as the spokesman for his people, was too old to tackle the task of ending segregation and prejudice based on race. When he died early in 1895, the Afro-American community was left without leadership capable of uniting the diverse elements within the movement. The pressing need was for black men and women to escape physical violence and to find acceptance with dignity, and it couldn't wait.

However, within this community there were many who were capable of leadership. What was lacking were the instruments of leadership. Money, power, and the press, for the most part, were in the hands of whites who had concluded that the ex-slave would have to solve his own problems. What this meant was that the whites wanted to be left in peace. Dozens of Afro-Americans, however, were not content to accept the degrading position which had been assigned to them. Utilizing the limited resources within

[121]

their own community, new leadership evolved and began to debate the issues of the day. Before Emancipation the problems had seemed simple. All attention was focused on the abolition of slavery, and the only point of controversy centered on the means by which it should be achieved. But segregation and discrimination were not so easily defined and attacked. The debates which ensued widened to include disagreement over both means and ends.

A vocal minority, discouraged by the emasculating effects of discrimination, believed that they should withdraw from white society altogether. Some of them wanted to return to Africa and to assist its inhabitants in their liberation from European imperialism. They planned to create an independent African nation. Others, while not wanting to leave America, still wanted to withdraw from white society into a world of their own choosing and making.

The majority, however, insisted that the African immigrant, like those from Europe, had the right to all the privileges of being American. Some of them wanted to join the white society, accept its Euro-American cultural values, forget their past, and assimilate into the mainstream of American life. Still others, while wanting to find their place within the American nation, insisted that the country must be transformed into a genuinely pluralistic society. While they wanted to be integrated into the nation, they did not want to join the white society. Instead of assimilating into Anglo-Saxon culture, they wanted American civilization to become multi-racial, multi-ethnic, and highly fluid.

The means which were proposed to achieve these differing ends were highly diverse. Some argued that the ex-slave must first demonstrate his readiness to be accepted within white society. Others claimed that they need only demand the rights which were legally theirs. In order to do this they planned to make aggressive use of the press and the courts. Mass organization to achieve economic and political pressure was also recommended as another technique.

There were scores of leaders representing dozens of differing positions. In the first half of the twentieth century, the spectrum was limited almost exclusively to the advocacy of nonviolent techniques. Four of these leaders will be discussed below. Their ideas present a broad overview of the concepts to be found within the Afro-American community. Booker T. Washington, W. E. B. Du-

Bois, Marcus Garvey, and A. Philip Randolph represented a wide variety of approaches, their ideas forming the total spectrum of the thrust for remaking the black role in white society.

Booker T. Washington: The Trumpet of Conciliation

Within a few months of Douglass's death, a new leader was thrust upon the Afro-American community. Unlike Douglass, who believed in self-assertion, Booker T. Washington developed a leadership style based on the model of the old plantation house servant. He used humility, politeness, flattery, and restraint as a wedge with which he hoped to split the wall of racial discrimination. His conciliatory approach won the enthusiastic support of the solid South as well as that of influential Northern politicians and industrialists. Their backing gained him a national reputation and provided him with easy access to the press. Members of his own community were filled with pride to see one of their own treated with such respect by wealthy and influential leaders of white America. When Theodore Roosevelt entertained Washington for dinner at the White House, the Afro-American community was overjoyed. However, some whites believed that it had been a dangerous breach of etiquette. Nevertheless, there were those within the Afro-American community who were not enthusiastic about their new leader. They believed that conciliation was the road to surrender and not the way to victory.

Booker T. Washington was born into slavery on April 5, 1858. His mother had been a slave in Franklin County, Virginia. The identity of his white father remains unknown. After Emancipation the family moved to West Virginia where it struggled to achieve a livelihood. Young Booker attended a school for the children of ex-slaves while, at the same time, holding down a full-time job in the mines. As a courteous, cooperative, hard-working young man he secured a job cleaning and doing other tasks around the house of one of the mine owners. This occupation was less strenuous than working in the mines, and it left him more energy to pursue his studies. In 1872, with nothing to help him besides his determination, he traveled and worked his way hundreds of miles to Hampton Institute. Undaunted by lack of tuition, he insisted that he could do some useful work to cover his expenses. When he was directed to clean the adjoining room as a kind of entrance test, his response was to apply himself to the task. When the teacher's white handkerchief could not discover any dirt in the room, she was so impressed with his work and with his genial personality that she admitted him to the institute and found janitorial jobs to ease his financial situation.[1]

Hampton Normal and Agricultural Institute had been started after the Civil War by General Samuel Armstrong to train ex-slaves to lead their people in pursuit of land and homes. Armstrong believed that they should not be given what they could earn for themselves. Therefore, the institute strove to teach the students manners, cleanliness, morality, and practical skills with which to make a living. He believed that hard work for its own sake developed moral virtue, and he tried to instill this respect for labor into his students.[2]

After graduating, Washington became an instructor at Hampton Institute. Then in 1881, he was invited to Tuskegee, Alabama, to found a similar school there. Louis Adams, a skilled freedman, had made a political deal which led to the establishment of the Tuskegee Institute. In return for his delivery of the Negro vote, the state legislature provided minimal funds for educating ex-slaves in practical skills. The school began with almost no facilities. The roof of the building which they were using leaked, and the students often had to study with umbrellas over their heads. In effect, the institute became a kind of commune. The students grew their own food on the adjoining land, and they erected their own buildings. They sold their excess produce to the citizens of Tuskegee. They also developed skills in carpentry, brick-making, and a score of other trades and sold their products to the community. Gradually, as the white citizens realized that the school was not developing aggressive blacks and that the students were providing a contribution to the community, they came to accept it and to help it to develop by contributing funds and supplies. They found that Tuskegee students were hard-working, courteous, and humble instead of being self-assertive and articulate. They realized that their fears of educating the ex-slave had been unfounded.

In an attempt to lure more business and industry into the South, political leaders scheduled a trade exposition for Atlanta, Georgia, in 1895. A delegation was sent to the nation's capital to request financial aid from a Congressional committee. Booker T. Washington was included in the delegation as a token that there was solid backing from all portions of the community for the project. Speaking to the committee, Washington said that:

". . . While the Negro should not be deprived by unfair means of the franchise, political agitation alone would not save him, and that back of the ballot he must have property, industry, skill, economy, intelligence, and character, and that no race without these elements could permanently succeed." [3]

The delegation admitted that his oratory had significantly helped their cause. They were impressed with his racial views, particularly when he stated that character development was more important than political agitation. This was a position which they could heartily endorse.

The Cotton States Exposition which was held in Atlanta in 1895 strove to project an image of the South as a peaceful and prospering region. It tried to represent the South as a desirable location for future financial investment. Part of the peaceful image which it tried to create was a picture of racial harmony. The Exposition had a pavilion which was built by ex-slaves and which displayed their products, and it was decided to invite a Negro to speak at the Exposition. The choice fell on Booker T. Washington. His famous speech, which later became known as The Atlanta Compromise, lay heavily on his mind for many weeks before its delivery. He wanted to cement racial relations as well as to advance the status of his people. He was afraid of saying something which might undermine the cause.

Washington's speech was built around two graphic images. In the first, he told the story of a ship at sea which was out of fresh water. It signaled a passing vessel that it needed fresh water. The other ship told them to let down their bucket. Finally, after much consternation, the crew complied. Instead of finding salt water as they had expected, the bucket was pulled up filled with fresh water from the mouth of the Amazon. Washington used this image to suggest that the racial situation could be improved if both races would begin from where they were. The second picture which he used was that of the hand. He pointed out that while the hand was one, the fingers were separate. Similarly, he suggested that national unity and social segregation could go together.

Washington built on the image of the ship's needing fresh water to persuade Negroes to start where they were in building their future. He said:

"To those of my race who depend on bettering their condition in a foreign land or who underestimate the importance of cultivating friendly relations with the southern white man, who is their next-door neighbour, I would say: 'Cast down your bucket where you are'—cast it down in making friends in every manly way of the people of all races by whom we are surrounded.

"Cast it down in agriculture, mechanics, in commerce, in domestic service, and in the professions. And in this connection it is well to bear in mind that whatever other sins the South may be called to bear, when it comes to business, pure and simple, it is in the South that the Negro is given a man's chance in the commercial world, and in nothing is this Exposition more eloquent than in emphasizing this chance. Our greatest danger is that in the great leap from slavery to freedom we may overlook the fact that the masses of us are to live by the productions of our hands, and fail to keep in mind that we shall prosper in proportion as we learn to dignify and glorify common labour and put brains and skill into the common occupations of life; shall prosper in proportion as we learn to draw the line between the superficial and the substantial, the ornamental gewgaws of life and the useful. No race can prosper till it learns that there is as much dignity in tilling a field as in writing a poem. It is at the bottom of life we must begin, and not at the top. Nor should we permit our grievances to overshadow our opportunities." [4]

Washington then turned to the whites in the audience and urged them to start where they were in building national prosperity and racial unity. He said:

"To those of the white race who look to the incoming of those of foreign birth and strange tongue and habits for the prosperity of the South, were I permitted I would repeat what I say to my own race, 'Cast down your bucket where you are.' Cast it down among the eight millions of Negroes whose habits you know, whose fidelity and love you have tested in days when to have proved treacherous meant the ruin of your firesides. Cast down your bucket among these people who have, without strikes and labour wars, tilled your fields, cleared your forests, builded your railroads and cities, and brought forth treasures from the bowels of the earth, and helped make possible this magnificent representation of the progress of the South. Casting down your bucket among my people, helping and encouraging them as you are doing on these grounds, and to education of head, hand, and heart, you will find that they will buy your surplus land, make blossom the waste places in your fields, and run your factories. While doing this, you can be sure in the future, as in the past, that you and your families will be surrounded by the most patient, faithful, law-abiding, and unresentful people that the world has seen. . . . so in the future, in our humble way, we shall stand by you with a devotion that no foreigner can approach, ready to lay down our lives, if need be, in defence of yours, interlacing our industrial, commercial, civil, and religious life with yours in a way that shall make the interests of both races one." [5]

He summed up his plea for racial cooperation with the second pictorial image. He told the audience that "In all things that are purely social we can be as separate as the fingers, yet as one as the hand in all things essential to mutual progress." [6] This proposal brought forth thunderous applause. He went on to say that the wisest in his race were aware that fighting for social equality was folly. The ex-slave, he believed, must first struggle and prepare himself for the assumption of his rights, which were privileges to be earned. While he did believe that his people would receive their full rights at some future date, he insisted that "The opportunity to earn a dollar in a factory just now is worth infinitely more than the opportunity to spend a dollar in an opera-house." [7] Economic opportunity was far more important than either social equality or political rights. He closed the speech by praising the Exposition for the effect it would have in bringing fresh material prosperity to the South, and added:

". . . yet far above and beyond material benefits will be that higher good, that, let us pray God, will come, in a blotting out of sectional differences and racial animosities and suspicions, in a determination to administer absolute justice, in a willing obedience among all classes to the mandates of law. This, this, coupled with our material prosperity, will bring into our beloved South a new heaven and a new earth." [8]

When he finished, the audience applauded wildly. Governor Bullock rushed across the platform and shook his hand. The next day he was greeted and praised enthusiastically on the Atlanta streets. President Cleveland, after having read the speech, wrote Washington and thanked him for what he had said. The following year

Harvard University granted him an honorary Master's degree. The press, both North and South, quoted all or parts of the speech, and most of the newspapers carried appreciative editorials. The Charleston *News and Courier*, for example, said, "His skin is colored, but his head is sound, and his heart is in the right place." [9] Money poured in to finance the Tuskegee Institute. Overnight Washington was skyrocketed to national fame.

However, there were those who did not appreciate their new leader's call to conciliation. In view of the growing virulence of racism and the spread of Jim Crow legislation, they believed that his refusal to demand their rights was, in fact, a form of self-emasculation.

John Hope was one of those who had heard the Atlanta speech and did not want to accept the compromise. He was a professor at Roger Williams University in Nashville, Tennessee, and later was to become president of Atlanta University. The following year, after carefully considering Washington's speech, he made an address of his own to his colleagues in Nashville. He bitterly attacked the compromise and said that he believed it to be cowardly for a black man to admit that his people were not striving for equality. If money, education, and honesty would not bring the black man as much respect as they would to another American citizen, they were a curse and not a blessing.

This was obviously an attack on Washington's statement that the right to earn a dollar was worth more than anything else. He said that if he did not have the right to spend a dollar in the opera house and to do those things that other free men do, he was not free. Hope was not content with demanding equality in vague terms. He insisted that what he wanted was *social* equality. Instead of urging conciliation, he advocated that the Afro-Americans should be restless and dissatisfied. When their discontent broke through the wall of discrimination, then there would be no need to plead for justice. Then they would be men.[10]

A decade later, those who opposed Washington's leadership decided that they needed to organize and coordinate their activities. John Hope, W. E. B. DuBois, Monroe Trotter, and several others wanted to speak out more vigorously against racial discrimination, segregation, and lynching. To do this, they created the Niagara Movement to challenge the political domination of Washington's Tuskegee machine. Because he was the recognized advisor to politicians and philanthropists, this was a difficult task. Hope's criticism resulted in the diminution of financial support to Atlanta University where Hope was president.

W. E. B. DuBois, who was a professor at Atlanta University at that time, charged that:

"Mr. Washington distinctly asks that black people give up, at least for the present, three things,—First, political power, Second, insistence on civil rights, Third, higher education of Negro youth,—and concentrate all their energies on industrial education, the accumulation of wealth, and the conciliation of the South. . . . As a result of this tender of the palm-branch, what has been the return? In these years there have occurred: 1. the disenfranchisement of the Negro. 2. The legal creation of a distinct status of civil inferiority for the Negro. 3. The steady withdrawal of aid from institutions for the higher training of the Negro. These movements are not, to be sure, direct results of Mr. Washington's teachings; but his propaganda has, without a shadow of a doubt, helped their speedier accomplishment. The question then comes: Is it possible, and probable, that nine millions of men can make effective progress in economic lines if they are deprived of political rights, made a servile caste, and allowed only the most meagre chance for developing their exceptional men? If history and reason give any distinct answer to these questions, it is an emphatic *No*." [11]

He believed that beginning at the bottom with a humble trade was the best way to stay at the bottom. Self-respect should be worth more than material advancement. He believed that Washington's policy had replaced manliness with a shallow materialism.

Monroe Trotter edited the *Boston Guardian* which was one of the most militant papers published in the Afro-American community. Trotter used it as a platform from which to attack Washington's leadership. On one occasion when Washington was speaking in Boston, Trotter was among those arrested for creating a disturbance during the lecture. When the Niagara Movement was dissolved in 1909 and most of its leaders joined with liberal whites in founding the National Association for the Advancement of Colored People, Trotter refused to follow them. Besides distrusting the conciliatory policies of Washington, he could not put his faith in any organization which had substantial white leadership.

In the years immediately preceding his death in 1915, Washington hinted at a growing disillusionment with the way in which his compromise had worked. In 1912 he wrote an article for *Century* magazine entitled "Is the Negro Having a Fair Chance?" In it he criticized the fact that more money was appropriated for the education of whites than of blacks. He also criticized the convict lease system which had developed in the South. His dissatisfaction with segregation became clear when he pointed out that although Jim Crow facilities might be separate they were never equal. Another article which he had written was published after his death in *The New Republic*. In it he described the terrible effects of segregation. He said that it meant inferior sidewalks, inferior street-lighting, inferior sewage facilities, and inferior police protection. Such lacks made for difficult neighborhoods in which to raise families in decency.

If Washington's program was a sellout, as many believed, it is becoming increasingly clear that he did not intend his compromise as an end in itself. He believed that it could be the means to a much broader future. When he spoke before the Congressional committee early in 1895, he expressed his opposition to disenfranchisement on a racial basis. His apparent acceptance of it at Atlanta was only a tactical maneuver. In an article which he wrote in 1898, he said that he believed that the time would come when his people would be given all of their rights in the South. He said that they would receive the privileges due to any citizen on the basis of ability, character, and material possessions. He was, in effect, approving disenfranchisement of the poor and ignorant in both races. When Negroes did receive what was due them as citizens, he said, it would come from Southern whites as the result of the natural evolution of mutual trust and acceptance. Artificial external pressure, he insisted, would not help.[12]

The Atlanta Compromise was to be the means to an end and not an end in itself. If the ex-slave would start at the bottom, develop manners and friendliness, Washington believed that he could make his labor indispensable to white society. Acceptance of segregation was, at that time, a necessary part of good behavior. If the whites, in turn, opened the doors of economic opportunity to the ex-slave instead of importing more European immigrants, Washington said that the nation would have an English-speaking non-striking labor force. Gradually, individual Afro-Americans would gain trust, acceptance, and respect. The class line based on color would be replaced by one based on intelligence and morality.

Washington seemed to be unaware that a race which began at the bottom could stay at the bottom. In an age of rapid urbanization and industrialization, a strategy which emphasized craft and agriculture was drastically out of step with the economic realities. Moreover, the nation did not accept its part of the compromise. The flood of immigration continued unabated for another two decades. When Afro-Americans were given opportunities in industry, it became clear that there were black jobs and white jobs. The former were always poorly paid.

There were two bases for Washington's belief that the Negro should start at the bottom and work his way up. The nineteenth-century economic creed had taught that hard work unlocked the door which led from rags to riches. This teaching was also reinforced by Washington's own experience. Born in slavery and poverty, he rose from obscurity to fame and influence through honesty and industry. However, Washington seemed unaware that the most which his policy could ever achieve was a token acceptance which would leave the Negro masses behind.

W. E. B. DuBois: The Trumpet of Confrontation

In contrast to Washington's policy of conciliation and compromise, W. E. B. DuBois believed that it was necessary to act like men in order to be accepted as men. Speaking the truth as he saw it, loudly, clearly, and fearlessly, was to him the minimum criterion for manliness. This led to a contrasting style of leadership. Where Washington had been polite and ingratiating, DuBois was self-assertive and, frequently, aggressive. Where Washington had tried to win the trust of white bigots, DuBois insisted on confronting them with the truth as he saw it. Where Washington had counseled peace, DuBois clamored for action.

The contrasting leadership styles of Washington and DuBois were rooted in their differing life experiences. DuBois was born in February, 1868, in Great Barrington, Massachusetts. His grandfather had procured his own freedom through participating in the American Revolution. DuBois received his elementary and secondary education in an integrated setting which prevented his becoming conscious of the color bar. However, receiving an integrated college education was not so simple. Instead he headed South to Fisk University to further his education. There, the daily insults of discrimination and segregation came to him as a shock. He had not been trained to accept them, and these daily harassments filled him with anger and hostility. He returned north to pursue his graduate education at Harvard University, and he also spent some time at the University of Berlin exploring the new field of sociology.[13]

DuBois's first-class education as well as his own scholarly bent led him to put considerable faith in reason and learning as the tools with which to rebuild the world. He came to believe that bigotry and discrimination were rooted in ignorance and that scholarship could destroy them by exposing them to the light of truth. He strove to demonstrate that the Afro-American was not innately inferior and that his inferior status sprang from his unequal and unfair treatment in America.

While at Harvard, he wrote *The Suppression of the African Slave Trade* which was of such high quality that it became the first volume in an important historical series published by Harvard. Soon afterwards, while teaching at the University of Pennsylvania, he conducted extensive sociological research which resulted in *The Philadelphia Negro*. This pioneering sociological work was valuable for the understanding of the Negro in Philadelphia and throughout the North. At that time sociology was a new field, and there was not a single institution of higher learning in the United States or the world which had adopted it as the tool for studying the problems of minority groups. Atlanta University invited DuBois to come there and teach and to conduct sociological studies. There he began a research department which was devoted to studying the problems of the Afro-American community and which resulted in the production of a dozen works.

Besides his interest in scholarly research, DuBois developed a theory of racial leadership. For a people to advance, he believed, they needed leaders. If they failed to develop such people of their own, they would be guided by others. DuBois was doubtful whether his people should entrust themselves to white leaders. He agreed with Washington that the masses would have to make their living with their hands, and he also believed that it was important for them to develop skills which would help them. While wanting to assist the masses, however, he argued that the important priority, at the beginning, must be given to training a leadership elite which he called "the talented tenth."

"The Negro race, like all races, is going to be saved by its exceptional men. The problem of education, then, among Negroes must first of all deal with the Talented Tenth; it is the problem of developing the Best of this race that they may guide the Mass away from the contamination and death of the Worst, in their own and other races." [14]

This influential aristocracy would include scholars who would unearth the facts about the race and its problems. It would provide leaders who would examine those facts, make key decisions, and lead the race forward. This elite would also include professionals and businessmen who would set an example of good citizenship for the whole community. Moreover, the achievements of "the talented tenth" would provide living evidence that the racial stereotypes held by white bigots were untrue. This would lead gradually to the acceptance of "the talented tenth" within the majority community, and they would provide the wedge which would break open the walls of prejudice and discrimination forever.

His work at Atlanta University was only one of the ways by which he strove to build "the talented tenth." In 1905 DuBois and several others had founded the Niagara Movement to provide a common platform from which to speak. They also intended it to become the framework within which they could exchange their ideas. In it "the talented tenth" tried to oppose the policies of conciliation and submission which were being propounded by Booker T. Washington. However, in 1906 Atlanta was rocked by a race riot which shook DuBois's faith in reason and scholarship as a panacea. In the very city in which he lived and where his influence should have been strongest, white bigotry exploded, and mobs roamed the streets for days beating Afro-American citizens and burning their homes. DuBois began to wonder whether scholarly discovery of the truth was enough.

Following another race riot in Springfield, Illinois, in 1908 and the founding of the National Association for the Advancement of Colored People, DuBois left his post at Atlanta to become the director of publicity and research for the N.A.A.C.P. While continuing his interest in scholarly research, his new job involved him in the aggressive exposure and condemnation of discrimination. He became editor of *Crisis* which he developed into a journal of protest. Instead of a scholar dispassionately unearthing and publishing his findings, DuBois's new position made him a passionate journalist and engaged him in a righteous crusade.

However, some blacks questioned the wisdom of entrusting their future to a biracial organization like the N.A.A.C.P. When it was formed, Monroe Trotter refused to join it, claiming that its white membership would blunt its efficiency and militancy. The fact that for many years DuBois was the only black on its executive board led many to wonder whether it had genuine biracial participation in its decision making.

Later, Ralph J. Bunche, professor of political science, U. N. diplomat, and winner of the Nobel Peace Prize, attacked the N.A.A.C.P. on the same grounds. He argued that its dependence on white middle-class leaders, white financial backing, the sympathy of a large segment of the public, and on favorable court decisions prevented it from achieving significant results. He claimed that whenever a controversial crisis arose, it would be prohibited from taking a truly militant position. Even if its white leadership was capable of making such a radical decision, it was always forced to consider the effect of an action on its white, middle-class, liberal financial backers.

Bunche also criticized the N.A.A.C.P. for relying on the courts and the Constitution for support. He claimed that the Constitution was a brief, general document which always required interpretation to relate it to specific, contemporary issues. This interpretation, he maintained, was always shaped by public opinion. While the courts' understanding of the Constitution might not always conform precisely to the majority opinion, the influential, vocal, and dominant segment of the public inevitably influenced the courts' thinking on important subjects. While in individual cases it might even contradict this force, in the long run the Constitution could never be more than what the vocal majority wanted it to be. Bunche believed that the N.A.A.C.P. thinking was always sensitive to the feelings of the white middle class, and therefore could never afford to alienate that group. At the same time, he believed that racism was so ingrained in the white mentality that it would have to receive a series of hard jolts if significant changes were to occur. In the final analysis, he said, the N.A.A.C.P. would have to bargain and conciliate. Like Booker T. Washington, he felt that it could not afford to be as militant as was necessary.[15]

At about the same time DuBois, himself, became disillusioned with the gradualist, conciliatory approach of the N.A.A.C.P. While he still wanted to work for an integrated society, he had lost faith in the effectiveness of a biracial organization to achieve significant change. In an article which he wrote in *Crisis* before resigning from the N.A.A.C.P., he suggested that black separatism or black unity could provide a more solid front with which to attack discrimination and segregation than cooperation with white society. His goal, he insisted, was still to make ten million of his people free. He wanted to help them break the bondage of economic oppression, to shake off the chains of ignorance, to gain their full political rights, and to become exempt from the insults of discrimination and segregation.

This kind of freedom, he maintained, was not inconsistent with self-organization for self-advancement. He wanted to see the Afro-American community develop control over its own churches, schools, social clubs, and businesses. This was not, DuBois insisted, a surrender to segregation. He believed that a community which controlled its own basic institutions was in a better position to make its own decisions and work for its own advancement. This kind of black unity or black separatism would provide the solidarity and cooperation necessary to achieve significant change resulting in an integrated society.

Indirectly, he admitted that this was a shift away from his concept of "the talented tenth." The assumption that an educated and cultured elite would be accepted within white society had proved to be erroneous. To the contrary, he noted, whites often feared educated blacks as much or more than uneducated ones. "The talented tenth" had not even gained token acceptance. Therefore DuBois shifted to a concept of a group solidarity instead of an elite leadership. This concept of group cooperation must not be confused with that of Washington. DuBois's type of solidarity was to be the platform from which to assert one's manhood even if it meant personal deprivation:

"Surely then, in this period of frustration and disappointment, we must turn from negation to affirmation, from the ever-lasting 'No' to the ever-lasting 'Yes.' Instead of sitting, sapped of all initiative and independence; instead of drowning our originality in imitation of mediocre white folks; instead of being afraid of ourselves and cultivating the art of skulking to escape the Color Line; we have got to renounce a program that always involves humiliating self-stultifying scrambling to crawl somewhere where we are not wanted; where we crouch panting like a whipped dog. We have got to stop this and learn that on such a program they cannot build manhood. No, by God, stand erect in a mud-puddle and tell the white world to go to hell, rather than lick boots in a parlor." [16]

Both Walter White and James Weldon Johnson took on the task of countering DuBois's position. Johnson argued that DuBois ended where Washington began. He noted that the conflict between integration into a biracial society and withdrawal into black separatism had existed throughout American history. There had always been a minority who wanted to build a separate community, but he said that what was favored by the majority was to gain entrance into American society. Yet the daily insults which were felt even by the most avid integrationists led them to curse white society and, at times, to consider retreat into isolationism.

According to his point of view, Johnson pointed out, isolationism had to be based on economics and although one could talk about black capitalism and could even develop some prospering businesses, the economic realities favored mass production and economic interdependence. Separate black institutions were always contingent institutions which were subservient to the country as a whole. Therefore they could never really be free or independent. The separate society would always be subject to external control by the larger economic and political institutions on which it relied. Johnson also noted that integrationists like himself had been charged with failing to see the intensity of the institutional racism which existed all about them. He denied this and claimed that racism and discrimination were patently obvious. To the contrary, he suggested that the real danger was in overemphasizing their importance and becoming paranoid. [17]

After the Second World War, DuBois joined the N.A.A.C.P. staff for another short period. However, his disillusionment with American society had deepened, and he was ready to consider even more radical solutions than before. He had become increasingly convinced that racism was a world problem and not merely an American problem. The series of Pan-African Congresses which he had helped to organize forced him to see a connection between American racism and European imperialism in Africa. At the same time, communism was representing itself as the foe of both racism and imperialism, and for many of the oppressed peoples throughout the world the communist claim had become attractive.

To the N.A.A.C.P. it seemed that DuBois's new "pink" ideas and associations were not good for its image, and it asked him to resign. The government charged DuBois with failing to register the Peace Information Center, where he was employed, as an agent for a foreign principal. Although acquitted, the harassment deepened his cynicism and hostility. Finally, he became a communist, and he moved to Ghana in 1960. He died there in 1963.[18]

As a young scholar, DuBois had begun by believing that reason and research would dispel ignorance and prejudice. Obviously, prejudice was not so easily eradicated by reason alone. "The talented tenth," which was to lead the Afro-American community into the mainstream of American life, had not been successful. White bigots were especially antagonized by educated blacks. When DuBois had advocated black solidarity, it had failed to take root because the intellectuals had become alienated from the masses. The black bourgeoisie had been hindered by their color from assimilating into white society, and their newly acquired education, values, and middle-class style of life prevented them from returning to their people. Finally, DuBois's work with the N.A.A.C.P., while it achieved some significant results, failed to bring about the kind of structural social change he desired. Despairing of bring about racial advancement in America, DuBois decided to work for it in Africa.

Marcus Garvey: The Trumpet of Pride

Marcus Garvey's personality differed markedly from that of both Booker T. Washington and W. E. B. DuBois. Washington's image was one of humility and courageousness bordering, many believed, on obsequiousness. DuBois projected the picture of a self-confident, hostile, and reserved individual. In contrast, Garvey was easy-going and flamboyant. The personalities of both Washington and DuBois minimized the fact that they were black. On one hand, Washington appeared to be a man who knew his place and who did not intrude as an individual or a Negro into any situation. On the other hand, DuBois had shaken off the habits of both the "house nigger" and the "field nigger" in order to adopt the characteristics of a cold intellectual which was more in keeping with the Anglo-Saxon character. Garvey, however, flaunted his blackness wherever he went. Black pride and black identity were the cornerstones of his philosophy, and they vibrated through everything he said and did. He was not ashamed of the personality characteristics of the lower classes, and he readily identified with them. It was the black middle class, which had adopted the life style of the mainstream of white society, that earned his scorn.

Marcus Garvey was born in St. Anne's Bay, Jamaica, in August, 1887. His parents were of unmixed African descent. His ancestors had belonged to the Maroons, a group of slaves who had escaped and established their own community in the Jamaican hills. They fought so well and had been so thoroughly organized that the British found it necessary to grant them their independence in 1739. Garvey was very proud of this heritage and of his unmixed ancestry. Jamaican society was structured hierarchically along color lines. The whites were at the top, mulattoes in the middle, and blacks at the bottom. The mulattoes enjoyed displaying and protecting their superiority over the blacks. In turn, Garvey was scornful of the mulattoes, and he distrusted all people with light skin throughout his life.[19]

As a young man, Garvey began making his living as a printer's helper in a large Kingston printing firm and worked his way up to foreman. His leadership ability became evident when, during a walkout, the workers chose him to lead the strike. He had been the only foreman to join the workers, and the company later blacklisted him for it. The union failed to come to his aid, and thereafter he distrusted labor organizations as a source of help for his people.

He then traveled extensively around Central and South America, staying briefly in several large cities and supporting himself by his trade. Wherever he went, he found blacks being persecuted and mistreated. In 1912 he crossed the Atlantic and spent some time in London. There he met large numbers of Africans and became interested in their plight as well. While he was there, he was influenced by a Negro Egyptian author named Duse Mohammed Ali. His ideas further intensified Garvey's interest in Africa. At the same time, Garvey read Booker T. Washington's *Up from Slavery* and was impressed with his philosophy of self-help and moral uplift.

By this time, Garvey had become aware that black people were persecuted all around the world, in the West Indies, in Central America, in South America, in the United States, and even in Africa, their homeland. When he returned to Jamaica, he determined to establish an organization to work for the improvement of the conditions of black people the world over. The result was the founding, in 1914, of the Universal Negro Improvement and Conservation Association and African Communities League. In 1916, Garvey came to the United States to solicit the support of Afro-Americans. He had hoped to get the backing of Booker T. Washington with whom he had already corresponded, but, unfortunately, Washington died the previous year.[20]

In the United States Garvey found the Afro-American community ready to support his program of encouraging aggressive racial pride. The hopes which had accompanied the end of slavery, half a century earlier, had turned to ashes. Then, thousands moved from the rural South to the urban North to escape the growth of segregation and to find economic advancement. In the "promised land," they were continually confronted by socially sanctioned segregation, constant racial insults, and relentless job discrimination.

In 1919 white race hatred exploded in race riots all across the country. In that year, there were also some seventy lynchings, mostly black, and some of them were soldiers who had just returned from defending their country. Urban whites resented the influx of rural blacks from the South who were pouring into their cities, and they tried to confine the newcomers to dilapidated, older neighborhoods. To do this, they were quite willing to resort to violence, and, between 1917 and 1921 Chicago was struck with a rash of house bombings as whites tried to hold the line. During these years, there was one racially motivated bombing every twenty days. In the midst of such conditions, white America did not seem very beautiful, and black pride, black identity, and black solidarity had an appeal which was novel.

Chapters of the Universal Negro Improvement Association sprang up all across the country. Although there has been considerable debate about the number of members in the U.N.I.A., it was clearly the largest mass organization in Afro-American history. Its membership has been estimated between two and four million. In any case, its sympathizers and well-wishers were ubiquitous. The "respectable" N.A.A.C.P. never reached such grass-roots support, and even with its white liberal financing, its capital was much smaller than that which Garvey was able to tap from the lower-class blacks alone.[21]

Garvey advocated a philosophy of race redemption. He said that blacks needed a nation of their own where they could demonstrate their abilities and develop their talents. He believed that every people should have its own country. The white man had Europe, and the black man should have Africa. Race redemption did not mean that all blacks must return to Africa. However, when there was a prosperous, independent African nation, blacks throughout the world would be treated with respect. He noted that Englishmen and Frenchmen were not lynched, but that blacks, in contrast, were treated like lepers. Garvey did plan to encourage those blacks who had particularly useful skills or who desired to return to Africa to do so, in order to become the backbone of this new prosperous black nation.[22]

Garvey was harshly critical of the leadership in the Afro-American community. With the exception of Booker T. Washington, they had all advocated social equality, intermarriage, and fraternization. Garvey said that these only led to increased racial friction. He argued that racial purity for both whites and blacks was superior to racial integration. Blacks should also be proud of their race and their ancestry. Africa was not a dark and degenerate continent; instead it was a place of which to be proud.

To demonstrate this, Garvey adopted African clothes and hair style long before they became popular. The black bourgeoisie was shocked and ashamed by his blatant display. Whites were totally incapable of understanding why anyone would try to glorify blackness and the African heritage. To them, he seemed merely a clown. However, to the black masses who had no hope of achieving middle-class respectability, his pride in blackness came as a release. Instead of a life buried in shame, he offered them pride and dignity. Instead of being considered "nobodies," he gave them a sense of identity. In place of weakness, he offered solidarity and strength. These ideas spread through the ghettoes of large American urban centers like a fever. In 1920 the Universal Negro Improvement Association held its annual convention at Madison

Square Garden in New York City. There were 25,000 delegates in attendance. Garvey told them that he planned to organize the four hundred million blacks of the world into one powerful unit and to plant the banner of freedom in Africa. In response, the convention elected him as the Provisional President of Africa.[23]

Garvey's black separatism led, naturally enough, to black capitalism. Businesses connected with the U.N.I.A. sprang up all across the country. They were usually small enterprises: grocery stores, laundries, and restaurants. Larger businesses included a printing house and a steamship line. The *New York World*, which was begun in 1918, was the only black daily in existence at that time. After its demise, Garvey began *The Black Man*, which was published monthly. Although most of these businesses only served to sink Negro roots deeper in American society, the purpose of the Black Star Steamship Line was, eventually, to provide a means of transportation for those who desired to return to Africa.

The black middle class felt that Garvey was hurting its image. White politicians were nervous about the existence of such a large and potentially powerful organization, especially when it was led by a man like Garvey whom they could not understand. When the steamship line ran into financial trouble, many were convinced that Garvey had been defrauding the ignorant masses.

After a power struggle within the U.N.I.A., Eason, who had led the fight, was murdered in New Orleans. Two Garveyites were accused of the crime, and opposition to the movement grew even stronger. Finally, with the urging of middle-class Negroes, the government brought Garvey to trial for using the mails to defraud. He insisted on being his own lawyer, and he took great pleasure in harassing the witnesses and haranguing the jury. When he realized that this was undermining his own case, he began taking advice from a white lawyer. Nevertheless, he was fined $1,000 and given a sentence of up to five years in prison. In 1925, he was sent to the Atlanta Penitentiary. At that point, many of his opponents joined his friends in claiming that the trial had not been fair. President Coolidge commuted the sentence, but as soon as he was released Garvey was again arrested and was deported as an undesirable alien.[24]

As the movement had been largely dependent on Garvey's magnetic personality, the organization began to dissolve as soon as he left the country. Garvey tried to establish a worldwide movement with its base in Jamaica, but a power fight for control with the New York leadership developed. The outbreak of the Second World War further diminished the influence of his organization. Garvey died in London in June, 1940.[25]

Both James Weldon Johnson and W. E. B. DuBois claimed that emigration of blacks from America to Africa was merely a form of escapism. (Ironically DuBois's disillusionment drove him to Africa some thirty years later.) Johnson argued that a small independent African nation would have to be dependent on Europe and America for capital. Therefore Garvey's program could not achieve the kind of freedom and equality which it claimed. Johnson maintained that it would still be subject to oppression from white imperialism. As such, the nation would only be an underdeveloped area dependent on external financing and continually subjected to economic exploitation. In foreign affairs it would always be small and weak, and it would have to depend on some stronger ally for its defense. It would only become a pawn for the great powers, all of which were white Europeans or Americans. Johnson claimed that a separate African nation would not provide the kind of power base which Garvey promised.[26]

Although Garvey had, overnight, created the largest mass organization in Afro-American history, it crumbled almost as quickly as it had been built. The movement had been overly dependent on his personality. However, Garvey cannot be dismissed so easily. Although his movement disintegrated rapidly, the interest in black identity and black pride which he had sparked, lingered on. Lacking a structure within which to operate, it was not very obvious to the external observer. Nevertheless, his ideas have clearly provided the spawning ground from which more recent organizations have developed.

A. Philip Randolph: The Trumpet of Mobilization

The leadership style of A. Philip Randolph differed from that of Washington, DuBois, and Garvey. His interest in providing jobs and skills for the working class was akin to that of Washington. His aggressive outspoken manner was more like that of DuBois. While lacking the flamboyant style of Garvey, he was able to work among the ranks of the working class and gain their acceptance. He, too, has demonstrated considerable ability in mass organization. Like DuBois, he wanted to use black solidarity as a wedge with which to break through discrimination into a biracial society and not as an end in itself.

Asa Philip Randolph was born in Crescent City, Florida, in 1889. He was raised in a strict religious home. His father was a local minister but he also had to hold down another full-time job in order to support his family. Early in the century, Randolph moved north and attended City College in New York.[27]

During the First World War, Randolph, with Chandler Owen, edited *The Messenger* and made it into an outspoken vehicle for their own opinions. In its pages, they espoused a radical, American brand of democratic socialism. They supported the International Workers of the World, which many viewed as being alien and communistic, and they questioned the advisability of Negroes' supporting the war effort. They were charged with undermining the national defense, and they spent some time in jail. Both advocated a working-class solidarity of blacks and whites which would resist exploitation by capitalism. In their view, every nonunion man, black or white, was a potential scab and a potential threat to every union man, black or white. While the white and black dogs were fighting over the bone, they pointed out, the yellow capitalist dog ran off with it. *The Messenger* encouraged blacks to join unions, and it tried hard to persuade the unions to eliminate discrimination. The view they propagated was that unions could not afford to be based on the color line; instead they should be based on a class line. Randolph and Owen attacked Samuel Gompers and the A. F. of L. for failing to be truly biracial.[28]

Randolph criticized DuBois and the N.A.A.C.P. for their lack of concern with the real day-to-day problems of the masses. He charged that the N.A.A.C.P. was led by people who were neither blacks nor workers, and that they were incapable, therefore, of articulating the needs of the masses. He argued that an organization for the welfare of the Irish would never be led by Jews. Therefore, he suggested that an organization for the welfare of blacks should not be led by whites. He was especially critical of the gradualist, peaceful policy which DuBois appeared to support during the early years of the N.A.A.C.P. He questioned DuBois's professed stand against violence and revolution. Randolph said: "Doubtless DuBois is the only alleged leader of an oppressed group of people in the world today who condemns revolution." [29] To Randolph, violence and revolution were not anti-American, but were justified by the Declaration of Independence.

During the twenties, Randolph tried several schemes to increase black and white cooperation in unions. Along with Chandler Owen, he founded the National Association for the Promotion of Unionism among Negroes. The most successful of Randolph's efforts came in 1925 when he established the Brotherhood of Sleeping Car Porters. The Brotherhood appeared to demonstrate the futility of his basic thesis. Randolph, who believed in biracial unionism, had established, in the Brotherhood, an organization which, by the nature of the occupation, was to be an exclusively black union. He found himself being pushed relentlessly away from biracial unionism into supporting racial organizations for racial advancements.

In 1936, he played a key role in forming the National Negro Congress. It was a broad alliance of all kinds of groups to advance the welfare of the race. Although it did not receive the backing of the N.A.A.C.P., the Urban League, an even more conservative organization, became a cornerstone in the Congress. The Urban League has always been primarily interested in securing employment for the Negro working class. During the thirties, the communists adopted a united-front policy, and they tried to infiltrate the N.N.C. Some of the left-wing unions which did support the N.N.C., were largely white.

Randolph's talent for mass mobilization was demonstrated most clearly in his efforts to organize two gigantic marches on Washington in order to dramatize Afro-American needs and to pressure the government into action. As American industry began to gear up for war production at the beginning of the Second World War, it needed to find new sources of labor. The Afro-American community was eager to support the war effort, particularly because it meant fighting Hitler's racism.

But they were also eager to find jobs. However, defense industries in America continued to display their own brand of racial discrimination. Many of them said quite openly that, while they were willing to hire blacks, they would only give them menial positions regardless of their skill and training. It became clear that racism had to be fought at home and abroad. Many tried to get the government to take action, but it seemed more concerned with protecting its political image and with avoiding alienating the party's financial backers.

In January, 1941, Randolph suggested a mass march on Washington to demand government action against discrimination both in government services and in defense industry. The idea took root, and a mass march was being organized for July. On June 25, 1941, President Roosevelt issued Executive Order 8802 which forbade further discrimination either in government services or defense industries, on the grounds of race, creed, or nationality. While some discrimination still continued, the order and the Fair Employment Practices Commission, which resulted from it, played an important role in opening large numbers of new jobs to the Afro-American community. The planned march, which will be discussed more fully in a later chapter, was then called off.

Although the march was canceled, Randolph hoped to keep the March on Washington Movement alive. He wanted to create a permanent mobilized community. This, too, failed to materialize, but, if it had not been for the war, his efforts might have been more successful. In September, 1942, Randolph called a meeting of the March on Washington Movement before which he outlined his program. He told the conference that slavery had not ended because it was evil, but because it was violently overthrown. Similarly, he said that if they wanted to obtain their rights, they would have to be willing to fight, go to jail, and die for them. Rights would not be granted; they must be taken if need be. His plan was to organize a permanent mass movement on a nationwide basis and to conduct protests, marches, and boycotts. This was an adaptation of some of Gandhi's techniques to the Afro-American problem.

The March on Washington Movement was to be an all-Negro movement. Yet, Randolph did not intend it to be anti-white. He pointed to the fact that every organization must have its own purposes, that Catholic groups concentrated on their interests in the same way as labor groups strove to gain their objectives. Any oppressed people must assume the major responsibility for furthering their goals. They might accept help and cooperation from outside, but they must, in the final analysis, rely on self-organization and self-help. One of the by-products of this, Randolph believed, would be the development of self-reliance within the Afro-American community and the destruction of the slave mentality. Although individual blacks within the community could join other organizations, and while the movement itself might cooperate with other organizations, the March on Washington Movement itself was to be exclusively for blacks. It was a racial movement for racial advancement.[30]

Randolph went on to envision an organization with a challenging action program. Millions of supporters would be divided into a network of small block units. Each would be headed by a block captain. This would facilitate instant, mass mobilization. At a moment's notice, a chain of command could be activated, and millions of marchers would be in the streets. Randolph also envisioned repeated, gigantic marches aimed at Washington and state capitals. He could also see smaller, regular marches on the city halls and other establishments in dozens of cities across the country. To him it was desirable for blacks to picket the White House, if need be, until the nation came to see that blacks were willing to sacrifice everything to be counted as men. Randolph also wanted to encourage the mobilization of registration and voting.

Besides being reminiscent of the Gandhi nonviolent campaign in India, Randolph's March on Washington Movement, although it never materialized, foreshadowed the civil rights movement of the late fifties and sixties. This later civil rights movement, however, was directed by several separate organizations which, at times, were involved in power fights with one another. It lacked the central organization and national, instant mobilization which Randolph had in mind. It also included a substantial number of white supporters and leaders which Randolph had excluded from his program. He had predicted that this kind of white participation would back down in times of crisis and thereby emasculate the movement. This is precisely what the Black Power advocates of the late sixties claimed had happened to the civil rights movement, and they gave the same reasons for its collapse.

In 1947, Randolph cooperated with Grant Reynolds in organizing the League for Non-Violent Civil Disobedience Against Military Segregation; its aim was to encourage draft resisters objecting to serving in a segregated army. Randolph was also one of a delegation which told President Truman that America could not afford to fight colored people in Asia with the army as it then existed. Truman, then, took the first real steps in ending military segregation. In 1963, Randolph and Bayard Rustin did organize a massive march on Washington. Most of the publicity, however, went to Martin Luther King, Jr., its main speaker. This march contributed significantly to the passage of civil rights legislation. However, most of Randolph's efforts continued to be in the realm of union organization. In 1957, he was made a vice president in the A.F.L.–C.I.O. and a member of its executive council. Two years later, he was censured for charging organized labor with racism.[31]

Although Randolph was not able to achieve his dream of mass mobilization, he did display considerable organizational ability. In part, his ideas have been put into effect by subsequent groups, and his philosophy was similar to that which became popular in the 1960s. The whole civil rights movement bore a marked resemblance to his philosophy, and undoubtedly it drew considerable motivation from it. The idea of an all-black mass organization, with a vast network of local action groups participating in it, is still alive. He had envisioned a grass-roots black power movement a quarter of a century before it became popular. Although dozens of such groups have sprung up across the country, they still lack the kind of mass mobilization and national coordination which he had planned. His was to have been a militant, all-black movement without its becoming anti-white. It was to teach self-reliance to the Afro-American community. Local control and power were to be used to achieve freedom and civil rights within a genuinely biracial society.

CHAPTER 9

The New Negro

Immigration and Migration

DURING the nineteenth century, the American racial dilemma had appeared to be a regional problem. The Northern states had abolished slavery early in the century, and the abolitionists self-righteously condemned Southern slave holders while remaining unaware of their own racism. However, the twentieth century showed that racism was really a national issue. Thousands of Afro-Americans moved from the rural South into the urban North, creating a more even distribution of that population throughout the country. At the same time, there was a fresh wave of voluntary immigration into America by peoples with an African heritage. Most of these newcomers also moved into Northern cities. As thousands of blacks spread into the North and West, the inhabitants there developed sympathies with Southern racists. Actually, this population shift only unearthed attitudes which had been there all the time. This gigantic migration of peoples was symptomatic of the change in the heart of the black community. It signaled a new dynamism and a new aggressiveness.

The voluntary black immigration which occurred during the twentieth century was a new and unusual phenomenon. Almost all blacks who had previously come to America had been brought in chains. Those who came voluntarily during this century came in spite of their knowledge that racism would confront them. Their awareness of American racism, however, was an abstraction and was only partially understood by them.

Nevertheless, they saw America as the land of prosperity and opportunity at a time when, for many of them, social and economic conditions in their homeland did not seem promising. While only a few came from Africa itself, except as students staying for a limited period, there was a swelling flow from the West Indies and the entire Caribbean area.

At the beginning of the 1920s, the United States imposed a quota system on new immigrants and this drastically slowed the influx of people from South and East Europe. In spite of the racist and ethnic overtones of this legislation, it failed to build significant barriers to movement by blacks within the western hemisphere. During the 1920s large numbers of blacks came to the United States from other parts of the Americas. By 1930 eighty-six percent of the foreign-born Negroes living in the United States were born in some other country in this hemisphere. By far the largest number of these, seventy-three percent, came from the West Indies, and most of them were from the British West Indies.

By 1940, there were some eighty-four thousand foreign-born Negroes living in the country. As large as this total might appear, however, it was still less than one percent of the twelve million Negroes recorded in the 1940 census. Most of these new immigrants went to live in large cities in the Northeast, with by far the majority being concentrated in New York City itself. At the point when the influx was at its highest, in 1930, seventeen percent of the Negroes in New York City were foreign born.

An unusually high percentage of these newcomers had held white-collar occupations—mostly young professionals with little hope of advancement in the static economy of the Islands. Although they were aware of the American racial situation, they were still unprepared to cope with it. Most of them were accustomed to being part of the majority in their homeland. They had experienced discrimination before, but it had not been as uncompromising as what they found on arrival in America. Society, as they knew it, was divided into whites, mulattoes, and blacks instead of into black and white. Many mulattoes were not psychologically ready for the experience of being lumped in with the blacks. Moreover, the racism they knew had been modified by an economic class system which left some of the poor whites with less status than that of professional blacks. Coming to America, for them, meant a loss of status although it might also mean an increase in affluence.[1]

James Weldon Johnson described the West Indian immigrants as being almost totally different from the Southern rural Negroes who had moved into New York City. He said that the West Indians displayed a high intelligence, many having an English common-school education, and he noted that there was almost no illiteracy among them. He also said that they were sober-minded and had a genius for business enterprise.[2] It has been estimated that one-third of the city's Negro professionals, physicians, dentists, and lawyers, were foreign born.

The West Indians had an ethos which stressed saving, education, and hard work. The same self-confidence and initiative which enabled substantial numbers of them to move into professional employment made others into political radicals. Unaccustomed to the intensity of racial hostility and harassment which they found in America, they reacted with anger. They had not been trained since birth in attitudes of submission and nonresistance. This was the phenomenon which created Marcus Garvey and the United Negro Improvement Association. The West Indian community had been gradually merging with the larger Afro-American society. It never established a separate place of residence, and the second generation became mixed with the larger Afro-American community. After the Second World War, there was a fresh wave of emigration from the West Indies to America, but the 1952 Immigration Act drastically reduced the West Indian quota, thereby deflecting this stream of emigrants to Britain.[3]

In contrast, the Spanish-speaking immigrants from the Caribbean did establish separate communities. After the United States acquired Puerto Rico, a sizeable number of Puerto Ricans moved to the mainland. This flow began as a trickle at the beginning of the century, and it has grown rapidly since. Most of the Puerto Ricans settled in urban centers in the Northeast, and they established a large, Spanish-speaking community in New York City. The migration of Cubans into America, while not as large, has been important in both Miami and New York. The largest number of Cubans came during the 1950s and 1960s.

In 1910, the Puerto Rican community in New York City numbered only five hundred, but by 1920 it had grown to seven thousand. In 1940, the number of New York residents who had been born in Puerto Rico reached seventy thousand, and in 1950, it jmped to one hundred eighty seven thousand. The 1960 census showed that the Puerto Rican community of New York City, including those born in Puerto Rico as well as those born in America of Puerto Rican parentage, had reached 613,000.[4]

The Spaniards in Latin America had intermarried with both

the Indians and Africans to a far higher degree than had the Anglo-Saxons in North America. For this reason, it is much more difficult to identify the racial background of individual Puerto Ricans. Certainly, there was a significant African influence on the entire population of the island. In 1860, it was estimated that almost 50 percent of the island's residents were Negro. In 1900, the percentage had dropped to 40 percent, and, by 1950, it had dropped to 20 percent. The change in these statistics was due to assimilation through intermarriage. Those who migrated to the continent did not include many with dominant negroid characteristics. The 1960 New York City census listed only 4 percent of its Puerto Ricans as being Negro. Nathan Glazer and Daniel P. Moynihan, in their study of this community, believed that the Puerto Rican racial attitudes may alter the racial views of the entire city and thereby have some effect on the nation. Puerto Ricans are not as race conscious as are most Americans. Most of them are not clearly either black or white. Intermarriage between color groups is common. The Puerto Rican community in New York City is more conscious of being a separate, Spanish-speaking community than it is of being either a black or white one.[5]

The other major Caribbean element in the American Spanish-speaking community comes from Cuba. In 1960, the Cuban community in the United States, including those born in Cuba as well as those born in America of Cuban parentage, totaled 124,416. Only 6.5 percent of this community is nonwhite, while 25 percent of the population in Cuba is nonwhite. The Cuban community in the United States has almost 46 percent of its number living in the Northeast, and it has another 43 percent living in Florida. Almost the entire community is divided between the cities of Miami and New York.[6]

This immigration of foreign-born blacks into the cities of the North and West was concurrent with a sizeable movement of American blacks from the rural South into these same cities. Actually, this internal migration was not new. As soon as the Northern states had begun to abolish slavery, runaways from the slave states in the South began to trickle into the North. As the underground Railway developed, this trickle swelled into a sizeable flow.

Immediately after the Civil War, the flow reversed directions for a short time. Many who had run away during the war returned home to be with friends and family. Thousands of others, born in the North, hurried south to help educate and rehabilitate their brothers. However, this flow was short-lived. As the South moved from slavery into segregation, hope slid into disillusionment and cynicism. In 1878–79 there was a wave of migration from the South into the West. "Pap" Singleton, an ex-slave from Tennessee, had come to the conclusion that the ex-slaveholder and the ex-slave could not live together in harmony, and he believed that the best solution was to develop a separate society. As a result, he formed the Tennessee Real Estate and Homestead Association, but there was not enough land available in Tennessee for the program. Finally, he decided that Kansas was the ideal location in which to build a separate Negro society. Various transportation companies saw this scheme as a way for them to make money, and they encouraged this westward migration.

Although the original migrants to Kansas were welcomed, opposition grew as their numbers increased. Before his death in 1892, Singleton became disillusioned with the possibilities of developing a separate society anywhere in the United States, and he came to favor a return to Africa. He believed that this was the only place where his people could escape racial discrimination. Nevertheless, Singleton took pride in his work, and he claimed, probably with some exaggeration, to have been responsible for transporting some 82,000 Afro-Americans from the South into Kansas.

Another ex-slave, Henry Adams, called a New Orleans Colored Convention in 1879 to examine the condition of the ex-slave throughout the South. A committee was formed for this purpose. It found the situation discouraging and recommended migration into other regions. Another convention held in Nashville reached similar conclusions, and it requested funds from Congress to assist in the process. Funds were not forthcoming. When Congress did investigate this vast migration, Southerners assured the committee that their Negroes were really very happy, and they claimed that the migration was a myth.[7]

In spite of this earlier migration, the 1900 census showed that 89.7 percent of the Afro-American community still resided in the South. One-third of the Southern population was nonwhite. The real exodus still lay ahead.

The migrants were moved both by forces within the South

which pushed them out and by those within the North which pulled them in. On one hand, continuing violence and segregation drove many to leave their homes. When the boll weevil spread across the Southern states like a plague, it wiped out many poor farmers, and it drove them to seek other means of livelihood elsewhere. On the other hand, the war had interrupted the flow of immigrants from Europe into the Northern industrial centers, and at the same time it created the need for even more unskilled labor in the factories. After the war, the restrictive immigration laws which were passed kept the flow of European immigration low, and Northern industry continued to draw labor from the Southern rural pockets of poverty.

Between 1910 and 1920, some 330,000 Afro-Americans moved from the South into the North and West. By 1940, the number of those who had left the South since 1910 had soared to 1,750,000. Between 1940 and 1950, there were another 1,597,000, and between 1950 and 1960, there were 1,457,000 more who left the South. The percentage of the Afro-American community living in the South had dropped from 89.7 percent in 1900 to 59 percent in 1960, and for the first time, more than half of them lived outside of the Deep South.

Another indication of the northward migration which had occurred was that a Northern state, New York, had acquired an Afro-American community which was larger than that of any of the Southern states. Much of this migration was also a move from the country to the city. In the South, 58 percent of the Afro-Americans live in cities. In the West, there are 93 percent who live in cities, and in the North, there are 96 percent. In the first half of the twentieth century, the Afro-American community had been transformed from a rural and regional group into a national and urban one.[8]

Harlem: "The Promised Land"

In 1925, Alain Locke edited a volume of critical essays and literature entitled *The New Negro*. In it, Locke heralded a spiritual and cultural awakening within the Afro-American community. This awakening was manifested by a creative outburst of art, music, and literature as well as by a new mood of self-confidence and self-consciousness within that community. The center of this creative explosion was located in Harlem. Famous personalities such as Claude McKay, Langston Hughes, Paul Robeson, James Weldon Johnson, Duke Ellington, and Louis Armstrong either moved to Harlem or visited it frequently in order to participate in the vigorous cultural exchange which took place there. The artists of the Negro Renaissance, as important as they might be in themselves, were merely symbolic of the new life which was electrifying the Afro-American community. This new life was also evident in the large urban centers of the North and particularly in Harlem.

Locke pointed out the significance of the great northward migration when he said that the Negro "in the very process of being transplanted," was also being "transformed." This migration was usually explained either in economic terms—jobs pulling Negroes northward—or in social terms—discrimination pushing them out. In both cases, the Afro-American was represented as the passive victim of external socio-economic forces. Locke insisted that, to the contrary, it was more accurate to understand this migration as a result of a decision made by the Negro himself. For the first time in history, thousands upon thousands of individual Afro-Americans had made a basic choice concerning their own existence. They refused to remain victims of an impersonal and oppressive system, and, as the result, they deliberately pulled up their roots, left their friends and neighbors and moved north to what they hoped would be "the promised land."

From this decision emerged the new Negro. If he was less polite and more aggressive than before, he was also more self-reliant and less dependent on pity and charity. This change, however, did not occur suddenly. The passive, well-behaved Negro, content to stay in his place, had largely been a myth. In part, he had been the product of a guilt-ridden white stereotype which found this myth comforting. The Negro himself had also contributed to this fiction by his custom of social mimicry, his habit of appearing to fill the role which whites expected of him. Since the end of slavery, however, a spirit of individuality had been growing within the Negro consciousness. The opportunity for industrial employment in the North which had resulted from the war and from the slowdown in European immigration along with the increase of racism and segregation in the South combined to open the way for the development of the growing spirit of self-determination.[9]

The new Negro was doing more than asserting his own individuality; the entire Afro-American community was developing a new sense of solidarity. The racist attitudes of mainstream America, both North and South, made it almost impossible for a Negro to conceive of himself purely in individualistic terms. Any Negro who thought of himself as an exceptional or unique individual was brought sharply back to reality by this racism which relentlessly and mercilessly depicted him as nothing more than a "nigger."

In spite of the individualism which was preached as a basic part of the American creed, the Afro-American community was forced to develop a strong sense of group cooperation. In the face of growing racism and segregation, the idealism of the new Negro was still based on the American ideal of democracy, and his goal was still to share fully, some day, in American life and institutions. The Afro-American's heightened sense of racial consciousness was not an end in itself. This racial self-consciousness gave him the strength to withstand the daily injustices which confronted him, and it provided him with faith in himself and hope in his future. Locke believed that the new Negro was taking the racial separatism which had been forced upon him by white society and was turning it to positive uses, transforming obstacles to his progress into "dams of social energy and power."

The factor which prevented this new, energetic Afro-American spirit from becoming alienated from America was that its goals were identical with the expressed ideals of the country. The racial discrimination and injustice from which Afro-Americans suffered, though deeply entrenched in national institutions, were themselves in contradiction to the American democratic philosophy. The Afro-American, besides having justice on his side, was comforted in knowing that his goals were sanctioned and hallowed by the nation's ideals. As Locke put it, "We cannot be undone without America's undoing." [10]

Thousands of Negro migrants poured north into Chicago. The new automobile factories in Detroit attracted thousands more, but Harlem became the center of "the promised land." James Weldon Johnson described the Harlem of the 1920s as the "culture capital of the Negro world." Its magnetism attracted Negroes from all across America, from the West Indies and even some from Africa itself. Harlem contained more Negroes per square mile than any other place on earth. It drew a bewildering and energizing diversity of peoples. Students, peasants, artists, businessmen, professional men, poets, musicians, and workers; all came to Harlem. It combined both the exploiters and the outcasts. Langston Hughes, in describing his first entrance into Harlem from the 135th Street subway exit, said that he felt vitality and hope throbbing in the air. In *Black Manhattan,* James Weldon Johnson said that Harlem was not a slum or a fringe. Rather, he insisted that it was one of the "most beautiful and healthful sections of the city."

According to Johnson, the stranger traveling through Harlem would be totally surprised by its appearance. Crossing 125th Street on his way up Seventh Avenue, Johnson said, the visitor would not expect to find himself in the midst of an Afro-American community. The character of the houses did not change. For the next twenty-five blocks the streets, stores, and buildings looked no different from those he had already passed. With the exception of their color, the appearance of the people on the streets was the same too. Moreover, Johnson insisted that Harlem was an integral part of metropolitan New York and was not just a quarter within the city in the sense that was true of the communities inhabited by recent European immigrants. Its citizens were not aliens. They spoke American; they thought American.

Harlem Negroes, claimed Johnson, were woven into the fabric of the metropolitan economy. Unlike the Negroes in other Northern cities, they did not work in "gang labor"; rather, they had individual employment here and there scattered throughout the city. He believed that this integration into the society as a whole made a difference in the kind of race relations which existed there, and he said that it explained why New York had not had a major race riot in the "bloody summer" of 1919. He contended that Harlem was a laboratory for the race problem. Many had argued that when Negroes moved north, the race problem would follow them. Johnson pointed out that 175,000 Negroes had recently moved into Harlem without any substantial racial friction and with no unusual increase in the crime rate. Unfortunately, Johnson's views were not to be fulfilled. Before long, crime rates rose in Harlem, and race riots occurred there as well as in other parts of New York City.[11]

Johnson was aware that there had been considerable racial

tension at an earlier date as Negroes first moved into Harlem. The community had been, in turn, Dutch, Irish, Jewish, and Italian. Originally, Negroes, living in New York, worked for wealthy aristocrats and lived in the shadows of the large mansions surrounding Washington Square. Several of the streets in Greenwich Village had been almost entirely inhabited by Negroes. About 1890 the community shifted its focus northward into the 20s and low 30s just west of Sixth Avenue. At the turn of the century, it moved again into the vicinity of 53rd Street. By this time, the city's Afro-American community was developing a small middle class of its own, and it contained its own fashionable clubs and night life. Visiting Negro entertainers from across the country usually performed at and resided in the Marshall Hotel. The Memphis Students, probably the first professional jazz band to tour the country, played at the Marshall. Shortly after 1900, Negroes began to move to Harlem.

Harlem had been overbuilt with large apartments which the owners were unable to fill. The Lenox Avenue subway had not yet been built, and there was inadequate transportation into the area. As a result, most tenants preferred to live elsewhere. Philip A. Payton, a Negro real estate agent, told several of the owners, located on the east side of the district, that he could guarantee to provide them with regular tenants if they were willing to accept Negroes. Some of the landlords on East 134th Street accepted his offer, and he filled their buildings with Negro tenants.

At first, whites did not notice. However, when Negroes spread west of Lenox Avenue, white resistance stiffened. The local residents formed a corporation to purchase the buildings inhabited by Negroes and to evict them. In turn, the Negroes responded by forming the Afro-American Realty Company, and they too bought out apartment buildings, evicted the white tenants, and rented the apartments to Negroes. White residents then put pressure on lending institutions not to provide mortgages to prospective Negro buyers. When one was able to buy a piece of property, regardless of how prosperous or orderly he might appear, local whites viewed it as an invasion, panicked, and moved out in droves. This left the banks, still unwilling to sell to Negroes, holding a large number of deserted properties. Eventually, they were compelled to sell these properties at deflated prices. During and immediately after the First World War, Negroes poured into Harlem, obtained high-paying jobs, and purchased their own real estate. Johnson believed that Harlem Negroes owned at least sixty million dollars worth of property, and this, he believed, would prevent the neighborhood from degenerating into a slum.[12]

However, the great migration from the rural South had only just begun. As thousands upon thousands more poured into Chicago, Detroit, Milwaukee, Newark, Boston, Harlem, and other Northern centers, housing became increasingly scarce. Harlem, like the other Negro communities of the North, became more and more crowded. At the same time, jobs became harder to obtain. Poor "country cousins" streamed into "the promised land" to share in the "milk and honey," but, unfortunately, there was not enough to go around. As the Negro population of Harlem grew, white resistance and discrimination also increased. Although Johnson had been impressed with the wealth contained in Harlem, it was infinitesimal compared to the great sums of money held by whites downtown.

Langston Hughes, who had also been impressed by the vitality of Harlem, came to realize that Negro Harlem was, in fact, dependent on downtown financing. As Harlem grew, downtown financiers became increasingly aware that money could be made there. In the 1930s, in contrast to Johnson's optimistic vision, Adam Clayton Powell, Jr. and others pointed out that almost all the stores on 125th Street, the major shopping district, were owned by whites and that they employed whites almost exclusively. Harlem soon became a center for both crime and exploitation.[13]

However, in the 1920s Harlem throbbed with vitality and hope. Besides attracting Afro-Americans from every walk of life, it became the focal point for young intellectuals whose creativity resulted in the Negro Renaissance.

The Negro Renaissance

In 1922, James Welden Johnson edited a volume of American Negro poetry, and in the same year Claude McKay, who had come to Harlem from Jamaica, published his first significant volume of poetry, *Harlem Shadows*. These twin events, however, were only the beginning of a vast outpouring of cultural activity, and Harlem became, as Johnson called it, the "culture capital" for this movement. Artists poured into Harlem from across the country. Night clubs rocked with music and dance. Publishers were besieged by eager young poets and novelists, and, surprising to the young writers, the publishers were eager to see Negro authors. Besides the new creative urge, thousands of Negroes and whites were hungry to consume the fruits of this new renaissance.

This artistic renaissance did not come out of a vacuum. Negroes had been publishing poetry for over a century and a half, since the time of Phillis Wheatley and Jupiter Hammon. Paul Laurence Dunbar was the first Negro poet to gain nationwide recognition, at the beginning of the twentieth century. While, on one hand, he captured and depicted the spirit of the Negro folk, on the other hand, he did it in such a way as to perpetuate black stereotypes and white prejudices. Actually, this aided his popularity, and he later came to regret it.

Negroes had also been dancing and creating music in America for over three hundred years. Vaudeville and minstrelsy were their first commercial products. Ironically, the first professional entertainers to perform in minstrel shows were whites who were imitating plantation slave productions. In the beginning, whites performed in blackface, and, only later, did Negroes themselves perform commercially. The spirituals were a religious manifestation of the Afro-American heritage. They appear to have been on the verge of disappearing when the Fisk University Singers, late in the nineteenth century, took steps to preserve them. A choral group from Fisk was touring the country in order to raise money for the school. They received only polite appreciation. When, on one occasion, they decided to offer one of their spirituals as an encore, the audience was enthusiastic. Since then, spirituals have become a standard part of American religious and concert music.

In short, even before the Negro Renaissance of the 1920s the Afro-American community had made a basic contribution to American culture, providing America with a peasant folk tradition of the greatest importance. The social mobility in the American scene had permitted each wave of European immigrants to move up the social ladder before it had time to develop into an American peasant class. However, this mobility was not extended to the Afro-American. Therefore, it was from the Afro-American peasant class that an indigenous American folk culture was to emerge. When minstrelsy and jazz spread around the world, they were seen as American productions. They were, at the same time, Afro-American creations.

The Afro-American folk culture must be seen as the product of the African's experience in America rather than as an importation into America of foreign, African elements. Although the content of the Afro-American folk culture grew out of the American scene, its style and flavor did have African roots. It was based on the artistic sense which the slave brought with him—a highly developed sense of rhythm which was passed from generation to generation, and an understanding of art which conceived of it as an integral part of the whole of life rather than as a beautiful object set apart from mundane experience.

Song and dance, for example, were involved in the African's work, play, love, and worship. In sculpture, painting, weaving, and pottery, the African used his art to decorate the objects in his daily life rather than to make art objects for their own sake. The African could not have imagined going to an art gallery or a musical concert. Art was produced by artisans rather than by artists. This meant that slave artisans in America could continue to produce decorative work, and slave laborers in the field could continue to sing. Art and life could still be combined, though in a highly restricted manner.

However, while the African brought his feeling for art with him, the content of his art was actually changed as the result of his American slave experience. The dominant African arts were sculpture, metal-working, and weaving. In America, the Afro-American created song, dance, music, and, later, poetry. The skills displayed in African art were technical, rigid, controlled, and disciplined. They were characteristically sober, restrained, and heavily conventionalized.

In contrast, the Afro-American cultural spirit became freely emotional, exuberant, and sentimental. This is to say that those Afro-American characteristics which have been generally thought of as being African and primitive—his naiveté, his exuberance, and his spontaneity—are, in reality, his response to his unique American experience and not part of his African heritage. They are to be understood as the African's emotional reaction to the American ordeal of slavery. Out of this environmental furnace, along with its suffering and deprivation, has evolved a unique Afro-American culture.[14]

LeRoi Jones, the contemporary poet, playwright, and jazz critic, points out in *Blues People* that the earliest Negro contributions to formal art did not reflect this genuine Afro-American culture. It was only with the emergence of the New Negro and the Negro Renaissance that this folk culture entered the mainstream of the art world. Previously, those Negroes who had gained enough education to participate in literary creation generally strove to join the American middle class, and tried to disavow all connections with their lower-class background. In doing this, they were only following the same route as that pursued by other ethnic minorities in America. They were ashamed of slavery as well as of everything African.

The folk culture, nevertheless, flourished within the music produced by the Afro-American community. The spirituals and work songs were the product of the slave. After Emancipation, work songs were replaced by the blues. Work songs had been adapted to the mass labor techniques of slavery, whereas the blues, which is a solo form, was the creation of a lone individual working as a sharecropper on his own tenant farm. It continued to express the earthy folk culture, and it, too, was woven into daily life. It expressed the daily tribulations, weariness, fears, and loves of the Afro-American after Emancipation. At the beginning of the twentieth century, blues along with ragtime, became popular, although not always respectable. They could be heard most often in saloons and brothels. Nevertheless, they were beginning to move out of the Afro-American subculture and into the white society. W. C. Handy, while by no means the father of the blues, became its best-known commercial creator. He is still remembered for the "Memphis Blues" and the "St. Louis Blues." [15]

In New Orleans, the folk tradition and formal music came together for the first time. There, the Latin tradition had permitted the Creoles to participate in education and culture. They had developed a rich musical tradition, and many of them had received training in French conservatories. However, they preferred the sophisticated European music to the more earthy sounds of their blacker brothers. With the growth of Jim Crow legislation, the Creoles lost their special position in society, and they found themselves forcibly grouped with the blacks, whom they had previously shunned. Out of this fusion of technical musicianship and folk creativity emerged a new, vigorous music which became known as jazz.

Jelly Roll Morton was one musician who had begun by studying classical guitar but preferred the music of the street. He became a famous jazz pianist and singer. Over the years, he played his way from night spots in New Orleans to those in St. Louis, Chicago, Los Angeles, and scores of smaller cities. The musical quality of jazz, instead of adopting the pure tones of classical music, was boisterous and rasping. Instruments were made to imitate the human voice, and they deliberately used a "dirty" sound. Both the trumpet playing and singing of Louis Armstrong illustrate this jazz sound paticularly well. When Armstrong appeared in Chicago with King Oliver as the band's second trumpeter, he was immediately recognized as a jazz trumpet virtuoso, and his playing sent an electric shock through the jazz world.

The most famous jazz musician and composer to appear in New York City during and after the Negro Renaissance was Duke Ellington. His well-known theme song "Take the A Train" made reference to the subway line which went to Harlem. By the time jazz had reached Harlem the Negro Renaissance was in full swing. This renaissance, unlike previous art produced by Negroes, consciously built on the Afro-American folk tradition.

Langston Hughes, the most prolific writer of the renaissance, wrote a kind of manifesto for the movement. He said that he was proud to be a black artist. Further, he said that he was not writing to win the approval of white audiences. At the same time he claimed that he and the other young Negro artists were not attempting to gain the approval of black audiences. They were writing to express their inner souls, and they were not ashamed that those souls were black. If what they wrote pleased either whites or blacks, Hughes said, they were happy. It did not matter to them if it did not.[16]

In "Minstrel Man" Hughes expressed the inner emotions of the stereotyped, well-behaved Negro which white America thought it knew so well:

> Because my mouth
> Is wide with laughter
> And my throat
> Is deep with song,
> You did not think

I suffer after
I've held my pain
So long.

Because my mouth
Is wide with laughter
You do not hear
My inner cry:
Because my feet
Are gay with dancing,
You do not know
I die.[17]

Claude McKay expresses an inner anger rather than a secret
pain felt by a contained and somewhat more sophisticated Negro
responding to segregation:

Your door is shut against my tightened face,
And I am sharp as steel with discontent;
But I possess the courage and the grace
To bear my anger proudly and unbent.[18]

In still more defiant tones, McKay expresses the aggressive response which many Negroes made during the race riots of 1919:

If we must die, let it not be like hogs
Hunted and penned in an inglorious spot,
While round us bark the mad and hungry dogs,
Making their mock at our accursed lot.

If we must die, O let us nobly die,
So that our precious blood may not be shed
In vain; . . . .[19]

Nevertheless, Langston Hughes made it clear that his bitter
hostility was aimed at injustice and inhumanity and not at American ideals when he wrote:

O, yes,
I say it plain,
America never was America to me,
And yet I swear this oath—
America will be!
An ever-living seed,
Its dream
Lies deep in the heart of me.[20]

Besides articulating the Negro's emotional reaction to prejudice and discrimination, the Negro Renaissance depicted other aspects of the Afro-American culture. The flavor of its religious life was captured best by James Weldon Johnson in his volume *God's Trombones: Negro Sermons in Verse,* which he published in 1927. Instead of resorting to the standard technique of using stereotyped dialect to capture the flavor, Johnson used powerful, poetic imagery to express its essence. In "The Creation" Johnson depicted a Negro minister preaching on the opening verses of Genesis:

> And God stepped out on space,
> And he looked around and said:
> I'm lonely—
> I'll make me a world.
>
> And far as the eye of God could see
> Darkness covered everything,
> Blacker than a hundred midnights
> Down in a cypress swamp.
>
> Then God smiled,
> And the light broke,
> And the darkness rolled up on one side,
> And the light stood shining on the other,
> And God said: That's good! [21]

The Negro Renaissance, besides losing its shame over its folk culture, developed a fresh interest in its African heritage. One of the many expressions of this was made by Countee Cullen:

> What is Africa to me:
> Copper sun or scarlet sea,
> Jungle star or jungle track,
> Strong bronzed men, or regal black
> Women from whose loins I sprang
> When the birds of Eden sang? [22]

The Renaissance also included an outcropping of Negro novelists. There had been Negro novelists before, and the best known of them were Charles W. Chestnut and, to some extent, Paul Laurence Dunbar. Chestnut's novels included *The Conjure Woman* and *The Wife of His Youth and Other Stories of the Color Line,* whereas Dunbar, who wrote mainly poetry, was known for his novel *The Sport of the Gods*. Chestnut's writing, though moving away from the plantation romanticism which had glorified slavery, developed a more realistic flavor, and it emphasized intergroup relations based on the color line rather than developing the interior lives of its characters.[23] Negro fiction came into its own in 1923 with Jean Toomer's publication *Cane*, and, in 1924, with Jessie Redman Fauset's *There is Confusion*. These works dealt with Negroes as people and not merely as objects to be manipulated for racial propaganda. Langston Hughes, in 1930, published *Not Without Laughter*, a novel to gain wide renown.

To catalog all the authors of the Negro Renaissance would become tedious. However, all the poets and novelists listed within these pages are generally accepted as having gained a place among America's significant writers. They were more than products of an Afro-American subculture; their work became part of the mainstream of American literature. These authors, along with other Negro artists, gained the respect of American art and literary critics. With them, the Afro-American folk culture made its way into the formal art of the nation.

The Negro Renaissance of the 1920s, however, was more than a literary movement. There was, as had been noted earlier, a vast outpouring of musical creativity. Besides the jazz composers and performers, many made their mark in classical concert music. The best known composer from the Afro-American community was William Grant Still. Many operatic and concert singers have been Negroes, and they include such well-known names as Paul Robeson, Marian Anderson, Leontyne Price, and William Warfield.

The most famous of the Afro-American painters was Henry O. Tanner, who had made his reputation before the Negro Renaissance. Tanner's paintings had been widely acclaimed at the Paris Exposition in 1900, the Pan-American Exposition in 1901, and the St. Louis Exposition in 1904. Tanner avoided Negro subjects and concentrated on biblical themes. In the field of sculpture, Meta Warrick Fuller was the first Negro to gain attention. Augusta Savage became well-known for her head of Dr. DuBois, and Richmond Barthe gained recognition for the bust of Booker T. Washington.

In retrospect, the Renaissance of the twenties can be seen as the beginning of a continuing, self-conscious cultural movement within the Afro-American community. During the 1930s, however, the outpouring diminished. The Depression affected the entire American scene, businessmen, workmen, and artists, and its impact on the Negro Renaissance was particularly severe. One of the New Deal measures which alleviated the situation considerably was the Federal Writers Project. Sterling Brown, literary critic and Howard University professor, headed the Negro section. Two of the better known authors who were helped by the Project were Arna Bontemps and Richard Wright.

Wright's novel *Native Son* was widely acclaimed. In it, he depicted the inner anger and hatred felt by many young Negro men as dominating characteristics of the hero's personality; eventually, his life was destroyed. The first Negro to win a Pulitzer Prize was Gwendolyn Brooks, who won it for her poetry. Later, Ralph Ellison was awarded a Pulitzer Prize for his novel *Invisible Man*.

Since the Second World War, innumerable Negroes have made significant contributions to American culture through the mass media: radio, television, and movies. Large numbers have also joined the ranks of professional athletes in every field from tennis to football. Nevertheless, complaints persist that prejudice continues in these areas. While they are often included as performers, rarely do Negroes achieve significant decision-making authority in their field. In the 1968 Olympics, several black athletes, especially Carlos and Smith, claimed that instead of being accepted on an equal basis, they were being exploited.

The decade of the 1960s has been marked by a militant spirit throughout the Afro-American community; this spirit was reminiscent of the new Negro of the 1920s although it appears to be more cynical and disillusioned. LeRoi Jones and James Baldwin are only the best known of dozens of contemporary black writers. Their bitterness, undoubtedly, springs partly from the dashed hopes of the new Negro. Unfortunately, at the very time that the Afro-American community was stepping forward with new confidence, the nation was tottering on the brink of economic disaster. The year 1929 brought a harsh end to the optimism of the 1920s.

Black Nationalism

Although Langston Hughes had been confident that the American dream could be made to include his people, thousands upon thousands of other Afro-Americans, especially among the lower classes, were extremely dubious. In 1916, Marcus Garvey came to Harlem, and before long his Universal Negro Improvement Association had opened chapters in urban centers all across the nation. As mentioned previously, Garvey did not believe that blacks could be taken into American society. Hundreds of thousands, who apparently agreed with him, followed his banner. Whatever was the actual number of members of the U.N.I.A., the movement gained more grass-roots support than had any other organization in Afro-American history. While the nation was willing to tolerate the Afro-American folk spirit, the people, themselves, did not believe that they would be accepted.[24]

Although Garvey's movement was by far the largest black nationalist organization in America, it was not the only one. In Chicago, Grover Cleveland Redding was preaching a Back-to-Africa philosophy of his own. He organized the Abyssinian Movement and urged Negroes living on the south side of Chicago to return to Ethiopia. On Sunday, June 20, 1920, Redding led a parade through the Chicago streets. He sat astride a white horse and wore what he claimed was the costume of an Abyssinian prince. At the corner of East 25th Street and Prairie Avenue he stopped the procession, poured a flammable liquid on an American flag, and burned it. A Negro policeman, who attempted to break up the demonstration, was shot by one of Redding's followers. In the course of the melee, a white storekeeper and a white soldier were killed. Redding and another Negro were later executed for their part in the affair.[25]

In 1925 Noble Drew Ali came to Chicago and established the Moorish American Science Temple. Actually, he had previously attempted to organize other temples in New Jersey, Pennsylvania, and Michigan. He claimed that American Negroes were of Moorish descent and, instead of being really black, were olive-hued. His movement had a banner which carried a Moorish star and crescent on a field of red. He also claimed that American Negroes, being Moors, had an Islamic heritage rather than a Christian one, and he endeavored to spread his particular version of that faith throughout the Afro-American community. By 1927 Ali had established branches in Pittsburgh, Detroit, Philadelphia, Kansas City, Lansing, and elsewhere. He wrote his own version of the Koran which combined passages from the Moslem Koran, the Christian Bible, and some of the writings of Marcus Garvey.[26]

Ali gave his followers a new sense of identity. Most of them wore a fez which set them apart from the typical urban black. Many were also bearded, and each one carried a membership card. Having a different religion from that of the typical ghetto black contributed further to their special sense of identity. Ali's teaching also made them feel that they had a special and unique heritage of which they could be proud. His emphasis on separatism instead of on integration struck a harmonious note with their disillusionment. Instead of leaving them in despair, it permitted them to face white America boldly.

In 1929 a power struggle broke out between Noble Drew Ali and Claude Green, one of his organizers. When Green was found murdered, the Chicago police charged Ali with the crime. While Ali was out on bond, he too died under mysterious circumstances. While some claimed that he had been beaten by the police, others said that he had been "mugged" by Green's followers. Before he was released on bail Ali wrote a letter from prison to his followers encouraging them to have faith in him and in their future. His letter bore distinctly messianic overtones. After assuring them that he had redeemed them, he concluded by extending to them his peace and by commanding them to love one another. His movement splintered after his death into innumerable competing factions.

In Detroit, sometime before 1930, a dark-skinned man appeared selling silk and raincoats. He said that he was W. D. Fard and that he had come from the Holy City of Mecca in order to save the American Negro. People generally described him as being unusually light-skinned for a Negro with perhaps an Oriental cast. Fard also taught that the American Negro was Islamic in origin and that he should return to his ancestral faith. Sometime in 1933 or 1934 he disappeared as mysteriously as he had come. While many believed that Fard and his movement must have been connected with Noble Drew Ali and the Moorish American Science Temple, the Black Muslims have always denied it.[27]

Fard founded, in Detroit, Muslim Temple Number One, and he acquired a handful of devout followers. He insisted that the Muslims should refrain from eating pork, should pray facing the East, and should practice a daily washing ritual. Muslim members were reminded that their last names had been imposed upon them by the white man whom Fard equated with the Devil. It is the practice among Muslims to drop their Christian name and, until their true names will be revealed to them, to substitute the letter X for their last name symbolizing the unknown. Fard insisted that the first man had been a black man and that whites were a corruption of humanity. The days of the White Devil, he said, were numbered. Blacks should deliberately withdraw from white society in order not to be caught in its final destruction.

The Muslim's life was rigidly disciplined. There were temple services almost every evening. Individual behavior and dress were carefully dictated. Besides forbidding the eating of pork, devout Muslims were not allowed to drink alcohol or smoke tobacco. Relationships between men and women were extremely puritanical. Each temple had special groups to prepare young men and women for manhood and womanhood. The Fruit of Islam was the young men's group, and it was a semi-military defense corps aimed at developing a sense of manhood and the ability for self-defense. The common belief that the Fruit of Islam was preparing for racial aggression has never been substantiated. The Muslim Girls' Training Classes taught cooking, sewing, housekeeping, and etiquette.

After Fard's disappearance, the leadership passed on to Elijah Muhammed, formerly Elijah Poole, whom Fard had been grooming as his successor. Elijah Muhammed moved to Chicago and began Temple Number Two and established his headquarters there. The Black Muslims, as well as other small, semi-religious, separatist groups, continued to exist unnoticed by the general public. When Malcolm Little, better known as Malcolm X,[28] was converted to the Nation of Islam, he gave the movement the organizational skill and the eloquence which it previously lacked. This brought it into national prominence.

Black Nationalism and the Negro Renaissance shared a strong sense of racial consciousness and racial pride. However, while the writers who expressed the spirit of the new Negro still believed in their future in America, the black nationalists enunciated a mood of alienation and despair. The Depression, which eroded the hopes of many Americans, hit the Negro unusually hard. It served to increase the level of bitterness in the Afro-American community as a whole.

CHAPTER 10

Fighting Racism at Home and Abroad

Hard Times Again

THE new Negro of the 1920s who had struck out for "The Promised Land" found, in the 1930s, that his old enemies of hunger, cold, and prejudice were lurking outside the door of his newly chosen home. Hope slid into despair and cynicism. The dynamic, self-confident Harlem which Johnson had described in 1925 as the Culture Capital of the Negro World became choked with disillusionment and frustration, and, in 1935, it was the scene of looting, burning, and violence.

While the Depression which swept America in 1929 was a national disaster, it did not hit all segments of society equally. In America, poverty and starvation are also discriminatory. To quote the old adage again, "The Negro is the last to be hired and the first to be fired." The Depression also proved that Harlem, like other Afro-American communities, was not as economically self-sufficient as Johnson had imagined. Although such communities had many Negro-owned businesses thriving on a Negro trade, these businesses were still dependent on the economy at large. Therefore, they were not at all free from the racial discrimination in the nation. Their clientele was largely employed in white-owned businesses. When Negroes were laid off, Negro-owned businesses immediately felt the pinch.

Although Negro businesses had grown significantly during the 1920s, most were small establishments and, in the age of mass production and mass marketing, always had to struggle hard in order to compete. In 1929, the Colored Merchants Association was established in New York City, and it attempted to buy goods for independent stores on a cooperative wholesale basis. This aided them in competing with chain stores. The Association also urged blacks to patronize stores owned by Afro-Americans. Nevertheless, the Association only survived for two years. The entire Afro-American community felt the Depression sooner and harder than did the rest of the country.

By 1932, the government believed that 38 percent of the Afro-American community was incapable of self-support and in need of government relief. At the same time, it considered that only 17 percent of the white community fell into this category. In October of 1933, between 25 percent and 40 percent of the blacks in many of the large cities, to which they had moved to find a brighter future, were on relief. This percentage was three or four times higher than that of the whites in the same cities. As affluent whites felt the economic pinch, one of the first items to be trimmed from their shrinking budgets was the maid or the gardener. In 1935 the number of unemployed Negro domestics was at least one and a half million. In that same year, the government estimated that 65 percent of the Negro employables in Atlanta were on public assistance while, in Norfolk, 80 percent of the Afro-American community was on relief.[1]

As Negro unemployment statistics skyrocketed in the early thirties, The-Jobs-for-Negroes Movement strove to alleviate the crisis. It was begun by the Urban League in St. Louis. A boycott was organized against white-owned chain stores which catered to Negroes, but refused to employ them. The movement spread throughout the Midwest and had some success in "persuading" white-owned stores in the heart of the ghettoes to hire Negro employees. When the idea reached Harlem, it resulted in the establishment of the Greater New York Coordinating Committee. One of its founders and organizers was the Rev. Adam Clayton Powell, Jr., and the Committee received considerable support from his church, the Abyssinian Baptist Church.

It was Powell's claim that the Committee was shunned by most "respectable" Negroes but that its supporters included an unusually wide variety of radicals. The group referred to its members as antebellum Negroes by which, Powell said, they meant before Civil War II. Some of them, he claimed, favored repatriation to Africa; others were for black capitalism; still another group, including Powell himself, wanted the Negro to achieve full dignity within the American system. In spite of the variety of their objectives, all of them believed that the Afro-American must first achieve economic security before any of these specific goals could be attained.

It was on this primary tactical necessity that they were able to coordinate their activities. They picketed white-owned stores on 125th Street. They carried signs advocating, "Don't buy where you can't work," and Powell maintained that they were able almost to stop trade totally at any target they chose to picket. He also claimed to be able to call a meeting with only forty-eight hours notice and have 10,000 persons in attendance. The 125th Street stores soon negotiated and began hiring Negro employees. Next, the Committee hit the city's utility companies. They urged Negroes not to use electricity on specified days. They harassed the telephone company by urging Negroes to demand that the operator place their calls instead of their dialing the number and utilizing the automatic exchanges. Both companies changed their employment patterns in response. The Committee also boycotted the bus company until it began employing Negroes as drivers as well as on other levels of the company's staff.[2]

By 1935 Harlem had become a pressure cooker which was heated to the boiling point by economic and racial frustrations. When a young Negro stole a knife from a 125th Street store, it became the incident which triggered a social explosion. Although he had escaped from the pursuing owner, a rumor spread around the community that he had been beaten to death. A mob soon gathered and began to protest everything from the discriminatory practices of merchants to slum landlords and police tactics. Window-breaking, looting, and burning soon followed. Before peace was restored, three Negroes had been killed, some two hundred stores smashed, and it was estimated that approximately $2,000,000 worth of damage had been done. Mayor Fiorello H. LaGuardia appointed a study commission which was headed by the noted black sociologist E. Franklin Frazier. The commission concluded that the causes of the riot were rooted in resentment against racial discrimination and poverty. The "promised land" of the large northern cities had not lived up to expectations.[3]

The Depression, however, brought its own kind of hope. Franklin Delano Roosevelt, who had been elected in 1932, promised the country a "New Deal." It was to be a new deal for the workers, the unemployed and, it seemed, for the Negro too. In response, black voters switched to the Democratic party in droves. While Franklin D. Roosevelt was not the first president to appoint Negroes to government positions, his appointments were different in two major respects. First, there were more of them. Second, instead of being political payoffs, the appointees were selected for their expert knowledge, and their intellectual skills became part of the government's decision-making processes.

This group, which became informally known as the "Black Cabinet," included such prominent Afro-American leaders as Robert L. Vann of *The Pittsburgh Courier*, William H. Hastie of the Harvard Law School, Eugene Kinckle Jones of the Urban League, Mrs. Mary McLeod Bethune of the National Council of Negro Women, Robert C. Weaver, and Ralph Bunche, who later became the first Negro to be awarded the Nobel Peace Prize. The number of Afro-Americans hired by the Federal Government mushroomed rapidly.

Between 1933 and 1946 the number rose from 50,000 to almost 200,000. Most, however, were employed in the lower, unskilled and semi-skilled, brackets. It was also during this period that the Civil Service terminated its policy of requiring applicants to state their race and to include photographs. Individual personnel officers, nevertheless, could and did continue to discriminate.[4]

In spite of the attempt of the Roosevelt Administration to elevate the status of the Afro-American, the New Deal itself became enmeshed in racial discrimination in three ways: through discriminatory practice within government bureaus, through exclusion carried on by unions, and also as an indirect by-product of the structure of the New Deal programs. In a government bureaucracy, power and authority are distributed throughout the administrative hierarchy. Officials at varying levels were still influenced by their personal prejudices, and they continued to use their positions in a discriminatory manner. Regardless of the intentions at the top, prejudice continued to exist in varying degrees throughout the lower levels of the structure.

In 1935 the Wagner Act protected the rights of labor unions, but because most unions practiced racial discrimination, it served indirectly to undercut the status of the Negro worker for a short time. Actually, with the heightened competition for jobs, unions tended to intensify their discrimination. The American Federation of Labor largely consisted of trade or skilled workers. Its member unions regularly practiced racial exclusion and kept blacks out of the trades. To the contrary, the United Mine Workers Union which had been organized on an industry-wide basis rather than a craft basis had encouraged the participation of Negroes within the union since at least 1890. In 1935, several union leaders, led by John L. Lewis of the United Mine Workers, decided that the union movement must break away from its craft orientation and begin to organize the new mass production industries on an industry-wide basis.

While the A. F. of L. dragged its feet, the dissidents withdrew and formed the Congress of Industrial Organizations. Immediately they began to organize the steelworkers, the meat packers, and the automobile workers. These were all industries which employed significant numbers of Afro-Americans, and the CIO followed an aggressive, nondiscriminatory policy. In the beginning, black workers were suspicious, but they soon joined the new unions in large numbers. In the long run, both black and white labor benefited from the Wagner Act.[5]

Finally, the New Deal failed to extend its program to include either agricultural or domestic workers. These were two areas in which Afro-Americans were employed in unusually high proportions, and this meant that a large portion of the Afro-American community was not covered by this legislation. For example, both the Social Security and the Minimum Wage laws excluded both agricultural and domestic workers. Nevertheless, it was estimated that in 1939 some one million Negroes owed their livelihood to the Works Progress Administration. If it had not been for the W.P.A., the National Youth Administration, the Civilian Conservation Corps, and other similar organizations, Afro-Americans would have suffered even more during the Depression.

Some relief was brought to farmers through the Agricultural Adjustment Administration. However, white landlords usually kept the checks which had been intended for the sharecroppers. This resulted in the formation of The Southern Tenant Farmers' Union, an interracial organization. Despite the landlords' attempts to use racism to destroy it, the Union showed that white and black farmers could cooperate on the basis of their common economic plight. This alliance of poor whites and poor blacks was reminiscent of the earlier Populist Movement.

Although the New Deal did much to help the Negro, it tended to further undercut his self-confidence and independence. Alain Locke has argued that the significant fact about the northward migration by blacks had been that the Afro-Americans had made a decision for themselves. The fact of having made a decision and of taking action on it, Locke maintains, was the event which created the aggressive self-confident New Negro. In helping him to survive the Depression, the New Deal turned him again into a passive recipient. The large number of Afro-Americans who were receiving government aid in one way or another were aware of their dependency. Afro-American communities, which had been regarded as "The Promised Land," slid into poverty and dejection.

The Second World War

As ominous war clouds began to gather over Europe in the late 1930s, most Americans were preoccupied with domestic problems resulting from the Depression. Those who took notice of the ascendency of Mussolini and Hitler were apt to be impressed with their successes in combatting the effects of the Depression in Italy and Germany. The Afro-American community, however, was more concerned with the imperialistic and racist elements in the teachings of Fascism and National Socialism. Usually, American Negroes were prevented from looking beyond their own problems by the immediacy of racial prejudice which they faced daily, but this time they were among the first to warn of impending danger.

Racist thought in Germany did not begin with the rise of Adolf Hitler. European anti-Semitism can be traced back into the past for centuries. Although it originally had its roots in a religious feeling, racism became secularized and, by the middle of the nineteenth century, took on political overtones and tried to assume a scientific foundation.

Aggressive nationalism began to bloom at the beginning of the nineteenth century and went on to spread across Europe. The political unification of Germany, instead of being the glorious culmination of this nationalistic drama, only signaled the end of one act and the beginning of another. Even the German defeat in the First World War did not persuade ardent nationalists to be content with the victories they had already achieved. Instead, they probed the heart of the nation to find an explanation for their defeat. These nationalists contended that the defeat had been due to pollution of racial purity by the presence of a large, alien element—the Jews. If it had not been for this impurity, it was argued, Germany would certainly have been victorious, and it would have demonstrated its global superiority. Aggressive nationalism became virulent racism.

Adolf Hitler exploited this need for a political scapegoat and turned it into a national, anti-Semitic campaign. The racial stereotypes and accompanying feelings were already widespread. Nineteenth-century popular German literature was full of such trite symbols. The Jew was always portrayed as a villainous merchant, shifty-eyed, large-nosed, unscrupulous, and wealthy. In contrast, the German was invariably portrayed as a solid, blond-haired peasant, hard-working, loyal, and exploited.

The drama in such literature sprang from the tension between the wealthy Jewish merchants and the hard-working but poor German peasants. Here could be found the same kind of exploitation which Hitler used to explain the German defeat in the war. These popular stereotypes were then joined to the teachings of Houston Stewart Chamberlain which had built on elements from biology, anthropology, sociology, and phrenology. In his book *Foundations of the Nineteenth Century*, Chamberlain had developed them into a philosophy of world history which centered on the concepts of racial conflict. Human progress and racial purity were equated. He predicted an eventual struggle to the death between the Jewish and the Teutonic races. The Germans, he believed, would emerge victorious. Through the survival of the fittest and the destruction of the weak, mankind would reach a higher stage of evolution. Although Nazi racist thought was concerned almost exclusively with the conflict between the Germans and the Jews, it was clear that the Negro race was, if anything, consigned to an even lower level of importance than the Jews. Certainly, in the survival of the fittest, Negroes were also destined for extermination in the name of human progress.

Afro-American suspicions about the nature of Mussolini's imperialism proved to be justified when Italy invaded Ethiopia. Mussolini's dream of reviving Roman glory included rebuilding a powerful empire. However, underdeveloped countries which were not already dominated by European nations and which could easily be colonized, were few in number. When Italy invaded Ethiopia, Afro-Americans saw it as another white nation subjugating another black nation. At the very time when Africans and Afro-Americans were looking forward to the liberation of

Africa from European domination, Italy was extending imperialism even further and conquering the last remaining independent supposedly black nation in Africa. Afro-Americans were outraged. They looked to the League of Nations hoping that it would take decisive action against the Italian aggression. Their hopes were in vain.

The war that began in 1939 came to be expressed in terms which were even more ideological than had been true of the First World War. The Allies depicted themselves as being the champions of freedom and humanity while they portrayed their enemies as tyrants and barbarians. Afro-Americans were painfully aware of some of the imperfections in this simple dichotomy. While aghast at the racist teachings propagated by Germany, they could not forget the racism which confronted them daily within the United States.

They were also aware of the imperialism which was practiced by both the British and the French who dominated and exploited Africa almost at will. Nevertheless, Hitler's form of brazen racism did give a note of validity to this ideological formulation. Afro-Americans viewed the war both with more enthusiasm and with more pessimism than they had felt at the outbreak of the First World War. On the one hand, they could eagerly support a war to defeat Hitler's racist doctrines. On the other hand, they did not believe that any display of patriotism on their part would significantly diminish racism at home. During the First World War they had thought that a demonstration of patriotism would help to knock down the walls of antagonism. Instead, they found that manliness on the part of Afro-Americans, even in the name of patriotism, was a threat to those whites who believed that Negroes should be kept in their place. Afro-Americans were prepared not to be disillusioned in that way again. For them, the war would still be a double struggle—fighting racism at home as well as abroad.

The Second World War began to affect Americans long before the country was actually drawn into the fighting. Although the American nation stood on the sidelines for the first two years, America became a major source of money, supplies, and encouragement for Britain and France. Providing matériel for the Allies gave new life to the sagging American economy. There were still some five million unemployed in the nation, and something more than New Deal pump-priming seemed to be needed. Unfortunately for the Afro-American, most of the new jobs were not open to him. Aside from the fact that he was the first to be fired and the last to be hired, many of the new defense industries made it clear that they would hire no Negroes at all or, at most, would restrict their employment to janitorial positions regardless of the training or education of the applicant.

Hostility was expressed quite openly by some leaders in the West Coast aircraft industry. As better jobs became available, they were quickly filled by white workers eager to improve their economic status. This left some of the more undesirable jobs to go begging, and, as the result, the war boom benefits began to trickle down to the Afro-American community. Afro-Americans, however, were not content with the crumbs from the industrial table. Complaints began to flood into Washington. Several government officials made pronouncements condemning discrimination in defense industries, but they were not heard. It became clear that nothing would change without strong government action, and it was also evident that this would not occur unless the entire Afro-American community could exert united, political pressure.

Early in 1941, A. Philip Randolph [6] put forth the idea of a gigantic March on Washington, and he expressed the belief that a hundred thousand Afro-Americans could be organized to participate in such an undertaking. The immediate response from most of the leaders of both black and white America was one of skepticism. Most of them felt that there was too much apathy in the Afro-American community for such a grandiose scheme to be taken seriously. Nevertheless, interest on the grass-roots level gradually grew and Randolph's idea was transformed into a project involving scores of organizers all across the country, all of whom were working diligently to enlist potential marchers. In the meantime, Randolph began to formulate the complex plans for organizing the actual march. By late spring, skepticism had turned to worry. Many government leaders and finally President Roosevelt himself tried to talk Randolph into canceling the march.[7] They suggested that such an aggressive protest would do more to hurt the Afro-American than help him.

Randolph remained unyielding. Others tried to suggest that the protest would be bad for the American image and therefore was unpatriotic. When they suggested that it would create a bad impression in Rome and Berlin, Afro-Americans retorted that white racism had already created such an image. Finally, Roosevelt contacted Randolph and offered to issue an executive order barring discrimination in defense industries and promised to put "teeth" in the order, provided Randolph call off the march. When Randolph became convinced that Roosevelt's intentions were sincere, he complied.

Roosevelt fulfilled his promise by issuing Executive Order 8802, which condemned discrimination on the grounds of race, color, or creed. Then, he established the Fair Employment Practices Commission and assigned to it the responsibility for enforcing the order. Many Afro-Americans felt that Executive Order 8802 was the most important government document concerning the Negro to be issued since the Emancipation Proclamation. Their immediate joy was somewhat dampened when they found that discrimination still continued in some quarters. Nevertheless, the F.E.P.C. did condemn discrimination when it found it, and, as the result, many new jobs began to open up for Negroes.

Once America was drawn into the fighting, Afro-Americans hurried to the enlistment centers to volunteer their services in the war against Hitler's philosophy. However, it soon became clear that America intended to fight racism with a segregated army. The fact that Negroes were confined to the more menial positions in the armed forces was what irritated Afro-Americans the most. The Negro army units were obviously going to be led by white officers. The Marine Corps was still not accepting any Negroes in its ranks at all. Complaints again began to pour into Washington.

Afro-Americans generally admitted that the Selective Service Act per se was not discriminatory and that it was applied impartially in most places. One of the reasons for this impartiality, undoubtedly, was the fact that both local and national Selective Service Boards included Afro-American representation. In the course of the war, about one million Afro-Americans saw service on behalf of their country. Their ratio within the armed forces was almost the same as that within the nation. This had been the stated goal of the Department of War.

Gradually, the armed forces modified their discriminatory policies in response to the flood of complaints. The Air Force began to train Negro pilots although they still received segregated training and served in segregated squadrons. The Marine Corps accepted Negro recruits for the first time in its history. They, too, served in segregated units. The Navy, which had restricted Negroes to menial positions, gradually began to accept them in almost all noncommissioned positions. Eventually, it even began to commission some Negro officers. The Army, too, introduced an extensive program to prepare Negro officers. It trained most of them in integrated facilities, but they continued to lead segregated units. As the war grew to a close, the Army announced that it intended to experiment with integration. However, when the experiment took place, the integration proved not to be quite what had been expected. Instead of putting individuals from both races together in the same unit, the Army took segregated black and white platoons and merged them into an integrated fighting force although the platoons themselves remained segregated.

This integrated unit did fight well in the field and made a significant contribution to the defeat of Germany in 1945. Negro units, as well as individual Negro soldiers, made outstanding contributions to the war effort both in Europe and in the Pacific, and they received numerous commendations and citations. Skeptics noted, however, that not a single Negro soldier had received the Congressional Medal of Honor in either the First or Second World Wars, and they suggested that the nation's highest award was being reserved for whites.[8]

Although most of the hostilities were focused on the enemy, racial tensions still ran very high within America. Southern whites were displeased with the self-confidence and manliness brought out in Negroes by military experience, and they were unhappy with the dignity which a military uniform conferred upon them.

At the same time, Negro soldiers in the South were angry over the harassment and segregation with which they were confronted. In particular, they were irritated by the fact that German prisoners of war were permitted to eat with white American soldiers in the same dining car on a railroad train traveling through the South, while Negro soldiers could not. Racial riots occurred at Fort Bragg, Camp Robinson, Camp Davis, Camp Lee, Fort Dix, and a notorious one at an American base in Australia. The policy of the War Department was to gloss over these events. Casualties which resulted from riots at bases in the United States were officially listed as accidental deaths. Those which resulted from riots overseas were officially reported as being killed in action. On several occasions, Negro soldiers refused to do work which they believed had been assigned to them purely because of their race. For this they were charged with mutiny.

There was also one serious civilian race riot during the war; it occurred on June 20, 1943, in Detroit. A fist fight between a white man and a Negro sparked the resentment which had been mounting in that city. Thousands of Afro-Americans had been moving again from the South into the North to fill vacant jobs in war industry, and this was resented by local white residents. Before the Detroit riot ended, twenty-five Negroes and nine whites had been killed. President Roosevelt had to send in federal troops to quell the disturbance.[9] Another factor which irritated Afro-Americans was that the Red Cross blood banks separated Negro and white blood. This was particularly humiliating in that it had been a Negro doctor, Charles Drew, who had done the basic research that made the banks possible.

In spite of this, Afro-Americans were eager to demonstrate their patriotism and to support the war effort. Besides the hundreds of thousands who were involved directly in the military, millions more supported the war effort in countless other ways. Besides growing their own vegetables, saving tin cans and newspapers, they were avid contributors to the War Bond issues. Others volunteered to serve as block wardens in case of enemy air raids. Negro newspapers had their own journalists at the front, and the Afro-American community eagerly kept up with the war news. They took special pride in stories of heroism about Negro soldiers. When Hitler and his racist philosophy went down in defeat, they felt that they had achieved a personal victory and that at the same time they had made a contribution to America and the world.

Thus, as the war came to a close and Afro-Americans looked forward to the postwar years with both apprehension and determination, they feared that, with the foreign antagonism eradicated, racist feeling at home might increase. At the same time, they were possessed by a new drive to make American democracy into a reality. The ideological character of the war had reminded them of America's expressed ideals of brotherhood and equality. Their participation in the war convinced them that they were worthy of full citizenship. Many had broken the bonds of tradition which had held them in fear and apathy. Some had left their communities to fight in the Army, and some had moved into large urban centers to work in defense industries. Although the war against racism abroad had ended, they were intent to see that the struggle for racial freedom and equality at home would continue.

The U.S. and the U.N.

The San Francisco Conference which founded the United Nations organization was looked upon by peoples around the world as the sunrise of a new day of peace and brotherhood. While hope ran high in most quarters, some of these same peoples were suspicious about its lofty ideological character. Humanitarian ideologies had made their appearance before, but there had always been a gap between theory and practice. Colored peoples and other minorities around the world observed the San Francisco Conference with hope mixed with caution. They wanted to see whether it was mere ideological rhetoric which would salve the consciences of the exploiters and dull the senses of the exploited, or whether, perhaps, its aims might spring from genuine conviction and become established in a framework which would be fully implemented.

The U.N. was to be more sweeping in its goals and programs than the League had been, and it was hoped that it would have more power to carry out its decisions. Its very initials signified that the peoples of the world were to be one people bound together in brotherhood, freedom, and equality. This should have meant the end of imperialistic exploitation as well as the end of minority persecutions. The Afro-American community wondererd if its government which was playing such a leading role in founding the U.N. would apply these principles to them. Many skeptics suggested that the U. S. initiative in founding the U.N. was only part of a plan to create a world image which would help America in her new role as a world leader.

Several Afro-Americans were accredited as official observers at the San Francisco Conference. Their number included Mrs. Mary McLeod Bethune, Dr. Mordecai W. Johnson of Howard University, W. E. B. DuBois and Walter White, both of the N.A.A.C.P. Ralph Bunche was an official member of the American staff. There were also a large number of Negro journalists, and the conference was widely covered in the Negro press. Once the U.N. was organized and in operation, several other Afro-Americans worked for it in a number of ways. While some held diplomatic posts, others used their specific scientific and scholarly skills to help various branches of the U.N. They were particularly interested in the departments concerned with the treatment of colonial nations and with the various scientific organizations involved in helping underdeveloped countries.

The United Nations Charter defended universal human rights more clearly than any previous political document in world history. The Charter proclaimed human rights and freedom for all without respect to "race, sex, language or religion." Minority groups were particularly interested in the work of UNESCO which, among other things, studied the nature of prejudice and racism and tried to develop programs to eradicate these evils. The U.N. also formed a Human Rights Commission, and Afro-Americans expected that whatever action the U.N. took to support human rights throughout the world would also have an impact on their situation.

The first test came in 1946 when India charged South Africa with practicing racial discrimination against Indian nationals and their descendants who were living within South Africa. Minority groups throughout the world eagerly waited to see what, if anything, the U.N. would do. When a resolution was passed by a two-thirds majority, charging South Africa with the violation of human rights, and requiring it to report back on what steps had been taken to alter the situation, religious and national minorities were overjoyed. However, the enthusiasm of Afro-Americans was dampened by the fact that both the United States and Britain had voted against the resolution. While posing as the leaders of democracy and humanitarianism, they seemed more concerned with protecting their sovereign rights as nations against similar future charges which might impinge on their sovereignty, than they were with protecting the human rights of oppressed peoples.[10]

The attitude which the U. S. Government took towards human rights sheds considerable light on the internal conflict concerning race within América itself. The U. S. led the fight at the U.N. for the approval of the Universal Declaration of Human Rights. Yet the American government has been reluctant to support the inclusion of specific economic and social rights in a draft treaty. The U.N. had endeavored to write a draft treaty which its member nations would sign and which would be binding on them. If the

U. S. Senate had ratified such a document, its terms presumably would then be binding on the entire nation. At that time, senators from the Southern states were still staunchly defending legal segregation and disfranchisement of Afro-Americans. The government found itself supporting human rights ideologically while backing down on them in practice.[11]

As the Cold War deepened, the U. S. became increasingly sensitive about its world image. While fighting for world leadership, Russia and America each claimed that its way of life was based on the principles of brotherhood and humanitarianism. Each, in turn, tried to prove to the rest of the world that its ideology was genuinely humane and democratic, while its opponent's ideology was, in reality, oppressive and dehumanizing. The communist bloc attacked the West for being purveyors of imperialism and racism. This forced the American government to face up to the discriminatory policies within the nation and, especially, to reexamine the legal discrimination existing within the Southern states. It was particularly embarrassing to the American ambassador to the United Nations to have to be berated by the Russian delegate concerning some unpleasant racial events which had happened somewhere in the South. The Federal Government had always followed a policy of "hands off," at least since the days of Hayes and the end of Reconstruction. Party politicians always opposed taking a strong federal stand against an established state policy within the South for fear of what would happen to that party within the South. Party unity had almost always been put above civil rights or justice.

However, these same party politicians could not ignore world opinion. Even from a narrow political point of view, a party could not permit the nation's world image to become tarnished, lest the electorate become dissatisfied. World leadership brought with it the need to be concerned with world opinion. Racism was no longer a local or state question. In fact, as W. E. B. DuBois had predicted, it had become the leading question of the twentieth century. At the end of the Second World War, Walter White, then executive director of the N.A.A.C.P., toured Europe and drew conclusions concerning the effect of the war and the course of the future. In his book *Rising Wind*, White demonstrated a relationship between the oppressed peoples of the world, racism, and imperialism. Though a relative moderate, White warned of a future worldwide racial conflict.

As the war was drawing to an end in the Pacific theater, the Japanese cautioned Asiatics about American racial oppression. What they called attention to was that the British dominated colored peoples in Africa and Asia and that the Americans persecuted their racial minority at home. White believed that this propaganda was taking root in the hearts of many Asiatics. He also believed that most of Asia would slide into the Russian camp, thereby preparing the way for a third world conflict. He contended that Britain and America had a choice between ending their policies of racial superiority and preparing for the next war.[12]

In 1948 A. Philip Randolph began to advocate civil disobedience on the part of Afro-Americans, rather than ever again allowing themselves to be part of a segregated army. He recommended that they refuse to serve in future wars, and the idea received widespread attention. In a Senate committee inquiry, Senator Wayne Morse from Oregon suggested to him that such civil disobedience in wartime could well be viewed as treason and not merely as civil disobedience. Clearly, Randolph's suggestion had hit a sensitive nerve. A nation which had been skeptical about permitting Afro-Americans in its armed forces was now becoming extremely uneasy at the thought that Afro-Americans might not want to serve.[13] In the same year President Truman appointed a commission to study race relations in the military. Its report, *Freedom to Serve,* recommended that the Armed Forces open up all jobs regardless of race, color, or creed. As a result, the military began to move slowly in the direction of integration. However, when the communists invaded South Korea, the issue quickly came to a head. Unless integration was achieved, America would have to fight communists and colored Asiatics with a segregated army and would have to do it in the name of the United Nations.

In 1950 General Matthew Ridgway began to accelerate integration in the forces under his command. He did this partly as a matter of philosophy and partly from necessity. The Army needed the fullest and most efficient use of the few troops available in order to stem the flow of a much larger communist force into South Korea. This integration proceeded very well, and when he was put in charge of all forces in the Far East, he asked the Defense Department for permission to integrate all of the forces in the area. Within three months, the extent of integration in the Armed Forces jumped from nine percent to thirty percent. While Afro-Americans were pleased, they were also convinced that it had been done more from the pressure of world opinion than from a genuine humanitarian conscience.[14]

During this period, the Federal Government took a more active role in several other ways in regard to improving race relations. How much of this action sprang from internal motivation and how much resulted from the pressure of world opinion is a matter of conjecture. In any case, the Truman Administration deliberately created an atmosphere favorable to changing race relations within America. In 1946 Truman appointed a committee on civil rights which, after intensive study, published its report, *To Secure These Rights*.

The report set forth that the Federal Government had the duty to act in order to safeguard civil rights when local or state governments either could not or did not take such action. The committe recommended enlarging the size and powers of the civil rights section of the Justice Department and also recommended that the F.B.I. increase its civil rights activity. The threat of federal intervention in state racial policies led to a revolt by several Southern Senators within the Democratic Party. In 1948 they formed the Dixiecrat Party and refused to support many of the policies and candidates of the Democratic Party. Truman also appointed a committee to study higher education in America, and its report recommended an end to discrimination in colleges and universities. In 1948 Truman issued an executive order aimed at achieving fair employment within government service. He also continued the practice of attacking discrimination within industries working under government contracts. In 1948 the Supreme Court declared that restrictive covenants in housing were unconstitutional. Many state and local governments across the country also took action against discrimination in the fields of housing and employment.

Thus the principles underlying the United Nations and the Declaration of Human Rights had the effect of stirring democratic and humanitarian ideals in many parts of white America. Sensitivity to world opinion had made all branches of the Federal Government more willing to act on racial matters. Although most

Americans would have insisted that these activities sprang from a genuine concern for racial justice, Afro-Americans were convinced that it had been the pressure of world opinion which had turned these humanitarian convictions into action.

CHAPTER 11

Civil Rights and Civil Disobedience

Schools and Courts

THE democratic idealism which had been fostered by the Second World War and the Cold War made many American citizens increasingly uncomfortable about the legal support given to racism in the Southern states. A wide variety of organizations—labor unions, religious and fraternal societies as well as groups specifically concerned with attacking racism—became increasingly active in trying to put democratic ideals into practice. America's competition with communism in gaining world leadership, made many Americans feels that it was necessary to prove, once and for all, the superiority of the American way of life. However, there was a growing concerted effort to destroy legal segregation because it was a serious blemish on this democratic image.

Believing strongly in the democratic process as these groups did, this attack was mounted within the framework of the legal system. The N.A.A.C.P. came to be the cutting edge of the campaign. In particular, the Legal Defense Fund of the N.A.A.C.P. and the small group of intelligent, dedicated Negro lawyers whom it financed, spearheaded the attack. It was clear that the legal system itself supported the position of Southern racists. Most Afro-Americans in the South could not vote, and Southern senators were in a position to sabotage any attempt to change the system through the legislative process. They were chosen through a white electorate, and Afro-Americans in the South could do little about that. Even if a favorable majority in Congress stemming from the North and West could be established, the one-party system in the South meant that Southern Senators were continually reelected and, therefore, had Congressional seniority. Consequently, they controlled most of the committees and were thereby in virtual control of the legislative process itself.

Although the courts had usually interpreted the Constitution so as to support segregation, much of that document's language supported democratic and equalitarian principles. If the courts could be persuaded to understand the Constitution differently, legal segregation might well be found to be unconstitutional. The judicial system to some degree reacts to popular pressure and events, and it too was influenced by the need to justify American democracy to the rest of the world.

The N.A.A.C.P. had already mounted a broad, concerted attack against legal segregation before the Second World War. When Walter White defeated W. E. B. DuBois in a struggle for leadership, he confirmed the Association's emphasis on striving for an integrated society. The number of white and middle-class black supporters of the N.A.A.C.P. grew, and its treasury prospered. The Association chose to concentrate its efforts on a gradual, relentless attack against segregation through the courts. Believing that education was an all-important factor in society, it decided that school desegregation should become the major target.

Thurgood Marshall was the master strategist in the school desegregation campaign. He decided that the attack should be a slow, indirect one. Most Southern school systems, although they had developed two separate institutions, had not established separate graduate and professional facilities for Negroes. Marshall decided to attack the school question on the graduate, professional, and law-school level. First, Southerners did not seem as frightened about racial mixing on the graduate school level, and second, the cost of developing separate graduate and professional schools for a handful of Negro students, it was reasoned, would be prohibitive.

In 1938, in *Gaines v. Canada*, the Supreme Court declared that Missouri's failure to admit a Negro, Lloyd Gaines, to the state law school, when the state did not have a comparable "separate but equal" institution for Negroes, constituted a violation of the "equal-protection" clause of the Fourteenth Amendment. Missouri wanted to solve the problem by paying the student's tuition in an integrated Northern law school, but the Court refused to accept that as a solution. It argued that the state had already created a privilege for whites which it was denying to Negroes. This, in itself, was a Constitutional violation.

A decade passed without any further action. In 1948, the Supreme Court attacked Oklahoma for its failure to permit a Negro to enroll in its state law school. The Oklahoma Board of Regents, then, decided to admit Negroes to any course of study not provided for by the state college for Negroes. This was a considerable step forward.

In 1950, in *Sweatt v. Painter*, the Supreme Court condemned an attempt by the state of Texas to establish a special law school overnight in which it could enroll a Negro applicant. The Court said that this fly-by-night institution was not equal, and it insisted that an equal institution must include equal faculty, equal library, and equal prestige. It argued that part of an equal degree was the prestige conferred on the graduate by the status of that institution. To be equal, the Court reasoned, the separate school must carry an equal degree of professional status. It also decided, in *McLaurin v. Oklahoma Regents*, that it was unconstitutional for a university to segregate a Negro student within its premises. Oklahoma had roped off part of its university's classrooms, library, and dining room as a means of accommodating a graduate student in the School of Education. The Court argued that this handicapped a student in his pursuit of learning and that part of a graduate education included the ability to engage in open discussion with other students.[1]

These decisions, in essence, meant that the South was compelled to integrate graduate and professional schools. In themselves, they did not constitute an attack on segregated education. They merely represented an attempt by the courts to guarantee that separate education was, in fact, equal education. Southern states, recognizing the trend of events, began crash programs to build and upgrade their Negro school systems. At this point, the N.A.A.C.P. was not certain whether to push on for total desegregation or whether temporarily to settle for quality education. However, the stubbornness of some Southern school boards in refusing to upgrade Negro schools forced the N.A.A.C.P. lawyers into their decision to make an outright attack on legal segregation.

In 1950 N.A.A.C.P. lawyers initiated a series of suits around the country attacking the quality of education in primary and secondary schools. Three of these suits—Topeka, Kansas, Clarendon County, South Carolina, and Prince Edward County, Virginia—became involved in the 1954 Supreme Court desegregation decision. The N.A.A.C.P. charged that these schools, besides being inferior, were a violation of the "equal-protection" clause of the

Fourteenth Amendment. All of the suits, as had been expected, were defeated in the local courts. However, they were appealed.

Though the Supreme Court had allowed the decision made in *Plessy v. Ferguson* in 1896 to stand, the Court was moving closer to a reexamination of the "separate but equal" clause. That decision had argued that separate facilities, if they were equal, did not violate a citizen's right to equal protection under the law. It had become the cornerstone on which a whole dual society had been built. The Court had made no attempt, however, to guarantee that these separate institutions would be equal, and clearly they were not. At mid-century, the Court began by challenging this dual system at points of blatant and obvious inequity. By 1950 in *Sweatt v. Painter,* the Court was attacking subtle inequalities such as that of institutional prestige. The next step was for the Court to ask whether in fact separate institutions could ever be equal. In other words, the question was whether segregation, in itself, constituted inequality and was an infringement on a citizen's rights.

On May 17, 1954, in *Brown v. Board of Education of the City of Topeka*, the Supreme Court declared that school segregation was unconstitutional and that the "separate but equal" doctrine, which the Court itself had maintained for half a century, was also unconstitutional. Although the decision referred directly only to school segregation, in striking down the "separate but equal" doctrine, the Supreme Court implied that all legal segregation was unconstitutional. It contended that to separate children from other children of similar age and qualifications purely on the grounds of race generated feelings of inferiority in those children. It argued that the segregation of white and colored children in schools had a detrimental effect on the colored children. Further, the Court insisted that the damaging impact of segregation was greater when it had the sanction of law. It pointed out that segregation was usually interpreted as denoting the inferiority of the colored child. This resulted in a crippling psychological effect on his ability to learn by undermining his self-confidence and motivation. Therefore, segregation with the sanction of law deprived the child of equal education, and the Court concluded that it was a violation of the "equal-protection" clause of the Fourteenth Amendment.[2]

Southern whites were outraged, and they dubbed May 17 as "Black Monday." Ninety Southern Congressmen issued the "Southern Manifesto" condemning the Court decision as a usurpation of state powers. They said that the Court, instead of interpreting the law, was trying to legislate. Southern states resurrected the old doctrine of interposition which they had used against the Federal Government preceding the Civil War. Several state legislatures passed resolutions stating that the Federal Government did not have the power to prohibit segregation. Other Southerners resorted to a whole battery of tactics. The Ku Klux Klan was revived along with a host of new groups such as the National Association for the Advancement of White People. The White Citizens' councils spearheaded the resistance movement. Various forms of violence and intimidation became common. Bombings, beatings, and murders increased sharply all across the South. Outspoken proponents of desegregation were harassed in other ways as well. They lost their jobs, their banks called in their mortgages, and creditors of all kinds came to collect their debts.

In 1955 the Supreme Court declared that its desegregation decision should be carried out "with all due speed." Southern school districts, however, became experts in tactics of avoiding or delaying compliance. It began to appear that each school board would have to be compelled to admit each individual Negro student. Even then, some officials said that they would never comply. They persisted in arguing that the Court had overstepped its constitutional functions. Again, the constitutional question of federal vs. state authority had come to a head just as it had a century earlier.

In 1957, the governor of Arkansas openly opposed a court decision ordering the integration of the Central High School in Little Rock. When federal marshals were sent to carry out the order, Little Rock citizens were in no mood to stand idly by and watch. Both the citizens and the local officials were united in opposing federal authority. Everyone watched to see what President Eisenhower would do in the face of this challenge. On the one hand, Eisenhower and the Republicans had condemned the increasing centralization of power in the federal government. On the other hand, Eisenhower had been a general who had been accustomed to having his subordinates carry out his orders. Eisenhower, the general, moved with decisiveness and sent troops into Little Rock to enforce the law.[3]

Although Eisenhower himself had said that men's hearts could not be changed by legislation, he diligently fulfilled his functions as the head of the Executive Branch of the government. Surprisingly enough, it was also under his administration that Congress passed the first Civil Rights Act since 1875. Although the bill was rather weak, it was an admission that the Federal Government had an obligation to guarantee civil rights to individual citizens and to act on their behalf when state and local governments did not. This was a reversal of the traditional "hands off" position.

It cannot be stated with certainty that these events were merely calculated responses to the changing world situation, but the Cold War and the emergence of an independent Africa were nevertheless realities which could not be overlooked. Ghana had gained its status as an independent nation. It had also sought and gained admission to the United Nations in 1957, and in that same year, opened an embassy in Washington. African diplomats, traveling through the United States, were outraged whenever they were confronted by humiliations which were the consequence of segregation. Communist leaders, at the same time, took great pleasure in pointing out to these Africans the mistreatments of Afro-Americans within the United States. Although many Southern whites continued to insist that their freedom to maintain a separate society apart from that of the blacks was an essential part of democracy as they understood it, most Americans found legal segregation to be embarrassing in the face of America's claim to the democratic leadership of the world. Afro-Americans exploited the situation in order to involve the Federal Government in their desegregation campaign.

The Civil Rights Movement

On December 1, 1955, an obscure black woman, Mrs. Rosa Parks, was riding home on a bus in Montgomery, Alabama. As the bus gradually filled up with passengers, a white man demanded that she give him her seat and that she stand near the rear of the bus. Mrs. Parks, who did not have the reputation of being a troublemaker or a revolutionary, said that she was tired and that her feet were tired. The white man protested to the busdriver. When the driver also demanded that she move, she refused. Then, the driver summoned a policeman, and Mrs. Parks was arrested.

None of this was unusual. Daily, all across the South, black women surrendered their seats to demanding whites. Although most of them did it without complaint, the arrest of an obstructionist was entirely within the framework of local laws and in itself was not a noteworthy event. However, the arrest of Mrs. Parks touched off a chain reaction within Montgomery's Afro-American community. If she had been a troublemaker, the community might have thought that she had only received what she deserved. On the contrary, its citizens viewed her as an innocent, hard-working woman who had been mistreated. Her humiliation became their own.

Spontaneous protest meetings occurred all across Montgomery, and the idea of retaliating against the entire system by conducting a bus boycott took hold. Almost immediately, the call for a black boycott of Montgomery buses spread throughout the community, and car pools were quickly organized to help people in getting to and from their employment. Whites refused to believe that the black community could either organize or sustain such a campaign. Nevertheless, Montgomery buses were running half empty and all white.

The man chosen to lead the Montgomery bus boycott was a young Baptist minister named Martin Luther King, Jr. He and ninety others were indicted under the provisions of an anti-union law which made it illegal to conspire to obstruct the operation of a business. King and several others were found guilty, but they appealed their case. As the boycott dragged on month after month, Montgomery gained national prominence through the mass media, and King quickly gained a national reputation. When the bus company was finally compelled to capitulate and to drop its policy of segregated seating, King had become a national hero. Mass resistance, including some forms of civil disobedience, became popular as the best way to achieve racial change.

King had already given considerable thought to the question of how best to achieve social change, and, more important, to do it within the framework of moral law. His experiences with direct action techniques in Montgomery helped him to confirm and to further elaborate his thinking. His philosophy had been influenced by the writings of Henry Thoreau and Mahatma Gandhi with the result that he developed an ideology of nonviolent resistance. Like Gandhi, King wanted to make clear that nonviolence was not the same as nonresistance. Both maintained that if it should come to a choice between submission and violence, violence was to be preferred. Both stressed that nonviolent resistance was not to be an excuse for cowardice. To the contrary, nonviolent resistance was the way of the strong. It meant willingness to accept suffering but not the intention to inflict it.

King believed in nonviolent resistance both as a tactic and as a philosophy—both as means and end:

". . . the nonviolent approach does something to the hearts and souls of those committed to it. It gives them new self-respect. It calls up resources of strength and courage that they did not know they had. Finally, it so stirs the conscience of the opponent that reconciliation becomes a reality." [4]

On the philosophical level, King said that nonviolent resistance was the key to building a new world. Throughout history, man had met violence with violence and hate with hate. He believed that only nonviolence and love could break this eternal cycle of revenge and retaliation. It was his hope that the Negro, through utilizing the philosophy of nonviolent resistance, could help to bring about the birth of a new day. To King, nonviolent resistance implied that the resister must love his enemy:

"When we allow the spark of revenge in our souls to flame up in hate toward our enemies, Jesus teaches, 'Love your enemies, bless them that curse you, do good to them that hate you, and pray for them which despitefully use you, and persecute you.' " [5]

To him, love, in the most basic and Christian sense, did not require that the resister had to feel a surge of spontaneous sentiment, but it did mean that he had made a deep and sincere commitment to the other person's best interest. From this point of view, helping to free a racist from the shackles of his own prejudice was construed to be in his best interest and, therefore, a loving act. The Biblical injunction "Love your neighbor as yourself" meant being as concerned for his well-being as for your own. King believed that, if injustice could be attacked and overcome through a policy of nonviolent resistance, it would then lead to the creation of the "beloved community." This philosophy would become the means of reconciliation and, to put it in religious terms, would be redemptive.

King made it clear that nonviolent resistance was concerned with morality and justice and not merely with obtaining specific goals. When laws, themselves, were unjust, nonviolent resistance could engage in civil disobedience as a means of challenging those laws. Civil disobedience was not to be understood merely as law-breaking. Instead, King said that it was based in a belief in law and also in a belief in the necessity to obey the law. However, when a particular law was grossly unjust, that unjust law itself endangered society's respect for law in general. If the unjust law could not be changed through normal legal channels, deliberate breaking of that specific law might be justified. Because the person engaging in civil disobedience did believe in the value of law, he would break the unjust law openly, and he would willingly accept the consequences for breaking it. He would participate in law-breaking and accept its penalty as a means of drawing the attention of the community to the immorality of that specific law.

Largely inspired by the successful Montgomery bus boycott, mass protests and other direct action techniques began to spread rapidly throughout the South and even into the North. King was concerned that those using the technique should fully understand its meaning and value. Otherwise, he feared that it might be used carelessly and thereby distort its moral and redemptive quality. Therefore, King and a number of his supporters formed the Southern Christian Leadership Conference as an organization to spread these ideas and to provide help to any community which became involved in massive, nonviolent resistance protests.

On February 1, 1960, four Negro students from the Agricultural and Technical College in Greensboro, North Carolina, entered a Woolworth's variety store and purchased several items. Then, they sat down at its lunch counter, which served whites only. When they were refused service, they took out their textbooks and began to do their homework. This protest immediately made local news. The next day, they were joined by a large number of fellow students.

In a matter of weeks, student sit-ins were occurring at segregated lunch counters all across the South. College and high school students by the thousands joined the Civil Rights Movement. These students felt the need to form their own organization to mobilize and facilitate the spontaneous demonstrations which were springing up everywhere. This resulted in the formation of the Student Non-Violent Coordinating Committee. The S.C.L.C. and S.N.C.C. came to be the leading organizations in the Southern states. C.O.R.E.—Congress of Racial Equality—carried on the militant side of the struggle in Northern urban centers, and it involved many Northern liberals in crusades to help the movement in the South.

The N.A.A.C.P. tended to be uncomfortable with the new direct action techniques and preferred more traditional lobbying and legal tactics. It did get involved on a massive scale in giving legal aid to the thousands of demonstrators who were arrested for various legal infractions such as marching without a parade permit, disturbing the peace, and for trespassing. To some extent, the N.A.A.C.P. resented the fact that it had to carry the financial burden for the legal actions resulting from these mass protests, while the other organizations received all the publicity and most of the financial aid inspired by that publicity.

By the time the 1960 Presidential election approached, both political parties had become aware that the racial issue could not be ignored. In several Northern states, Afro-Americans held the balance of power in close elections. Also, by that year, over a million Afro-Americans had become eligible to vote in the Southern states. John F. Kennedy, the Democratic candidate, easily outmaneuvered his Republican opponent, Richard M. Nixon, in the search for Afro-American votes. Kennedy had projected an image of aggressive idealism which captured the imagination of white liberals and of Afro-Americans.

The move which guaranteed the support of most Afro-Americans for Kennedy came in October, a mere three weeks before the election. Martin Luther King, Jr., and several other Negroes had been arrested in Atlanta, Georgia, for staging a sit-in at a department store restaurant. While the others were released, King was sentenced to four months at hard labor. Kennedy immediately telephoned his sympathy to Mrs. King. Meanwhile, his brother and campaign manager, Robert Kennedy, telephoned the judge who had sentenced him and pleaded for his release. The next day, King was freed. The news was carefully and systematically spread throughout the entire Afro-American community. When Kennedy defeated Nixon in November, Afro-Americans believed that their vote had been the deciding factor in the close victory.[6]

Two months after Kennedy took office, C.O.R.E., under the leadership of James Farmer, began an intensive campaign, involving "freedom rides." Scores and scores of whites and blacks were recruited from Northern cities and sent throughout the South to test the state of desegregation of travel facilities as well as of waiting rooms and restaurants. As the campaign reached a climax, Attorney General Robert Kennedy became annoyed with its intensity. Apparently, he had hoped that the direct actionists would wait for the new Administration to take the lead in Civil Rights. Instead, they chose to try to make the new Administration live up to the image which it had projected. Kennedy requested a cooling-off period, but the freedom riders would not listen. But when the freedom riders were attacked in Montgomery, Alabama, without receiving adequate local police protection, Kennedy sent six hundred federal marshals to escort them on the rest of their pilgrimage.[7]

The year 1963 was a target date for the Civil Rights Movement. It was the centennial of the Emancipation Proclamation, and the Movement adopted the motto, "free in '63." In the spring, the S.C.L.C. spearheaded a massive campaign in Birmingham for desegregation and fair employment. Marches occurred almost daily. The marchers maintained their nonviolent tactics in the face of many arrests and much intimidation. In May, when the police resorted to the use of dogs and high-pressure water hoses, the nation and the world were shocked. Sympathy demonstrations occurred in dozens of cities all across the country, and expressions of indignation resounded from all around the world. In June, the head of Mississippi's N.A.A.C.P., Medgar Evers, was shot in the back outside his home and killed. Scores of sympathy demonstrations again reverberated throughout the country. Violence in the South was on the increase.

Although President Kennedy had intended to use his executive authority as his main weapon in securing civil rights, the mounting pressure on both sides of the conflict forced him to take more drastic action, and he submitted a Civil Rights Bill to Congress. Opponents of the Bill were particularly perturbed by the section which sought to guarantee the end of discrimination in all kinds of public accommodations—stores, restaurants, hotels, motels, etc. They claimed that this was an invasion of the owners' property rights. It soon became clear that the Bill would be entangled in a gigantic Congressional debate for months. Civil Rights supporters looked for new techniques which would bring added pressure on Congress. Again, the idea of a March on Washington was proposed, and this time it was carried through. The demonstration on August 28, 1963, was larger than any previous one in the history of the capital. At least a quarter of a million blacks and whites, from all over America, representing a wide spectrum of religious, labor, and civil rights organizations, flooded into Washington.

The occasion was peaceful and orderly. The marchers exuded an aura of interracial love and brotherhood. The emotional impact on the participants was almost that of a religious pilgrimage. President Kennedy, instead of trying to block the march as demanded by many Congressional leaders, aided it by providing security forces, and he also met personally with a delegation of its leaders. The high point of the demonstration was Martin Luther King's famous speech:

"Now is the time to make real the promise of democracy. Now is the time to rise from the dark and desolate valley of segregation to the sunlit path of racial justice. Now is the time to lift our nation from the quicksands of racial injustice to the solid rock of brotherhood. Now is the time to make justice a reality for all of God's children.

"Now, I say to you today, my friends, so even though we face the difficulties of today and tomorrow, I still have a dream. It is a dream deeply rooted in the American dream. I have a dream that one day this nation will rise up and live out the true meaning of its creed: 'We hold these truths to be self-evident, that all men are created equal.'

"I have a dream that one day on the red hills of Georgia the sons of former slaves and the sons of former slave-owners will be able to sit down together at the table of brotherhood.

"I have a dream that one day even the state of Mississippi, a state sweltering with the people's injustice, sweltering with the heat of oppression, will be transformed into an oasis of freedom and justice.

"I have a dream that my four little children will one day live in a nation where they will not be judged by the color of their skin, but by the content of their character.

"This is our hope. This is the faith that I go back to the South with —with this faith we will be able to hew out of the mountain of despair a stone of hope." [8]

In November, Congressional debate on the Civil Rights Bill was still continuing, but the President had now made the passage of the Civil Rights Bill one of the most urgent goals of his Administration. But on the 22nd of November, John F. Kennedy was gunned down in the Presidential limousine in Dallas, Texas. The nation and the world were struck dumb with disbelief. Even those who had disliked his politics were horrified at the assassination of a President in a democratic state. His supporters felt that they had lost a friend as well as a leader. In fact many regarded Kennedy as a savior.

The sense of shock caused despair and gloom. The fact that his successor, Lyndon B. Johnson, was a Southerner led most civil rights supporters to feel that there would be a reversal of federal policies on the racial question. However, Johnson immediately tried to reassure the nation that his intention was to carry on with the unfinished business of the Kennedy era. By the time the Bill passed in the spring of 1964, civil rights supporters felt that Johnson was as dependable an ally as Kennedy had been. Instead of the vehement opposition to the public accommodations provision of the Bill which had been expected, compliance was fairly widespread and came with relatively little opposition.

It soon became clear, however, that the passage of the Civil Rights Act was not the victory which would end the racial conflict. In fact, violence on both sides escalated. A Washington, D. C., Negro educator, Lemuel Penn, was gunned down by snipers as he drove through Georgia on his way home from a training session for reserve officers. Two Klansmen were charged, but they were acquitted. In Philadelphia, Mississippi, three civil rights workers—two white and one black—disappeared. The youths were later found brutally murdered. In spite of national protests, local justice was not forthcoming.

At the same time, forewarnings of anger and violence had begun to rumble in many Afro-American communities across the land. In spite of the legislative victories, most ghetto Negroes found that their daily lives had not changed. In fact, the economic gap between blacks and whites had tended to increase as whites received the benefits of prosperity in larger portions than did the blacks. Also, many ghetto residents, whose lives were surrounded with crime and violence, were further angered when they watched the evening news showing their Southern brothers kicked and clubbed by sheriffs. These ghetto residents had not been schooled in the tactics of nonviolent resistance. In the summer of 1964, race riots occurred in Harlem and Rochester, N.Y., as well as in several cities in New Jersey.

In the spring of 1965, Selma, Alabama, was the scene of a concentrated voter registration drive. The campaign was once again spearheaded by Martin Luther King and the S.C.L.C. During the demonstrations, a black civil rights worker and a Northern Unitarian clergyman were both killed. Finally, a gigantic march was planned between Selma and the state capitol at Montgomery. State officials sought to prohibit the march. The U. S. District Judge at Montgomery, however, ordered officials to permit the march and to provide protection for the marchers. President Johnson federalized the Alabama National Guard and used it to guarantee the maintenance of law and order. When the procession reached the state capitol building, the demonstraters were addressed by two Afro-American Nobel Peace Prize winners. Ralph Bunche, who had received the award for mediating the Middle Eastern crisis, lamented the fact that he had to address an audience while standing under a Confederate flag. Dr. Martin Luther King, Jr., who had just received the award himself for his work in nonviolent resistance, told the marchers to take heart because they were on the road to victory:

"We are on the move now. The burning of our churches will not deter us. We are on the move now. The bombing of our homes will not dissuade us. We are on the move now. The beating and killing of our clergymen and young people will not divert us. We are on the move now. The arrest and release of known murderers will not discourage us. We are on the move now.

"Like an idea whose time has come, not even the marching of mighty armies can halt us. We are moving to the land of freedom.

"Let us therefore continue our triumph and march to the realization of the American dream. Let us march on segregated housing, until every ghetto of social and economic depression dissolves and Negroes and whites live side by side in decent, safe and sanitary housing.

"Let us march on segregated schools until every vestige of a segregated and inferior education becomes a thing of the past and Negroes and whites study side by side in the socially healing context of the classroom.

"Let us march on poverty, until no American parent has to skip a meal so that their children may march on poverty, until no starved man walks the streets of our cities and towns in search of jobs that do not exist.

"Let us march on ballot boxes, march on ballot boxes until race baiters disappear from the political arena. Let us march on ballot boxes until the Wallaces of our nation tremble away in silence.

"Let us march on ballot boxes, until we send to our city councils, state legislatures, and the United States Congress men who will not fear to do justice, love mercy, and walk humbly with their God. Let us march on ballot boxes until all over Alabama God's children will be able to walk the earth in decency and honor.

"For all of us today the battle is in our hands. The road ahead is not altogether a smooth one. There are no broad highways to lead us easily and inevitably to quick solutions. We must keep going." [9]

Later that evening, a white woman from Detroit was shot and killed on the highway between Montgomery and Selma as she was ferrying marchers back home.

President Johnson sent a new voting rights bill to Congress which gave sweeping powers to the Attorney General's office allowing it to send federal registrars into localities to register voters when local officials were either unable or unwilling to do so. In the course of a television appearance in which Johnson announced this legislation and in which he expressed his own indignation at the events in Selma and Montgomery, he acknowledged the impact of demonstrations in pushing both the country and the Congress into taking positive action to remedy injustices. He implied that, while he did not always approve of the methods used, the demonstrators had done a positive service for justice and for the country. He promised to see the fight through to the end, and he said that it was the obligation of all good men to see that the battle was fought in the courts and through the legislative process rather than forcing it into the streets. He ended his speech by quoting the lead line from the popular civil rights hymn, "We Shall Overcome."

By 1965, the Federal Government had enacted legislation guaranteeing almost all the citizenship rights of America to Negroes and had also provided mechanisms with which to enforce this legislation. Nevertheless, the passage of a bill in Washington did not immediately secure the same right in Selma, Montgomery, or in Philadelphia, Mississippi. Each right, so it seemed, had to be fought for and won over and over again in almost each locality. Although discrimination continued and even seemed to intensify at times, it no longer carried with it the force of law. The Civil Rights Movement had, no matter what its critics said of it, accomplished one sweeping victory—the destruction of legal segregation in the United States.

CHAPTER 12

The Black Revolt

Civil Disorders

THE smoldering tensions and frustrations which lay just below the surface in the Afro-American community exploded into a racial holocaust on August 11, 1965, in Watts—a black ghetto just outside of Los Angeles. When the smoke finally subsided several days later, more than thirty people were dead, hundreds had been injured, and almost four thousand had been arrested. Property damage ran into the millions.

The nation was shocked. The mass communications media tended to exaggerate the amount of damage done and also conjured up visions, in the mind of white America, of organized black gangs deliberately and systematically attacking white people. Many felt that it had been the worst racial outbreak in American history. In fact, it was not. The 1943 riot in Detroit and the 1919 riot in Chicago had both been more violent. The 1917 race riots in East St. Louis, Illinois, had outdone the Watts outburst in terms of the amount of personal injury. The violence in most previous riots had been inflicted by whites against blacks, and perhaps this was why white America did not remember them very clearly. The violence in Watts, though not directed against white persons as many believed, was still accomplished by blacks and aimed against white-owned property. White Americans were confused because they felt they had given "them" so much. Whites could not understand why blacks were not thankful instead of being angry.

In spite of the rumors that the riot was the result of conspiratorial planning, the activities of the rioters and of the law enforcement units displayed a crazy, unreal quality as the riot unfolded. It began with a rather routine arrest for drunken driving. Marquette Frye, a young black, was stopped by a white motorcycle officer and asked to take a standard sobriety test. In the course of arresting Frye, along with his brother and mother who were both objecting to the police action, the officers resorted to more force than many of the bystanders thought was necessary. The spectators became transformed into a hostile mob. As the police cars departed, youths began to pelt the vehicles with rocks and bottles. They continued to harass other traffic passing through the area. For a time, the police stayed outside the area, hoping that it would cool down. Then, believing that it was time to restore order, a line of police charged down the street clearing the mob. The police clubbed and beat anyone who did not get out of the way. The guilty usually ran the fastest, and the innocent and the physically disabled received most of the punishment. Instead of clearing the mob, the police charge only served to further anger the bystanders.[1]

The rage of the black ghetto had been accumulating against all the symbols of oppression. The police, of course, were the most obvious and visible manifestation of this power, and in a riot they were one of the most convenient targets for the rioters. Newsmen and firemen also became victims of rock and bottle throwing. White-owned stores throughout the ghettoes formed another target for this anger. Before long, rioters were breaking into stores and carrying off everything from beer to television sets and clothing. Breaking and looting was shortly followed by burning. The center of the action was soon nicknamed "Charcoal Alley."

After a couple of days when the riot continued to grow, Los Angeles officials began to consider calling in the National Guard. Police Chief Parker did not know that it was necessary for him to contact the Governor's office and ask the Governor to call out the Guard. Unfortunately, Governor Brown was in Greece. The Lieutenant Governor was afraid to make such an important decision on his own initiative. Finally, Los Angeles officials phoned Governor Brown in Athens, and he gave his authority for calling out the Guard.[2]

By the time the Guard arrived, all of Watts was covered with billowing clouds of smoke. The looting and burning were no longer confined to roving gangs of youths. Angry adults, who had previously only urged them on, had become intoxicated by the mood of destruction. People of all ages, many of whom had had no previous police record, began to join. The pressure chamber had blown its valve and was now letting off steam. Watts abandoned itself to an emotional orgy.

The National Guard had not been adequately trained to handle civil disorders. It also came with a point of view which was unsuited to a civilian outburst. They had been trained to work against an enemy, and had a tendency to interpret every action in this way and to view all the residents of Watts as enemies. When two drunks in a car refused to stop at a Guard roadblock and ran into a line of soldiers, the Guard interpreted it as a deliberate and malicious suicide attack. The Guard was convinced that they were being personally threatened, and the officers issued live ammunition to all the men.[3]

By the end of the riot, the Guard had fired thousands of rounds of ammunition. The press portrayed Watts as an armed camp with scores of black snipers systematically trying to pick off the police and the Guard. In retrospect, both the police and the Guard came to believe that most of the snipers had really been the police and the Guardsmen unknowingly shooting at each other. When all of the evidence was examined in the calm light of day, very little of it pointed to the existence of snipers. Gradually, the Guard gained confidence in itself and in the situation. The more that it acted in calm and deliberation, the more quickly peace was restored to the area. Finally, eleven days after the Frye arrest the last members of the Guard withdrew, and the next day the police returned to normal duty.[4]

In the light of the victories of the Civil Rights Movement, whites were bewildered by the anger which exploded from the black ghetto. They thought of their concessions to blacks as gifts from a generous heart. Blacks, to the contrary, viewed these concessions as the tardy surrender of rights which should have been theirs all along. Moreover, the effects of the civil rights victories had been largely limited to the Deep South and almost entirely to changes in legal status. The day-to-day realities of education, housing, employment, and social degradation had hardly been touched. Finally, life in an urban ghetto, though lacking the humiliation of legal segregation, had brought another harsh reality into Afro-American life. Survival for the individual as well as for the family came under fresh stress in urban slum situations. This had also been true for immigrant groups from Europe. Urban slum conditions created tremendous economic, social, and psychological strains. Ghetto life added a new dimension of social disorganization to an already oppressed community. The anonymity of life in large urban centers tended to remove many of the social constraints to individual behavior. Crime and delinquency increased. Actually, America had been deluded by the Civil Rights Movement into thinking that genuine changes were taking place for most Afro-Americans. Watts became a living proclamation that this was not true.

Early in 1967, violence began to reverberate throughout the ghettoes all across the nation. The earliest disturbances occurred at three Southern universities. Then, violence exploded in Tampa, Florida, in June. The following day, June 12, Cincinnati, Ohio, experienced a racial outburst. On June 17, violence began in Atlanta, Georgia.

The worst riots of that long hot summer occurred in Newark, New Jersey, and in Detroit, Michigan, during the month of July. Racial hostilities in Newark had been boiling for several months. In spite of the black majority in Newark, a predominantly white political machine still ran City Hall. Blacks were only given token recognition. The event which actually triggered the riot was, again, a relatively meaningless arrest. Bystanders assumed, probably mistakenly, that the black taxi driver who was being arrested, was also being beaten by the arresting officer. Bit by bit, again in a crazy pattern, the fires of frustration flared throughout the city. At almost the same time, ghetto violence began to rock several other northern New Jersey communities: Elizabeth, Englewood, Plainfield, and New Brunswick.

Looting and burning began to occur in Newark on a wide-scale basis. Before long, the Guard was called in, and the shooting increased. The chief of staff of the New Jersey National Guard testified that there had been too much shooting at the snipers. His opinion was that the Guard considered the situation as a military action. Newark's director of police offered the opinion that the Guard may have been shooting at the police with the police shooting back at the Guard. "I really don't believe," he said, "there was as much sniping as we thought." [5]

By the time the shooting had ended, twenty-three people had been killed. Of these, one was a white detective, one was a white fireman, and twenty-one were Negroes. Of the twenty-one Negroes killed, six were women, two were children, and one was an elderly man seventy-three years old. The Kerner Report also stated, as did the New Jersey report on the riot, that there had been considerable evidence that the police and the Guard had been deliberately shooting into stores containing "soul brother" signs. Instead of merely quelling a riot or attacking rioters, some of them were apparently exploiting the situation to vent their own racial hatreds.[6]

The violence in Detroit exploded on July 22. Again, it unfolded in an irrational, nightmarish fashion. The police had been making some rather routine raids on five illegal after-hours drinking spots. At the last target, they were overwhelmed to find eighty-two "inmates." They neded over an hour in which to arrest and remove all of them. This created considerable local disturbance and attracted an ever-growing crowd of onlookers.

In Detroit, the black community had been upset for some time by what it believed had been a selective enforcement of certain laws aimed at them. Apparently, many of the observers believed that these raids were intended to harass the black community. Small-scale looting and violence began. After sputtering and flaring for a few hours, the riot began to grow and spread rapidly. By that night, the National Guard was activated.

By Monday morning, the Mayor and the Governor had asked for federal help. The Governor had the impression that, in order to secure it, he would have to declare a state of insurrection. He was further led to believe that such an action would mean that insurance companies would not pay for any damage. For this reason, he refused to act. All day, burning and looting continued and grew. Shooting became increasingly widespread, and the number of deaths began to soar rapidly. Finally, before midnight on Monday, President Johnson sent in federal troops on his own initiative.

When the federal troops arrived, they found the city full of fear. The Army believed that its first task was one of maintaining its own order and discipline. Second, it strove to establish a rapport between the troops and the citizens as a basis on which to build an atmosphere of calm, trust, and order. The soldiers provided coffee and sandwiches to the beleagered residents, and an atmosphere of trust gradually developed.

It became clear that the mutual fear between the police and the citizens had only intensified the catastrophe. Lessons which had been learned two years earlier in Watts by the police and the Guard had not been applied in Detroit. Law enforcement officials again overreacted and used high-powered military weapons in a crowded civilian situation. This overreaction presented as much danger to innocent, law-abiding citizens as did the violence of the rioters. There had also been a tendency to treat the residents, en masse, as enemies and thereby to weld them into a hostile community. The federal troops demonstrated that a calm, deliberate, and open display of force was much more effective in restoring order than shooting at any frightening or suspicious target.

By the time order was restored to Detroit, forty-three people had been killed. Thirty-three were black, and ten were white. One Guardsman and one fireman were among the casualties. Some of the other white victims had been killed while they were engaged in looting. Damages were originally estimated at five hundred million dollars, but later estimates reduced the damage drastically.

Again, as in Newark, there was evidence of police brutality during the riot. The police were charged with brutality and murder in an incident which occurred at the Algiers Motel. After hearing that there had been a sniper in the building, the police riddled it with bullets. Then, they entered and searched it. In the course of questioning its inhabitants, three youths were shot and killed.

In turn, the police and the Guard accused the rioters of widespread sniping. Twenty-seven rioters were charged with sniping, but twenty-two of these charges were dropped at the preliminary hearings for lack of evidence. Later, one pleaded guilty to possessing an unregistered gun, and he received a suspended sentence.[7]

President Johnson appointed a commission, headed by Governor Otto Kerner of Illinois to investigate the causes of the riots. In particular, he wished to ascertain whether any subversive or conspiratorial elements were involved. Although many did not like the report, particularly because of the blame it laid on the white community, it clearly proved that there had been no subversive or conspiratorial elements in these riots. The report warned that America was splitting into two nations: one black and one white. It believed that racism and hatred were growing deeper and that communication between the two communities was breaking down. The Commission made several recommendations for change in government, business, and society at large. These changes, however, would be very expensive. Government at all levels largely ignored the report. Liberals applauded it. Blacks felt that it was merely another report; they wanted action. Conservatives claimed that it was a prejudiced and unfair study.

In April of 1968, another rash of riots swept through the Afro-American community. This time there was a clear and obvious cause. Dr. Martin Luther King, Jr., who was visiting Memphis in support of a garbage workers' strike, was leaning over his motel's second-floor balcony railing talking to a colleague below when suddenly he was struck by a sniper's bullet and killed. Shock and outrage swept across the nation. Many Afro-Americans felt that they had been robbed of a friend as well as of their only hope for a better future.

Robert Kennedy took to the campaign trail for the 1968 Presidential election in order to bring justice to the poor, both black and white, and in order to reunite America behind a new sense of purpose and idealism. In June, after a rally in Los Angeles, he too was shot and killed. The nation was filled with horror and disbelief. Robert Kennedy had gained the trust of Afro-Americans more than almost any other white man of his generation. Violence seemed to reign supreme, and idealists, both black and white, were paralyzed by a feeling of futility.

Black Power

Even before the assassination of Martin Luther King, the Civil Rights Movement was disintegrating. Many believed that it was being killed by the riots. In fact, the Civil Rights Movement had already come under sharp attack both from within and from without. The urban riots of the sixties, instead of being the cause of its demise, were symptoms of the disease in the urban, Afro-American communities—a disease for which the Civil Rights Movement had not been able to effect a cure. In retrospect, it appears that there had always been voices from within the Afro-American community which had maintained that the Civil Rights Movement was not the panacea that many believed it to be. To the contrary, militant blacks maintained that the Civil Rights Movement itself was one of the primary causes of the urban riots. Stokeley Carmichael pointed out:

"Each time the people . . . saw Martin Luther King get slapped, they became angry; when they saw four little black girls bombed to death, they were angrier; and when nothing happened, they were steaming. We had nothing to offer that they could see, except to go out and be beaten again. We helped to build their frustration." [8]

As early as 1957, Robert F. Williams, then the N.A.A.C.P. leader in Monroe, North Carolina, concluded that nonviolence could not be looked upon as a cure-all for all the problems of the Afro-American community. In his opinion the right for an Afro-American to sit in the front of the bus in Montgomery was not so spectacular a victory:

"The Montgomery bus boycott was a victory—but it was limited. It did not raise the Negro standard of living; it did not mean better education for Negro children, it did not mean economic advances." [9]

Williams compared the Montgomery boycott to an incident in Monroe:

"It's just like our own experience in Monroe when we integrated the library. I just called the chairman of the board in my county. I told him that I represented the NAACP, that we wanted to integrate the library, and that our own library had burned down. And he said, 'Well, I don't see any reason why you can't use the same library that our people use. It won't make any difference. And after all, I don't read anyway.'" [10]

Williams claimed that a racist social system existed because the violence at the heart of that system went unchallenged. Violence was an integral part of the racial system, and it had not been introduced into the system by Afro-Americans.

"It is precisely this unchallenged violence that allows a racist social system to perpetuate itself. When people say that they are opposed to Negroes 'resorting to violence' what they really mean is that they are opposed to Negroes defending themselves and challenging the exclusive monopoly of violence practiced by white racists. We have shown in Monroe that with violence working *both ways* constituted law will be more inclined to keep the peace." [11]

Williams urged Monroe Negroes to carry guns and other weapons and to defend themselves when attacked. He defended his position by invoking the teachings of Henry Thoreau who had also been used as an authority by the pacifists. Although Thoreau usually supported pacifism, according to Williams, Thoreau also believed that there were occasions which justified violence. Thoreau, who had defended John Brown's attack on Harpers Ferry, had made the statement that guns, for once, had been used for a righteous cause and were being held in righteous hands. In integrating his theory in regard to self-defense with the teachings of Thoreau, Williams was obviously attacking the philosophy of nonviolent resistance taught by Martin Luther King who also drew on Thoreau.

Even during the peak of the Civil Rights Movement, in the background there was a constant, irritating opposition. While the movement grew, the Black Muslims also grew. Not only did they challenge the tactics of nonviolent resistance, they disagreed totally with its goals. While Elijah Muhammed constantly opposed aggression, he did preach the need for self-defense. To him it was not necessary for a man to turn the other cheek when he was hit. He also ridiculed the Civil Rights goal of integration. Instead of losing themselves in white America, Muslims believed in finding their own identity and in maintaining a separate society. They claimed that blacks should not be ashamed of either their color or their heritage. They taught that the black man had had a history of which to be proud. The sense of self-acceptance and pride which they taught came as good news to ghetto residents who realized that they could never be assimilated into white, middle-class America.[12]

With the conversion of Malcolm Little, better known as Malcolm X, the Muslims gained a dynamic speaker who did much to popularize and spread their teaching. Although the peculiar doctrines and puritanical practices of the Muslims prevented many from joining the movement, the number of its sympathizers grew rapidly. Malcolm X was able to appeal to ghetto residents in a way that Martin Luther King could not.

King, obviously, had had all the advantages of a middle-class home. Malcolm, however, had started at the bottom, and ghetto residents could readily identify with him. King had gone to college and had even earned a doctorate. Malcolm gained his reputation "hustling" on the streets of Boston and New York and also from teaching himself while serving a sentence in prison.

In 1964 Malcolm X was forced to break with Elijah Muhammed. Apparently, Elijah Muhammed had become threatened by

Malcolm's charismatic appeal, and he feared he might lose his leadership in the movement. After a pilgrimage to Mecca as well as visits to several newly independent African nations, Malcolm returned to America ready to start a movement of his own. Although he believed more strongly than ever in Islam, he came to feel that several of the teachings of the Black Muslims were erroneous. One reason was that in Mecca he had worshiped with people from all races. As a result, he no longer felt that the white man, per se, was the "devil":

"In the past, yes, I have made sweeping indictments of *all* white people. I never will be guilty of that again—as I know now that some white people *are* truly sincere, that some truly are capable of being brotherly toward a black man. The true Islam has shown me that a blanket indictment of all white people is as wrong as when whites make blanket indictments against blacks." [13]

Malcolm intended to continue teaching Islam in America, and he insisted that a religious faith was a help to any political movement. Nevertheless, he also intended to form a secular organization, which could appeal to a wide variety of persons, and form the center of a new black militancy. Before any of these activities could get under way he was killed. Malcolm X was gunned down by four blacks, probably associated with the Black Muslims, while addressing a meeting in New York City early in 1965.[14]

To Malcolm X the Civil Rights Movement was in need of a new interpretation. The degree of segregation existing in schools and in the rest of society, he contended, had actually increased in the decade since the Supreme Court decision in 1954. It seemed to him to be particularly true in the case of the de facto segregation practiced in the North. The spirit of the Civil Rights Movement, he pointed out, had been one of asking and pleading for rights which should have belonged to Afro-Americans by birth:

"I said that the American black man needed to recognize that he had a strong, airtight case to take the United States before the United Nations on a formal accusation of 'denial of human rights'—and that if Angola and South Africa were precedent cases, then there would be no easy way that the U.S. could escape being censured, right on its own home ground." [15]

Malcolm was also critical of the Civil Rights Movement, contending that its interracial makeup and its emphasis on integration undercut the real goals of the black masses. "Not long ago," he said, "the black man in America was fed a dose of another form of the weakening, lulling and deluding effects of so-called 'integration.' It was that 'Farce on Washington,' I call it." [16] Malcolm held that the famous March on Washington in 1963 had begun as a very angry, grass-roots movement among poor black people. He said that whites took it over and turned a genuine protest into a sentimental, interracial picnic.

Finally, Malcolm made it clear that he, too, was willing to resort to violence although he did not favor initiating it. He held that, when the rights of blacks were violated, they should be willing to die in the struggle to secure them:

"If white America doesn't think the Afro-American, especially the upcoming generation, is capable of adopting the guerrilla tactics now being used by oppressed people elsewhere on this earth, she is making a drastic mistake. She is underestimating the force that can do her the most harm.

"A real honest effort to remove the just grievances of the 22 million Afro-Americans must be made immediately or in a short time it will be too late." [17]

The slogan "Black Power" exploded from a public address system in Greenwood, Mississippi, in the summer of 1966, and as it reverberated across America Stokeley Carmichael's motto spontaneously took on the dimensions of a movement. James Meredith, who had become famous for initiating federally backed integration of the University of Mississippi, was making a one-man freedom march across the South. He sought to demonstrate that blacks could walk through the South without fear. When he was shot, civil rights leaders from across the land felt compelled to continue his demonstration.

Martin Luther King representing S.C.L.C., Floyd McKissick from C.O.R.E., Stokeley Carmichael of S.N.C.C. and several others discussed the meaning and direction of the movement as they marched along the road by day and as they sat together in motels at night. Their discussion became a heated debate about both the tactics and the goals of their struggle. McKissick and Carmichael questioned the worth of nonviolence as a tactic and the value of integration as a goal. When the marchers reached Greenwood, Mississippi, a S.N.C.C. stronghold, Carmichael seized the microphone, and instead of using the traditional civil rights slogan of "Freedom Now," he began chanting "Black Power!" [18]

Many whites assumed that the phrase meant black violence, and they assumed further that black violence meant black aggression. They conjured up pictures of bloody retaliation. Others saw it as a rejection of white allies, and they insisted that the freedom struggle could not be won without white help. To Carmichael, the Civil Rights Movement as it existed was "pleading and begging." It also had been wrong, he said, in assuming it was possible to build a working coalition between a group which was strong and economically secure—middle-class white liberals—and one which was insecure—poor blacks. In his opinion, "there is in fact no group at present with whom to form a coalition in which blacks will not be absorbed and betrayed." [19] Two such differing groups had different sets of self-interest in spite of their similar sentiments. Carmichael contended that a genuine coalition had to be built between groups with similar self-interests. Further, he argued that each group must have its own independent base of power from which to negotiate the terms of a working alliance. Black power, he said, was an attempt to build the strength on which future coalitions could be established.

Carmichael also attacked the concept of integration. If blacks wanted good housing or good education, integration meant leaving a black neighborhood and finding these things in white institutions. "This reinforces, among both black and white," he argued, "the idea that 'white' is automatically better and 'black' is by definition inferior. This is why integration is a subterfuge for the maintenance of white supremacy." [20] If blacks could gain control of their own neighborhoods, each community, black and white, could define its own goals and be responsible for achieving its own standards. When both societies had built the kind of communities they wanted, meaningful integration between equal, though different, communities could occur, Carmichael contended. Integration, instead of being a one-way street, would be reciprocal.

Carmichael believed the existing political structure must be changed in order to overcome racism:

" 'Political modernization' includes many things, but we mean by it three major concepts: (1) questioning old values and institutions of the society; (2) searching for new and different forms of political structure to solve political and economic problems; and (3) broadening the base of political participation to include more people in the decision-making process." [21]

Black power meant two things: the end of shame and humiliation, and black community control. Blacks should be proud of being black, and they should be proud of their African past. Instead of using skin lighteners and hair straighteners, black power advocates began adopting a style of dress with an African flavor. To Carmichael there was still one other aspect to the black power philosophy. It should accentuate human values and human dignity. The prevailing system, besides being racist, put a primary emphasis on property rather than on humanity. Carmichael wanted the black-controlled community to act for the benefit of all blacks and not merely for the advantage of a handful of exploiting black capitalists.

What he advocated was the development of black cooperatives, not the building of black capitalism. He referred to this new political system as "political modernization." Its key was community, cooperative control of all the important things in people's lives. In addition to building a more participatory kind of democratic government, and developing cooperative enterprises, it meant that people renting houses or apartments must have rights and protection. He encouraged consumers and apartment dwellers to develop organizations which could fight for their special interests. He also wanted the community to gain local control of its police force. [22]

The black power ideology spread across the nation rapidly, providing the movement with fresh impetus and a philosophical framework. Many had lost faith in the effectiveness of marches, demonstrations, appeals to white consciences and other direct action techniques. Black Americans were also growing weary and frustrated over the amount of violence which was being heaped upon nonviolent resisters. In Bogalusa, Louisiana, blacks were intimidated daily by the local Ku Klux Klan. Law enforcement officials never provided help either in terms of protection or in prosecuting wrongdoers. In fact, the law enforcement officials themselves were increasingly suspected of belonging to the Klan. Bogalusa blacks came to feel that arming themselves for self-defense was their only solution. In 1966 a number of them armed themselves, and founded the Deacons for Defense and Justice.

Also in 1966, young blacks in Oakland, California, became extremely angry at what they believed to be police harassment. This resulted in their forming the Black Panther Party.

Huey P. Newton and Bobby Seale, both of whom had been raised under ghetto conditions, felt that there was a need for an organization which could communicate with poor blacks instead of merely appealing to the black bourgeoisie. The symbol of the black panther had been used by an independent, black political party which S.N.C.C. had helped to found in Lowndes County, Alabama.

The black panther had special appeal as a symbol because, though it rarely or never attacked another animal, it would defend itself ferociously whenever it was challenged. In Oakland, the Black Panthers began by keeping the police under surveillance as a means of limiting their alleged brutality. Panther members carried registered guns and displayed them openly as the law permitted. Whenever the police stopped to question someone, the following Panther car also stopped. Then, the Panthers would stand nearby displaying their weapons, and someone who had some legal training, would inform the individual being questioned by the police what his legal rights were. The police were extremely angry at this harassment and looked for ways to retaliate. The best-known Panther recruit was Eldridge Cleaver who, like Malcolm X, had educated himself while in prison. Cleaver wrote several articles for *Ramparts* magazine, and became well known for his book *Soul on Ice*. His vivid writing helped the Panthers in spreading their ideas widely. Gradually, chapters of the Black Panther party were established in ghettoes all across America.[23]

Besides demanding legal rights for blacks, the Black Panthers developed a ten-point program demanding decent jobs and decent housing. Also, arguing that most black prisoners had been convicted in courts by people conspicuous for their racial prejudice, they advocated that all black inmates of American jails should immediately be released and granted amnesty. Because blacks were not properly represented in the country and were not treated fairly as citizens, the Panthers contended that they should be exempted from all military service. Blacks fighting in the Vietnam war, they pointed out, were represented in numbers above their national proportion and were being used to fight a racist war against colored people in Asia.[24] Carmichael had previously made this same point and had popularized the motto, "Hell No! We Won't Go!"

Although the Black Panthers believed in black power, they were willing to cooperate with some extremist whites, and they wanted the entire political system restructured to remove power from the rich and put it in the hands of the masses of citizens. They expressed this teaching with the slogans, "All power to the people" and "Black power to the black people." Eldridge Cleaver had also concluded that some young whites could be trusted to support the black cause. He had been impressed with the commitment of some of the white college students, especially those connected with Students for a Democratic Society. He recognized that there were some modern John Browns who could be depended on to help the cause. In the 1968 election, the Panthers joined with militant white groups which were seeking both racial justice and an end to the war in Vietnam and formed the Peace and Freedom Party. Although he was not old enough to meet the constitutional requirements, Eldridge Cleaver was nominated as the party's presidential candidate. In spite of the fact that the Peace and Freedom Party received only a handful of votes, it was a means of communicating its message to the American people.

In spite of President Nixon's appeal to the American people to "lower their voices" of protest so that they might better be heard, many believed that he only wanted quiet in order not to be disturbed. With Nixon's election, black and white radicals felt that the white and conservative backlash had taken over the "Establishment" and that official repression was bound to follow. Vice President Agnew's anti-liberal attacks were taken by many as an expression of Nixon's feelings which he preferred not to express himself.

The Black Panthers and the police became involved in a number of confrontations or "shoot-outs" which the former believed to be the result of a nationally organized, official repression. The police, at the same time, accused the Panthers of deliberately trying to kill "pigs," the Panthers' name for the police, and the Panthers accused the police of deliberately creating situations which would allow them to kill the Panther leadership. Before long, most of the Panther leaders were either under arrest, had been killed, or had fled into exile to avoid being arrested.

As civil disorders diminished in the ghettoes, college campuses were increasingly rocked by student riots. In part, it was because students asked for changes in the university structure. Black students demanded that courses in black studies be initiated and that colleges aggressively recruit new black students even if their grades were below admission standards. Some urban schools, like Columbia University, were accused by black and white students of diminishing the housing of ghetto residents to make the university's expansion possible. Other campus riots were aimed against the war in Vietnam. In May of 1970, when President Nixon sent American troops into Cambodia supposedly in the process of de-escalating the war in Vietnam, protests spread all across the country, and several campuses exploded with riots.

At Kent State University in Ohio, the National Guard shot and killed four white student protesters. At Jackson State in Mississippi, the police killed two black students. Campus riots escalated, and dozens of colleges and universities were compelled to close their doors for the remainder of the academic year. While some Americans felt that these killings were a result of government repression of the freedom of speech, others believed that more action of this kind was necessary to curb what they viewed as extremist protest. Blacks again noticed that it had been the death of four white students which brought forth the widespread indignation. They believed that killings of blacks by police and Guardsmen were usually taken for granted or ignored. Even liberals, they believed, were only really stirred by repressive measures aimed against whites.

When the Nixon Administration still refused to change its policies in response to these violent confrontations, radicals turned increasingly to the use of terrorist violence. Bombings had been on the increase for a couple of years, and during the summer of 1970, they became even more frequent. But the walls of the Establishment still did not come tumbling down. Members of the Panthers, S.N.C.C., and the Weathermen—the left-wing of the Students for a Democratic Society—were generally thought to be responsible for much of this terrorism. Instead of rallying fresh supporters to the cause of the radical left, their terrorism only served to alienate other moderates and radicals. Although the violence of this left fringe increased, their numbers appeared to decrease, and because of this the terrorist fringe began to reevaluate its tactics and the whole situation.

In February of 1971, when the Army of South Vietnam crossed into Laos with heavy American air support, campuses across the country remained quiet. At the same time, when Bobby Seale of the Black Panthers was brought to trial for allegedly participating in the murder of an ex-Panther, only a handful of spectators attended the opening of his trial. A year before when another Panther had gone on trial for his alleged involvement in the same crime, New Haven, Connecticut, experienced a series of demonstrations which culminated in a mass protest meeting of some fifteen thousand people.

By early 1971, terrorism, violent confrontation, and peaceful protests had withered considerably. Pessimism, cynicism, and despair were widespread, and many advocates of change had become paralyzed by futility, but neither black nor white protesters had surrendered to the status quo. Both groups were rethinking their attitudes. Instead of using massive campaigns with mass media coverage, the Movement had switched its emphasis to the routine, day-by-day organization of support. In 1966 the Black Power Movement had contained more rhetoric than power. In 1971 it was still alive, but blacks were working in practical ways, limiting themselves to workable objectives. The Afro-American community was quietly building community organizations to create the economic and political foundations necessary for the future. Mass protests and radical slogans, even when they received worldwide attention, had not had enough muscle to change power relationships. Afro-Americans, then, turned to the more grueling and inglorious job of trying to put their theories into practice.

Epilogue

What insights can the study of history bring to the understanding and solution of the American racial situation? How can the knowledge of yesterday's events help us to face tomorrow's decisions? The fact is, whether we know it or not, that the past is always with us and clings tightly to us like a cloak. We have the choice of either recognizing it and dealing constructively with it or of ignoring it and remaining in bondage to it.

The heritage of the American slave system is still part of our lives. Racial attitudes of white superiority and black inferiority became an integral part of the American cultural climate, and it is still part of the air we all breathe. All Americans, black and white, inhale and assimilate more racism than we care to admit. Denying that we are still infected by prejudice, however, does not help us to deal creatively with it. The drive to create a black identity which can be worn with pride and the emergence of independent African nations already have made a significant impact in altering American racial stereotypes.

History is one of the disciplines concerned with understanding how social processes operate. On this point, the study of Afro-American history raises a particular question about the means of social change. There have been those who sought to achieve it through appeals to conscience and idealism, others have turned to the use of physical force, and there have also been those who worked for it through mobilizing economic and political power.

The black experience in the United States leaves one either disillusioned or cynical concerning the value of conscience and idealism in erasing American racism. These factors, however, have not been totally irrelevant. The American democratic creed has prevented the nation from building a permanent legal caste system based on color. As a legal structure, Jim Crow lasted less

[221]

than a century and was limited to the Deep South. Idealism has made it impossible for America to rest comfortably while pursuing its racist policies.

Violence is a tempting technique for the frustrated and angry. In fact, it often has accompanied rapid social change, but it is usually a by-product of shifting power relationships in society rather than the cause of change itself. Trusting in violence is a form of revolutionary romanticism, a seductive shortcut to other, more basic kinds of social power. The history of the Black Panthers would seem to be an example of this point. Their appeal to violence attracted angry youths who were eager for quick results. Although the party gained a lot of publicity, and, in some quarters, received a lot of applause, its desire for rapid success kept it from building a solid, mass base. Apparently its leaders believed that violence made this kind of mobilization unnecessary. Its publicity and quick successes were superficial and failed to achieve basic social transformation. On Wednesday, May 19, 1971, Huey Newton, the Black Panther Minister of Defense, declared that the Panthers had been wrong in confronting the police: "All we got was a war and a lot of bloodshed." He said that they had been mistaken in disregarding the church and in thinking that they could change things without the people's changing them:

"We'll be criticized by the revolutionary cultists for trying to effect change by stages, but to do all we want to do, we just have to go through all the stages of development. We cannot jump from A to Z as some thought." [1]

Throughout history almost all social transformations have been the result of shifts in basic power relationships. The attempt to build political and economic power on a nationwide basis within the black community is a relatively new phenomenon. Reconstruction had attempted to do it earlier, but it was destroyed before it could be tested. Almost all other black economic and political involvement has been dependent on sizable white support. This was true both of the policies of Booker T. Washington and of the Civil Rights Movement. In fact, this meant a reliance on white power and on white conscience. The new spirit of black pride and self-reliance along with the new voting rights has already created pockets of black political strength in many Northern cities and in parts of the rural South. It is also being reflected in the Congress with the election of more blacks and with their creation of the Black Caucus, presently consisting of thirteen black congressmen. After submitting a list of their demands to President Nixon, their spokesman, Representative William Clay, D-Mo., said:

"We are going to set the tone for the black liberation struggle in this country. . . . Black people in this country have no permanent friends, no permanent enemies, only permanent interests. . . . I think we've reached the point in black America where we've completely given up on the mass demonstrations, sit-ins and boycotts. We've come to the basic conclusion that America has no conscience. Anybody who still appeals to what they think is a conscience is either stupid or frustrated. The only possible avenue for the achievement of equal rights for all in this country is through the exertion of political power. We have actual power, and even greater potential power, more than we've ever had in history." [2]

As Representative Clay maintains, striving for racial change through an appeal to conscience has been found woefully inadequate. The resort to physical force has not been followed very often and, when it has, it has been used sporadically. To succeed, it obviously requires its own kind of mass power base to bring about lasting results. The creation of genuine black political power which was preached in 1966 is only being achieved now. It has already gained significant local results. In the Black Caucus, it promises broader national influence. Trusting to white consciences has been proven naive. Looking to terrorism for quick results has only led to publicity and bloodshed. Building genuine political power, however, is producing results now and promises to create more social transformation in the immediate future.

Notes and References

Chapter One

1. Basil Davidson, *Africa in History* (New York, 1968), pp. 6–10.
2. Roland Oliver and J. D. Fage, *A Short History of Africa* (Baltimore, 1962), p. 21.
3. S. and F. Ottenberg, *Cultures and Societies of Africa* (New York, 1960), p. 18.
4. Oliver and Fage, *op. cit.*, pp. 16–17.
5. *Ibid.*, pp. 25–28.
6. Basil Davidson, *The Lost Cities of Africa* (Boston, 1959), pp. 40 ff.
7. *Ibid.*, pp. 217 ff.
8. Basid Davidson, *The African Past* (New York, 1964), p. 70.
9. *Ibid.*, pp. 72–73.
10. *Ibid.*, p. 74.
11. *Ibid.*, p. 79.
12. J. D. Fage, *A History of West Africa* (Cambridge, 1969), p. 22.
13. *Ibid.*, pp. 27–28.
14. Basil Davidson, *The African Slave Trade* (Boston, 1961), p. 13.
15. Basil Davidson, *A History of West Africa* (Garden City, N. Y., 1966), pp. 40–47, 151–57.
16. *Ibid.*, pp. 169–72.
17. *Ibid.*, pp. 165–71, 190–91.
18. *Ibid.*, pp. 167–68.
19. *Ibid.*, pp. 174–89.
20. *Ibid.*, p. 176.

Chapter Two

1. Davidson, *The African Slave Trade*, pp. 21–221.
2. *Ibid.*, pp. 23–24.
3. *Ibid.*, pp. 50–53.
4. *Ibid.*, p. 79.
5. *Ibid.*, pp. 80–81.

6. Eric Williams, *Capitalism and Slavery* (Chapel Hill, N.C., 1944), p. 25.

7. D. A. G. Waddell, *The West Indies* (New York, 1967). Contains a full description of the subject.

8. John E. Fagg, *Latin America: A General History* (New York, 1969), pp. 146–49.

9. Herbert S. Klein, *Slavery in the Americas: A Comparative Study of Virginia and Cuba* (Chicago, 1967), pp. 57–68.

10. Ralph Korngold, *Citizen Toussaint* (Boston, 1944). Contains a full treatment of the slave revolution in Haiti.

Chapter Three

1. David Brion Davis, *The Problem of Slavery in Western Culture* (Ithaca, N.Y., 1966), pp. 29, 60.

2. *Ibid.*, p. 46.

3. Williams, *loc. cit.*

4. Susie M. Ames, *Studies of the Virginia Eastern Shore in the Seventeenth Century* (Richmond, Virginia, 1940), pp. 100–106.

5. Ulrich B. Phillips, *American Negro Slavery: A Survey of the Supply, Employment and Control of Negro Labor as Determined by the Plantation Regime* (New York, 1918), p. 75.

6. Oscar and Mary F. Handlin, "Origin of the Southern Labor System," *William and Mary Quarterly*, Third Series, VII, (April, 1950), 212.

7. Thomas J. Wertenbaker, *Planters of Colonial Virginia* (Princeton, 1922), pp. 96–100.

8. Kenneth M. Stampp, *The Peculiar Institution: Slavery in the Ante-Bellum South* (New York, 1956), pp. 144–48.

9. Wertenbaker, *op. cit.*, p. 138.

10. Frank Tannenbaum, *Slave and Citizen: The Negro in the Americas* (New York, 1947), p. 45.

11. *Ibid.*, p. 89.

12. *Ibid.*, p. 62.

13. *Ibid.*, pp. 50–58.

14. *Ibid.*, p. 56.

15. Stanley M. Elkins, *Slavery: A Problem in American Institutional and Intellectual Life* (Chicago, 1963), pp. 57, 73–74.

16. Tannenbaum, *op. cit.*, pp. 58–61.

17. Elkins, *op. cit.*, pp. 82–87.

18. *Ibid.*, p. 88.

19. *Ibid.*, pp. 105–18.

20. *Ibid.*, pp. 98–102.

21. *Ibid.*, p. 117.

22. *Ibid.*, pp. 119–22.

23. *Ibid.*, pp. 123–27.
24. *Ibid.*, p. 86.
25. Herbert Aptheker, *American Negro Slave Revolts* (New York, 1943). Contains a full description of the subject.
26. Elkins, *op. cit.*, pp. 88–93.
27. Eugene Kinkead, *In Every War but One* (New York, 1959). Contains a full description of the subject.
28. Elkins, *op. cit.*, p. 94.
29. Stampff, *op. cit.*, pp. 34 ff.
30. *Ibid.*, pp. 101–109.

Chapter Four

1. James Boswell, *Life of Samuel Johnson* (New York, ND), pp. 747–48.
2. Leon F. Litwack, *North of Slavery: The Negro in the Free States, 1790–1860* (Chicago, 1961), pp. 12–13.
3. William Jay, *The Life of John Jay* (New York, 1833), I, 231.
4. James Otis, *The Rights of the British Colonies Asserted and Proved* (Boston, 1766), pp. 43–44.
5. Charles F. Adams (ed.), *Letters of Mrs. Adams* (Boston, 1841), I, 24.
6. Benjamin Quarles, *The Negro in the American Revolution* (Chapel Hill, N.C., 1961). Contains a full description of the subject.
7. Litwack, *op. cit.*, p. 7.
8. William F. Cheek, *Black Resistance Before the Civil War* (Beverly Hills, Calif., 1970), pp. 107–11.
9. *Ibid.*, pp. 111–16.
10. Herbert Aptheker, *Nat Turner's Slave Rebellion* (New York, 1966).
11. Litwack, *op. cit.*, pp. 5, 162 ff.
12. *Ibid.*, pp. 20–29.
13. *Ibid.*, pp. 30 ff.
14. *Ibid.*, pp. 64 ff.
15. *Ibid.*, pp. 72–73.

Chapter Five

1. Margaret Just Butcher, *The Negro in American Culture* (New York, 1956), pp. 117–18.
2. Richard Bardolph, *The Negro Vanguard* (New York, 1959), pp. 30–32.
3. *Ibid.*, pp. 38–43.
4. *Ibid.*, pp. 35–36.
5. E. Franklin Frazier, *The Negro Church in America* (New York, 1969), pp. 26–35.

6. Litwack, *op. cit.*, p. 187.
7. *Ibid.*, pp. 244–45.
8. *Ibid.*, pp. 139, 232.
9. Frederick Douglass, *The Life and Times of Frederick Douglass, written by Himself* (New York, 1962).
10. Walter Merrill, *Against Wind and Tide, a Biography of William Lloyd Garrison* (Cambridge, 1963). Contains a description of his life philosophy.
11. Litwack, *op. cit.*, pp. 216–18.
12. Martin R. Delany, *Condition, Elevation, Emigration, and Destiny of the Colored People* (Philadelphia, 1852), pp. 10–27.
13. Larry Gara, *The Liberty Line: The Legend of the Underground Railroad* (Lexington, Ky., 1961). Contains a full description of the subject.
14. Litwack, *op. cit.*, pp. 248 ff.
15. Delany, *op. cit.*, pp. 14–15, 30–35, 159–98.
16. *Proceedings of the National Emigration Convention of Colored People; held at Cleveland, Ohio . . . the 24th, 25th, and 26th of August, 1854* (Pittsburgh, 1854), pp. 16–18, 23–27, 33–37, 40–41, 43–46, 55–56, 71–77.
17. Litwack, *op. cit.*, p. 266.
18. Herbert Aptheker (ed.), *A Documentary History of the Negro People in the United States* (New York, 1951), p. 368.
19. Litwack, *op. cit.*, p. 265.
20. Richard Hinton, *John Brown and His Men* (New York, 1968).

Chapter Six

1. Roy P. Basler, *The Collected Works of Abraham Lincoln* (New Brunswick, N.J., 1953), II, 256, III, 145–46.
2. Benjamin Quarles, *The Negro in the Civil War* (Boston, 1953), pp. 59 ff.
3. *Ibid.*, pp. 66, 93–99.
4. *Ibid.*, pp. 200–202.
5. *Ibid.*, pp. 108–20, 183 ff.
6. John Hope Franklin, *From Slavery to Freedom* (New York, 1969), p. 279.
7. John Hope Franklin, *The Emancipation Proclamation* (Garden City, 1963). Contains a detailed analysis of Lincoln's views and of the events surrounding the proclamation.
8. John Hope Franklin, *Reconstruction After the Civil War* (Chicago, 1961), pp. 15 ff.
9. W. E. B. DuBois, *Black Reconstruction in America* (New York, 1935), pp. 352–58.

10. Eric L. McKitrick, *Andrew Johnson and Reconstruction* (Chicago, 1960). Presents a fresh analysis of the conflict between the President and the Congress.

11. Franklin, *Reconstruction After the Civil War*, pp. 127 ff.

12. Rayford W. Logan, *The Betrayal of the Negro* (London, 1965), pp. 77–126.

13. Franklin, *Reconstruction After the Civil War*, pp. 152 ff.

14. Logan, *op. cit.*, pp. 17–18.

15. DuBois, *op. cit.*, pp. 352–58.

16. *Ibid.*, pp. 212–19, 345–79.

17. Logan, *op. cit.*, pp. 29–30.

18. C. Vann Woodward, *Reunion and Reaction: The Compromise of 1877 and the End of Reconstruction* (Boston, 1951), pp. 8, 195–96, 202 ff.

19. Logan, *op. cit.*, pp. 26–33.

20. *Ibid.*, p. 104.

21. *Ibid.*, pp. 115–21.

22. *Ibid.*, p. 118.

23. *Ibid.*, pp. 244–45.

24. *Ibid.*, pp. 221–23.

25. Richard Hofstadter, *Social Darwinism in American Thought, 1860–1915* (Philadelphia, 1944). Contains a detailed description of the development of American racial theories.

26. Theodore Roosevelt, "Kidd's 'Social Evolution,'" *North American Review*, CLXI (July, 1895), 94–109.

27. Josiah Strong, *Our Country* (New York, 1885), pp. 175–78.

28. Logan, *op. cit.*, p. 172.

Chapter Seven

1. Robert Kinzer and Edward Sagarin, *The Negro in American Business* (New York, 1950), pp. 92–101.

2. U.S. Bureau of the Census, abstract Eleventh and Twelfth Censuses.

3. Jessie P. Guzman, ed., *Negro Year Book* (New York, 1952), p. 278.

4. Mary W. Ovington, *How the National Association for the Advancement of Colored People Began* (New York, 1914). Provides a first-hand description of the subject.

5. George E. Haynes, *The Negro at Work in New York City* (New York, 1912).

6. Edward A. Johnson, *History of Negro Soldiers in the Spanish American War and Other Items of Interest* (Raleigh, 1899).

7. Theodore P. Wright, Jr., "United States Electoral Intervention in Cuba," *Inter-American Economic Affairs*, XIII, (3, 1959), 40–71.

8. Dana G. Munro, *Intervention and Dollar Diplomacy in the Caribbean 1900–1921* (Princeton, N.J., 1964). Contains a full description of the subject.

9. Logan, *op. cit.*, p. 362.

10. Emmett J. Scott, *The American Negro in the World War* (Washington, 1919). Contains a thorough account of the subject.

11. Arthur W. Little, *From Harlem to the Rhine. The Story of New York's Colored Volunteers* (New York, 1936), and Charles H. Williams, *Sidelights on Negro Soldiers* (Boston, 1923). Both contain accounts of the conflicts confronting Negro soldiers at home and overseas.

12. Francis L. Broderick, *W. E. B. DuBois: Negro Leader in a Time of Crisis* (Stanford, 1949), pp. 129–30.

13. Elliott W. Rudwick, *Race Riot at East St. Louis July 2, 1917* (Cleveland, 1966). Presents a detailed description of the riot, its causes, and its aftermath.

14. Chicago Commission on Race Relations, *The Negro in Chicago, A Study of Race Relations and a Race Riot* (Chicago, 1922) is the official report on the 1919 riot.

15. David M. Chalmers, *Hooded Americanism, the First Century of the Ku Klux Klan 1865–1965* (Garden City, N.Y., 1965), pp. 22–28.

16. *Ibid.*, pp. 28–33.

17. *Ibid.*, pp. 35–38.

18. *Ibid.*, pp. 202–212, 281–90.

Chapter Eight

1. Booker T. Washington, *Up From Slavery* (Garden City, N.Y., 1900), pp. 1–53.

2. *Ibid.*, pp. 54–56.

3. *Ibid.*, p. 208.

4. *Ibid.*, pp. 219–20.

5. *Ibid.*, pp. 220–21.

6. *Ibid.*, pp. 221–22.

7. *Ibid.*, p. 224.

8. *Ibid.*, pp. 224–25.

9. Charleston *News and Courier*, Sept. 19, 1895, p. 1.

10. Ridgely Torrence, *The Story of John Hope* (New York, 1948). Contains a thorough biography of John Hope.

11. W. E. B. Dubois, *The Souls of Black Folk* (Greenwich, Conn., 1961), pp. 48–49.

12. Booker T. Washington, "Education and Suffrage for Negroes," *Education* XIX, (Sept., 1898), 49–50.

13. W. E. B. DuBois, *Dusk of Dawn* (New York, 1968), pp. 3–49.

14. W. E. B. DuBois, "The Talented Tenth," in Francis L. Broderick and August Meier (eds.), *Negro Protest Thought in the Twentieth Century* (Indianapolis, 1965), p. 41.

15. Ralph J. Bunche, "A Critical Analysis of the Tactics and Programs of Minority Groups," *Journal of Negro Education*, IV, 3 (July, 1935), 308–20.

16. W. E. B. DuBois, "The Need for Racial Pride," *Crisis*, XLI (June, 1934), 182.

17. James Weldon Johnson, *Negro Americans, What Now?* (New York, 1935), pp. 12–18.

18. Peter M. Bergman, *The Chronological History of the Negro in America* (New York, 1969), pp. 260–61.

19. E. David Cronon, *Black Moses, The Story of Marcus Garvey* (Madison, Wis., 1969), pp. 3–11.

20. *Ibid.*, pp. 12–20.

21. *Ibid.*, pp. 204–07.

22. Marcus Garvey, "Aims and Objects of Movement for Solution of Negro Problem," in Amy Jacques-Garvey (ed.), *Philosophy and Opinions of Marcus Garvey* (New York, 1925), pp. 37–43.

23. Cronon, *op. cit.*, p. 69.

24. *Ibid.*, p. 142.

25. *Ibid.*, pp. 167–68.

26. Johnson, *op. cit.*, pp. 3–18, 35–40, 98–103.

27. Bergman, *op. cit.*, p. 302.

28. A. Philip Randolph and Chandler Owen, "Our Reason for Being," Editorial, *The Messenger* (August, 1919), pp. 11–12.

29. A. Philip Randolph and Chandler Owen, "DuBois Fails As a Theorist," Editorial, *The Messenger* (December, 1919), pp. 7–8.

30. A. Philip Randolph, "Keynote Address to the Policy Conference of the March on Washington Movement," in *March on Washington Movement: Proceedings of Conference Held in Detroit, September 26–27, 1942* (no imprint), pp. 4–11.

31. Bergman, *op. cit.*, p. 302.

Chapter Nine

1. Ira De Augustine Reid, *The Negro Immigrant, His Background, Characteristics, and Social Adjustment, 1899–1936* (New York, 1949), pp. 235–47.

2. James Weldon Johnson, *Black Manhattan* (New York, 1930), p. 153.

3. Reid, *op. cit.*, p. 121.

4. Nathan Glazer and Daniel P. Moynihan, *Beyond the Melting Pot: The Negroes, Puerto Ricans, Italians, and Irish of New York City* (Cambridge, 1963), pp. 91–94.

5. *Ibid.*, pp. 115, 133.

6. Clarence Senior, *Our Citizens from the Caribbean* (New York, 1965), pp. 110–11.

7. Carter G. Woodson, *A Century of Negro Migration* (Washington, 1918), pp. 126–42.

8. Bergman, *op. cit.*, pp. 327–28, 395–96, 486, 522, 563.

9. Alain Locke, "The New Negro," in Alain Locke, *The New Negro, An Interpretation* (New York, 1968), pp. 3–16.

10. *Ibid.*, p. 14.

11. James Weldon Johnson, "Harlem: the Culture Capital," in Locke, (ed.), *op. cit.*, pp. 301–11.

12. *Ibid.*, p. 307.

13. Gilbert Osofsky, *Harlem: The Making of a Ghetto* (New York, 1963). Presents a detailed description of Harlem's evolution from a residential neighborhood into an urban slum.

14. Locke, "The Legacy of the Ancestral Arts," in Locke (ed.), *op. cit.*, pp. 254–55.

15. LeRoi Jones, *Blues People: Negro Music in White America* (New York, 1963) is a highly interpretive history of the Afro-American community from the standpoint of its music.

16. Langston Hughes, "The Negro Artist and the Racial Mountain," *The Nation*, CXXII (June 23, 1926), 692–94.

17. Sterling A. Brown (ed.), *The Negro Caravan* (New York, 1969), p. 370.

18. Claude McKay, "White Houses," in Claude McKay, *A Long Way from Home* (New York, 1937), p. 332.

19. Claude McKay, "If We Must Die," *Ibid.*, p. 333.

20. Langston Hughes, "Let America Be America Again," in Walter Lowenfels (ed.), *The Writing on the Wall* (Garden City, N.Y., 1969), p. 26.

21. James Weldon Johnson, "The Creation," in James Weldon Johnson, *God's Trombones: Negro Sermons in Verse* (New York, 1927), p. 28.

22. Countee Cullen, "Heritage," in Countee Cullen, *Color* (New York, 1925), p. 121.

23. Hugh M. Gloster, *Negro Voices in American Fiction* (Chapel Hill, N.C., 1948), pp. 34–43.

24. For a full treatment on Garvey see Chapter 8.

25. Arna Bontemps and Jack Conroy, *Anyplace But Here* (New York, 1966), pp. 204–205.

26. *Ibid.*, pp. 205–208.

27. C. Eric Lincoln, *The Black Muslims in America* (Boston, 1961), and Essien-Udom, Essien U., *Black Nationalism: A Search for an Identity in America* (Chicago, 1962). Both contain a full account of the origins of the Nation of Islam.

28. Malcolm X is discussed more fully in the final chapter.

Chapter Ten

1. Franklin, *From Slavery to Freedom*, pp. 494–95.

2. Adam Clayton Powell, Jr., *Marching Blacks: An Interpretive History of the Rise of the Black Common Man* (New York, 1945), pp. 95–103.

3. Franklin, *From Slavery to Freedom*, p. 540.

4. Laurence J. W. Hayes, *The Negro Federal Government Worker* (Washington, 1941) is a study of the Negro in the Roosevelt Administration.

5. Horace Cayton and George S. Mitchell, *Black Workers and the New Unions* (Chapel Hill, N.C., 1939) contains a full description of the subject.

6. Randolph is discussed more fully in Chapter 8.

7. James MacGregor Burns, *Roosevelt: The Soldier of Freedom* (New York, 1970), p. 124.

8. Ulysses Lee, *The Employment of Negro Troops* (Washington, 1966) is a volume in the Special Studies Series of the United States Army in World War II, and presents the official account.

9. "Detroit—The Storm Bursts," *The Christian Century*, LX (June 30, 1943), 759–61.

10. *The New York Times* (November 22, 1946), p. 17.

11. *U.S. National Commission for UNESCO*, XC (50) 65, (September 12, 1950), and XC (51) 18, (April 5, 1951).

12. Walter White, *A Rising Wind* (New York, 1945), pp. 144–45.

13. 80th Congress, 2nd Session, *Congressional Record (1948)*, Part IV, 4312–18.

14. Franklin, *From Slavery to Freedom*, p. 609.

Chapter Eleven

1. Alfred H. Kelly, "The School Desegregation Case," in John A. Garraty (ed.), *Quarrels That Have Shaped the Constitution* (New York, 1964), pp. 243–68.

2. *Brown v. Board of Education of Topeka*, 347 U.S.—483 (1954).

3. *The New York Times*, (September 25, 1957), 1.

4. Martin Luther King, Jr., *Strength to Love* (New York, 1963), p. 139.

5. *Ibid.*, p. 10.

6. *The New York Times* (October 26, 1960), 1; (October 27, 1960), 22; (October 28, 1960), 1.

7. *Ibid.*, (May 21, 1961), p. 1.

8. *Ibid.*, (August 29, 1963), p. 21.

9. *Ibid.*, March 26, 1965), p. 22.

Chapter Twelve

1. Robert Conot, *Rivers of Blood, Years of Darkness* (New York, 1967), pp. 3–44, 50–55.

2. *Ibid.*, pp. 214–25.

3. *Ibid.*, pp. 274–76.

4. *Ibid.*, pp. 351–53, 373–75.

5. *Report of the National Advisory Commission on Civil Disorders* (New York, 1968), p. 66.

6. *Ibid.*, pp. 56–69.

7. *Ibid.*, pp. 84–108.

8. Stokeley Carmichael, "What We Want," *New York Review of Books*, (September 22, 1966), 5.

9. Robert F. Williams, *Negroes With Guns*, as quoted in Floyd B. Barbour (ed.), *The Black Power Revolt* (New York, 1969), p. 179.

10. *Ibid.*, pp. 179–80.

11. *Ibid.*, pp. 177–78.

12. The Black Muslims are treated more fully in Chapter 9.

13. Malcolm X, *The Autobiography of Malcolm X* (New York, 1966), p. 362.

14. *Ibid.*, pp. 434–37.

15. *Ibid.*, p. 361.

16. *Ibid.*, p. 278.

17. Malcolm X, "Racism: The Cancer That is Destroying America," *Egyptian Gazette* (August 25, 1964), in John Henrik Clarke (ed.), *Malcolm X, The Man and His Times* (New York, 1969), p. 306.

18. *The New York Times* (June 18, 1966), 28.

19. Carmichael, *op. cit.*, p. 6.

20. *Ibid.*

21. Stokeley Carmichael and Charles V. Hamilton, *Black Power: The Politics of Liberation in America* (New York, 1967), p. 39.

22. *Ibid.*, pp. 39–44.

23. Bobby Seale, *Seize the Time* (New York, 1970), pp. 59–110.

24. *Ibid.*, pp. 66–69.

Epilogue

1. Rochester *Democrat and Chronicle* (May 21, 1971), 1.

2. Rochester *Times-Union* (June 1, 1971), 1.

Bibliography

ADAMS, CHARLES F. (ed.) *Letters of Mrs. Adams.* Boston, 1841.

AMES, SUSIE M. *Studies of the Virginia Eastern Shore in the Seventeenth Century.* Richmond, 1940.

APTHEKER, HERBERT. *American Negro Slave Revolts.* New York, 1943.

APTHEKER, HERBERT. *Nat Turner's Slave Rebellion.* New York, 1966.

APTHEKER, HERBERT (ed.) *A Documentary History of the Negro People in the United States.* New York, 1951.

BARBOUR, FLOYD B. (ed.) *The Black Power Revolt.* New York, 1969.

BARDOLPH, RICHARD. *The Negro Vanguard.* New York, 1959.

BASLER, ROY P. *The Collected Works of Abraham Lincoln.* New Brunswick, 1953.

BERGMAN, PETER M. *The Chronological History of the Negro in America.* New York, 1969.

BONTEMPS, ARNA, AND JACK CONROY. *Anyplace But Here.* New York, 1966.

BOSWELL, JAMES. *Life of Samuel Johnson.* New York, ND.

BRODERICK, FRANCIS L. *W.E.B. DuBois: Negro Leader in a Time of Crisis.* Stanford, 1959.

BRODERICK, FRANCIS L., AND AUGUST MEIER. (eds.) *Negro Protest Thought in the Twentieth Century.* Indianapolis, 1965.

BROWN, STERLING A. (ed.) *The Negro Caravan.* New York, 1969.

Brown v. Board of Education of Topeka, 347 U.S.-483. 1954.

BURNS, JAMES MACGREGOR. *Roosevelt: The Soldier of Freedom.* New York, 1970.

BUTCHER, MARGARET JUST. *The Negro in American Culture.* New York, 1956.

BUNCHE, RALPH J. "A Critical Analysis of the Tactics and Programs of Minority Groups," *Journal of Negro Education,* IV (July, 1935), 308–20.

CARMICHAEL, STOKELEY. "What We Want," *New York Review of of Books* (September 22, 1966), 5.

CARMICHAEL, STOKELEY, AND CHARLES V. HAMILTON. *Black Power: The Politics of Liberation in America.* New York, 1967.

CAYTON, HORACE, AND GEORGE S. MITCHELL. *Black Workers and the New Unions.* Chapel Hill, 1939.

CHALMERS, DAVID M. *Hooded Americanism, the First Century of the Ku Klux Klan 1865–1965.* Garden City, 1965.

CHEEK, WILLIAM F. *Black Resistance Before the Civil War.* Beverly Hills, 1970.

CHICAGO COMMISSION ON RACE RELATIONS. *The Negro in Chicago, A Study of Race Relations and a Race Riot.* Chicago, 1922.

CLARKE, JOHN HENRIK (ed.) *Malcolm X, The Man and His Times.* New York, 1969.

CONOT, ROBERT. *Rivers of Blood, Years of Darkness.* New York, 1967.

CRONON, E. DAVID. *Black Moses, The Story of Marcus Garvey.* Madison, 1969.

CULLEN, COUNTEE. "Heritage," in Countee Cullen, *Color.* New York, 1925.

DAVIDSON, BASIL. *Africa in History.* New York, 1968.

DAVIDSON, BASIL. *The Lost Cities of Africa.* Boston, 1959.

DAVIDSON, BASIL. *The African Past.* New York, 1964.

DAVIDSON, BASIL. *The African Slave Trade.* Boston, 1961.

DAVIDSON, BASIL. *A History of West Africa.* Garden City, 1966.

DAVIS, DAVID BRION. *The Problem of Slavery in Western Culture.* Ithaca, 1966.

DELANY, MARTIN R. *Condition, Elevation, Emigration, and Destiny of the Colored People.* Philadelphia, 1852.

"Detroit—The Storm Bursts," *The Christian Century,* LX (June 30, 1943), 759–61.

DOUGLASS, FREDERICK. *The Life and Times of Frederick Douglass, written by Himself.* New York, 1962.

DuBOIS, W.E.B. *Black Reconstruction in America.* New York, 1935.

DuBOIS, W.E.B. *The Souls of Black Folk.* Greenwich, 1961.

DuBOIS, W.E.B. *Dusk of Dawn.* New York, 1968.

DuBOIS, W.E.B. "The Need for Racial Pride," *The Crisis,* XLI (June, 1934), 182.

ELKINS, STANLEY M. *Slavery: A Problem in American Institutional and Intellectual Life.* Chicago, 1963.

ESSIEN-UDOM, ESSIEN U., *Black Nationalism: A Search for an Identity in America.* Chicago, 1962.

FAGE, J.D. *A History of West Africa.* Cambridge, 1969.

FAGG, JOHN E. *Latin America: A General History.* New York, 1969.

FRANKLIN, JOHN HOPE. *From Slavery to Freedom.* New York, 1969.

FRANKLIN, JOHN HOPE. *The Emancipation Proclamation.* Garden City, 1963.

FRANKLIN, JOHN HOPE. *Reconstruction After the Civil War.* Chicago, 1961.

FRAZIER, E. FRANKLIN. *The Negro Church in America.* New York, 1969.

GARA, LARRY. *The Liberty Line: The Legend of the Underground Railroad.* Lexington, 1961.

GARRATY, JOHN A. (ed.) *Quarrels that Have Shaped the Constitution.* New York, 1964.

GLAZER, NATHAN, AND DANIEL P. MOYNIHAN. *Beyond the Melting Pot: The Negroes, Puerto Ricans, Italians, and Irish of New York City.* Cambridge, 1963.

GLOSTER, HUGH M. *Negro Voices in American Fiction.* Chapel Hill, 1948.

GUZMAN, JESSIE P. (ed.) *Negro Year Book.* New York, 1952.

HANDLIN, OSCAR, AND MARY F. HANDLIN, "Origin of the Southern Labor System," *William and Mary Quarterly,* Third Series, VII (April, 1950), 212.

HAYES, LAURENCE J.W. *The Negro Federal Government Worker.* Washington, 1941.

HAYNES, GEORGE E. *The Negro at Work in New York City.* New York, 1912.

HINTON, RICHARD. *John Brown and His Men.* New York, 1968.

HOFSTADTER, RICHARD. *Social Darwinism in American Thought, 1860–1915.* Philadelphia, 1944.

HUGHES, LANGSTON. "The Negro Artist and the Racial Mountain," *The Nation,* CXXII (June 23, 1926), 692–94.

JACQUES-GARVEY, AMY (ed.) *Philosophy and Opinions of Marcus Garvey.* New York, 1925.

JAY, WILLIAM. *The Life of John Jay.* New York, 1833.

JOHNSON, EDWARD A. *History of Negro Soldiers in the Spanish American War and Other Items of Interest.* Raleigh, 1899.

JOHNSON, JAMES WELDON. *Negro Americans, What Now?* New York, 1935.

JOHNSON, JAMES WELDON. *Black Manhattan.* New York, 1930.

JOHNSON, JAMES WELDON. *God's Trombones: Negro Sermons in Verse.* New York, 1927.

JONES, LEROI. *Blues People: Negro Music in White America,* New York, 1963.

KING, MARTIN LUTHER, JR. *Strength to Love.* New York, 1963.

KINKEAD, EUGENE. *In Every War but One.* New York, 1959.

KINZER, ROBERT, AND EDWARD SAGARIN. *The Negro in American Business.* New York, 1950.

KLEIN, HERBERT S. *Slavery in the Americas: A Comparative Study of Virginia and Cuba.* Chicago, 1967.

KORNGOLD, RALPH. *Citizen Toussaint.* Boston, 1944.

LEE, ULYSSES. *The Employment of Negro Troops.* Washington, 1966.

LINCOLN, C. ERIC. *The Black Muslims in America.* Boston, 1961.

LITTLE, ARTHUR W. *From Harlem to the Rhine, The Story of New York's Colored Volunteers.* New York, 1936.

LITWACK, LEON F. *North of Slavery: The Negro in the Free States, 1790–1860.* Chicago, 1961.

LOCKE, ALAIN. *The New Negro, An Interpretation.* New York, 1968.

LOGAN, RAYFORD W. *The Betrayal of the Negro.* London, 1965.

LOWENFELS, WALTER (ed.) *The Writing on the Wall.* Garden City, 1969.

March on Washington Movement: Proceedings of Conference Held in Detroit, September 26–27, 1942.

McKAY, CLAUDE. *A Long Way from Home.* New York, 1937.

McKITRICK, ERIC L. *Andrew Johnson and Reconstruction.* Chicago, 1960.

MERRILL, WALTER. *Against Wind and Tide, a Biography of William Lloyd Garrison.* Cambridge, 1963.

MUNRO, DANA G. *Intervention and Dollar Diplomacy in the Caribbean 1900–1921.* Princeton, 1964.

The New York Times. 1946–1966.

News and Courier. (Charleston, South Carolina). 1895.

OLIVER, ROLAND, AND J. D. FAGE. *A Short History of Africa.* Baltimore, 1962.

OSOFSKY, GILBERT. *Harlem: The Making of a Ghetto.* New York, 1963.

OTIS, JAMES. *The Rights of the British Colonies Asserted and Proved.* Boston, 1766.

OTTENBERG, S. AND F. *Cultures and Societies of Africa.* New York, 1960.

OVINGTON, MARY W. *How the National Association for the Advancement of Colored People Began.* New York, 1914.

PHILLIPS, ULRICH B. *American Negro Slavery: A Survey of the Supply, Employment and Control of Negro Labor as Determined by the Plantation Regime.* New York, 1918.

POWELL, ADAM CLAYTON, JR. *Marching Blacks: An Interpretive History of the Rise of the Black Common Man.* New York, 1945.

Proceedings of the National Emigration Convention of the Colored People; held at Cleveland, Ohio . . . the 24th, 25th, and 26th of August, 1854. Pittsburgh, 1854.

QUARLES, BENJAMIN. *The Negro in the American Revolution.* Chapel Hill, 1961.

QUARLES, BENJAMIN. *The Negro in the Civil War.* Boston, 1953.

RANDOLPH, A. PHILIP, AND CHANDLER OWEN. "Our Reason for Being." *The Messenger* (August, 1919), 11–12.

RANDOLPH, A. PHILIP, AND CHANDLER OWEN. "DuBois Fails as a Theorist," *The Messenger* (December, 1919), 7–8.

REID, IRA DE AUGUSTINE. *The Negro Immigrant, His Background, Characteristics, and Social Adjustment, 1899–1936.* New York, 1949.

Report of the National Advisory Commission on Civil Disorders. New York, 1968.

ROOSEVELT, THEODORE. "Kidd's 'Social Evolution,'" *North American Review,* CLXI (July, 1895), 94–109.

RUDWICK, ELLIOTT W. *Race Riot at East St. Louis July 2, 1917.* Cleveland, 1966.

SCOTT, EMMETT J. *The American Negro in the World War.* Washington, 1919.

SEALE, BOBBY. *Seize the Time.* New York, 1970.

SENIOR, CLARENCE. *Our Citizens from the Caribbean.* New York, 1965.

STAMPP, KENNETH M. *The Peculiar Institution: Slavery in the Ante-Bellum South.* New York, 1956 .

STRONG, JOSIAH. *Our Country,* New York, 1885.

TORRENCE, RIDGELY. *The Story of John Hope.* New York, 1948.

TANNENBAUM, FRANK. *Slave and Citizen: The Negro in the Americas.* New York, 1947.

U.S. BUREAU OF THE CENSUS. *Abstract Eleventh and Twelfth Censuses.*

U.S. NATIONAL COMMISSION FOR UNESCO. 1950–1951.

WADDELL, D. A. G. *The West Indies.* New York, 1967.

WASHINGTON, BOOKER T. *Up From Slavery.* Garden City, 1900.

WASHINGTON, BOOKER T. "Education and Suffrage for Negroes," *Education,* XIX (Sept. 1898), 49–50.

WERTENBAKER, THOMAS J. *Planters of Colonial Virginia.* Princeton, 1922.

WHITE, WALTER. *A Rising Wind.* New York, 1945.

WILLIAMS, CHARLES H. *Sidelights on Negro Soldiers.* Boston, 1923.

WILLIAMS, ERIC. *Capitalism and Slavery.* Chapel Hill, 1944.

WOODSON, CARTER G. *A Century of Negro Migration.* Washington, 1918.

WOODWARD, C. VANN. *Reunion and Reaction: The Compromise of 1877 and the End of Reconstruction.* Boston, 1951.

WRIGHT, THEODORE P., JR. "United States Electoral Intervention in Cuba," *Inter-American Economic Affairs,* XIII (1959), 40–71.

X, MALCOLM. *The Autobiography of Malcolm X.* New York, 1966.

80TH CONGRESS, 2ND SESSION, *Congressional Record (1948),* Part IV, 4312–18. U.S. *Congressional Record.* 1948.

Democrat and Chronicle (Rochester, New York). 1971.

Times-Union (Rochester, New York). 1971.

Index